D0990631

WITHDRAW:

The 'Puritan' Democracy of Thomas Hill Green

British Idealist Studies Series 3: Green
1: Matt Carter, *T.H. Green and the Development of Ethical Socialism*
2: Denys Leighton, *The Greenian Moment*
3: Ben Wempe, *T.H. Green's Theory of Positive Freedom*
4: Alberto de Sanctis, *The 'Puritan' Democracy of Thomas Hill Green*

Series Editor:
Peter Nicholson, University of York (retd.)
Editorial Board:
G.F. Gaus (Tulane)
John Morrow (Auckland)
Lord Plant (King's College, London)
Avital Simhony (Arizona State)
Geoffrey Thomas (Birkbeck)
Andrew Vincent (Sheffield)

imprint-academic.com/idealists

The 'Puritan' Democracy of Thomas Hill Green

With Some Unpublished Writings

Alberto de Sanctis

ia

imprint-academic.com

Published in the UK by Imprint Academic
PO Box 200, Exeter EX5 5YX, UK

Published in the USA by Imprint Academic
Philosophy Documentation Center
PO Box 7147, Charlottesville, VA 22906-7147, USA

ISBN 1 84540 038 0

A CIP catalogue record for this book is available from the
British Library and US Library of Congress

imprint-academic.com/idealists

"If God reveal anything to you by any other instrument of his, be as ready to receive it as ever you were to receive any truth by my ministry; for I am verily persuaded the Lord has more truth yet to break forth out of his holy word. For my part, I cannot sufficiently bewail the condition of the reformed churches, who are come to a period in religion, and will go at present no farther than the instruments of their reformation. The lutherans cannot be drawn to go beyond what Luther saw; whatever part of his will God has revealed to Calvin, they will rather die than embrace it; and the calvinists, you see, stick fast where they were left by that great man of God, who yet saw not all things. This is a misery much to be lamented . . . Remember that ... for it is not possible the christian world should come so lately out of such thick anti-christian darkness, and that perfection of knowledge should break forth at once."

J. Robinson, *Exhortation*,
quoted by Green in
'Four Lectures on the English Revolution'

Contents

Preface

This monograph is a revised version of a book published in Italian (*La democrazia "puritana" di Thomas Hill Green. Con alcuni scritti inediti*, Florence, 2002), which was adapted from a doctoral thesis (Dipartimento di Studi Politici, University of Rome, La Sapienza, 1998). The central concern of my doctoral thesis was already the relationship between Puritanism and idealism in Green's thought, but the material was not very well organised so that I entirely overlooked that Green's main objective was the achievement of democracy in his own country. The Italian version of this book resulted from an effort to offer better evidence for some central points of my work, for instance how Green managed to make the teaching of Vane consistent with that of F.C. Baur. The opportunity for an English translation of the book was the chance of a lifetime. I have tried to sharpen the focus of my analysis further, revising the structure of the book as well as consulting the latest scholarship. My main concern is to show the significant role which the Puritan element played in the working out of Green's view of democracy. The book focuses on a reconstruction of Green's political thought which is meant to illuminate facets usually regarded as inconsistent with both the English and the German philosophical traditions. It provides an examination of Green's position based on the assumption that Puritanism gave him the clue for harmonising idealism and empiricism and for attuning their differences and incompatibilities.

The central concern of the present study is to demonstrate how Puritanism was a theme which ran through all Green's biography and political philosophy. It thereby reveals how Green's connections with Evangelicalism and his known affinities with religious dissent came from his way of conceiving

Puritanism. In Green's eyes, its anti-formalist viewpoint made Puritanism the most suitable tool for avoiding the drawbacks of democracy. The key objective of the book is to illustrate how the philosophy elaborated by Green aimed to encapsulate the best of Puritanism whilst eschewing the dangerous abstractions of both Puritan philosophy and German idealism. It follows that Green's conception of positive and negative freedom, and his vision of political obligation, stemmed from his effort to revive the Puritan heritage rather than from an ambiguous flirtation with idealism.

The book purports to show how the influence of Puritanism in Green's political thought is an element which can help to integrate the literature in the area, contributing to a better comprehension of a philosopher who, despite being unanimously considered as the founder of the so-called Oxford idealist school, had a very difficult and sometimes obscure connection with idealism. It has been widely argued that Green's relationship with idealism seemed to be infected by a religious germ which, because it was unrelated to German idealism, gave it a bad taste. This study aims to encourage further investigation of the nature and propagation of that germ in the British idealist School.

Acknowledgements

This book was originally conceived whilst I was a Ph. D. student at the University of Rome, where my feeling that the religious element embedded in ethics and therefore in politics needed to be investigated further was fully confirmed by attending the seminars of Mario D'Addio and Gaetano Calabrò. D'Addio's analysis of the religious factor taught me that religion so concerns the inner life that it has to be seen in the light of a variety of complex and different attitudes. As a result, it can be classified according to preconceived typologies only with difficulty. This led me to investigate Green's political thought against his Puritan background.

There are many people who provided me with help and assistance. To them all I would like to express my warmest thanks. To Anna Maria Lazzarino Del Grosso who always trusted in me and my research; to Maria Antonietta Falchi Pellegrini who first introduced me to Green; to Salvo Mastellone who was for me a sort of a Socratic teacher well able to make me give my best; to Claudio Palazzolo who offered me his suggestions; and to Peter Nicholson, the person I am most indebted to for my work on Green. By talking to him, I gained the impression of having really been introduced into the Greenian world. Apart from being a sort of additional supervisor for my doctoral thesis, Peter very patiently helped me to turn my Italian English into something more like English.

I owe much to the staff of the Balliol College Library, Oxford, to Alan Tadiello and its director, Dr Penelope Bulloch, who were always willing to help me when I was working on Green's papers; and to that of the University Library of Genoa, particularly Claudio Risso. Special thanks go to the scholars with whom I discussed my work: Richard Bellamy, Maria Dimova-Cookson, Avital Simhony, Colin Tyler, Andrew Vincent; also to Giorgio Sola and the Department of Politics of the University of Genoa. This study has also benefited from comments and constructive suggestions from John Morrow. I am very grateful to the Department of Politics of the University of York, which hosted me as a visiting fellow and offered me the opportunity to give a paper on Green, and to the colleagues who invited me to give a paper on Green at the Political Studies Association conference held at the London School of Economics in 2000. These were important stages in advancing my reasearch.

The book is dedicated to my parents and Angela, who nourished my efforts with their love.

Introduction

Although Thomas Hill Green (1836–1882) was classified as an idealist thinker, most commentators noticed that his idealism was quite atypical. Seth, following Balfour's footsteps, already realized the oddness of Green's dialectic.[1] According to Milne, the notion of the concrete universal, which the British idealists took over from Hegel, revealed a certain ambiguity in their work.[2] As a result of its ambiguous character, if Green's political philosophy has usually been investigated in the light of its relationship with idealism,[3] continuity with the previous British tradition has not been denied.[4] At the same time, those who, like Milne, Plamenatz and Mabbott, pointed out that there was a mingling of hedonism and idealism in Green, corroborated Collingwood's view of the autochthonous character of British idealism.[5] Similarly, Monro argued that Green's conception of general will was not incompatible with a utilitarian

[1] A. Seth, *Hegelianism and Personality* (London, second edition 1893 [1887]), pp. 27–8 and A. J. Balfour, 'Green's Metaphysics of Knowledge', *Mind*, 9 (1884), pp. 73–92.
[2] A. J.M. Milne, *The Social Philosophy of English Idealism* (London, 1962), p. 15.
[3] See A.B. Ulam, *Philosophical Foundations of English Socialism* (Cambridge, 1951); J. Passmore, *A Hundred Years of Philosophy* (London, 1957); A. Quinton, 'Absolute Idealism', *Proceedings of the British Academy*, 57 (1971), pp. 303–29; C. Camporesi, *L'uno e i molti: l'idealismo britannico dal 1830 al 1920* (Florence, 1980); P. Robbins, *The British Hegelians, 1875–1925* (London, 1982); P. Nicholson, *The Political Philosophy of the British Idealists: Selected Studies* (Cambridge, 1990).
[4] See D.G. Ritchie, *The Principles of State Interference: Four Essays on the Political Philosophy of Mr. Herbert Spencer, J.S. Mill, and T.H. Green* (London, 1891); A.D. Lindsay, 'T.H. Green and the Idealists' in F.J.C. Hearnshaw, ed., *The Social and Political Ideas of Some Representative Thinkers of the Victorian Age* (New York, 1933); F.P. Harris, *Neo-Idealist Political Theory: Its Continuity with the British Tradition* (New York, 1944).
[5] Milne, *The Social Philosophy of English Idealism*, pp. 103–4; J.P. Plamenatz, *Consent, Freedom and Political Obligation* (London, 1968), p. 73; J.D. Mabbott, *The State and the Citizen: An Introduction to Political Philosophy* (London, 1967), p. 41; R.G. Collingwood, *An Autobiography* (London, 1939), pp. 15–6.

compromise which resulted from a multiplicity of contrasting interests cementing themselves through tradition and custom.[6] Alessandro Passerin d'Entrèves emphasised the inadequacy of an interpretation of Green's political philosophy which exaggerated its idealism.[7] In this vein, Pringle-Pattison's judgement, dating back to the end of the nineteenth-century, appears to be quite insightful. He observed that:

> It is a serious mistake to suppose that, in Green, for example, we have simply a revival of Kant, or a revival of Hegel, or a combination of the two. Materials certainly have been drawn from both these thinkers; but the result is a type of thought which has never existed before, and of which it is absurd, therefore, to speak as an importation from Germany.[8]

Almost everybody agreed that Green's relationship with German idealism, and particularly with Hegel, was a very controversial one.

Whilst those who favoured Green's inclination to justify State intervention affirmed that Kant's influence was more important than that of Hegel,[9] critics like Berlin claimed that Green added a religious dimension which made Hegel's position much more dangerous as regards the problem of freedom.[10] Richter had reduced Green's liberalism to a surrogate faith.[11] Richter realized that religion was a key element for understanding Green's connection with idealism, but he missed the point. Richter correctly stated that Green saw in

[6]   D.H. Monro, 'Green, Rousseau and the Culture Pattern', *Philosophy*, 26 (1951), p. 347.

[7]   A. Passerin d'Entrèves, 'Il problema dell'obbligazione politica nel pensiero inglese contemporaneo', *Rivista Internazionale di Filosofia del diritto*, 8 (1928), p. 29. Vittorio Frosini stated that Green owed much to Hume: *La ragione dello stato: Studi sul pensiero politico inglese contemporaneo* (Milan, 1976), pp. 23–4. In a similar way, Jellamo maintained that in Green's philosophy empiricism played an important role: *Interpretazione del bene comune: Saggio su Thomas H. Green* (Milan, 1993), p. 4.

[8]   Quoted in A.P.F. Sell, *Philosophical Idealism and Christian Belief* (Cardiff, 1995), p. 47. See also A. Jellamo, 'Da Mill a Green: osservazioni su liberty e freedom', *I problemi della pedagogia*, 41 (1995), p. 199.

[9]   See O. Bellini, 'La società civile secondo Thomas Hill Green', *Nuovi Studi Politici*, 6 (1976), pp. 114–8; C. Palazzolo, *Idealismo e liberalismo: La filosofia pratica di T.H. Green* (Carrara, 1983), pp. 103–5; G. Thomas, *The Moral Philosophy of T. H. Green* (Oxford, 1987), pp. 52–4, 286–7.

[10] I. Berlin, 'Two Concepts of Liberty' in *Four Essays On Liberty* (Oxford, 1969), p. 50.

[11] M. Richter, 'T.H. Green and His Audience: Liberalism as a Surrogate Faith', *Review of Politics*, 18 (1956), pp. 444–72.

"Philosophical Idealism, the fulfilment and correction of Puritanism."[12] However, Richter overlooked that the Puritan element was to be viewed as an instrument that could make a foreign philosophy which was considered abstract and authoritarian, more liberal and democratic. Consistently with this hypothesis, it seems as if Green sifted German idealism with a particular target in sight, because he was able to pick out what he needed to preserve and to reject what he did not.

Though some scholars showed themselves aware of the importance of the link between Green's idealism and protestant theology,[13] the connection between the Puritan background of Green and his idealism has not been examined. At the same time, it was almost universally recognized that Puritanism was a theme which underpinned Green's political thought. His contemporaries noted this too. One fellow member of the Old Mortality Essay Society in the early 1860s reported that "T. H. Green preached Hegel, with the accent of a Puritan."[14] Richter himself admitted that Puritanism played an important role in the formation of Green's ideas, and Frosini confirmed that Green owed much to Puritanism.[15]

The present study deals with the complex relationship between Puritanism and idealism in Green's thought. The book aims to prove that Green's main purpose was to promote the achievement of democracy in his own country, and that he used Puritanism in order to make German idealism consistent with English democracy. For Green, the anti-formalist attitude which characterized Puritanism stemmed from a quite concrete way of living and thinking which could be set in opposition to the abstractness of German idealism. It is worth remembering the judgement of John Addington Symonds on the nature of Green's Puritanism. Symonds, who was not only

---

[12] M. Richter, *The Politics of Conscience: T.H. Green and His Age* (London, 1964), p. 41; see also pp. 210–1.

[13] See, for instance, '"The Word is Nigh Thee": The Religious Context of Idealism' in A. Vincent and R. Plant, *Philosophy, Politics and Citizenship: The Life and Thought of the British Idealists* (Oxford, 1984), pp. 6–17; B.M.G. Reardon, 'T.H. Green as a Theologian' in A. Vincent, ed., *The Philosophy of T.H. Green* (Aldershot, 1986), pp. 36–47; A. Vincent, 'T.H. Green and the Religion of Citizenship' in *ibid.*, pp. 48–61.

[14] The Rev. W. Berkley, quoted in William Knight, *Memoir of John Nichol* (Glasgow, 1896), p. 150.

[15] Richter, *The Politics of Conscience*, pp. 40–1; V. Frosini, 'Sul problema dell'obbligazione politica nel pensiero di Green' in T.H. Green, *L'obbligazione politica*, trans. G. Buttà (Catania, 1973), pp. 63–4, 67–8.

one of Green's closest friends but also his brother-in-law, wrote that Green had taught him that the principles of democracy and socialism were active factors in modern politics which had to be accepted as actualities, and that they should not be taken up in any revolutionary or extreme way but grasped with "the spirit of a philosophical Puritan & a Christian who loved his fellow-men."[16]

In this sense, though Puritanism was viewed as similar to that typical English background from which empiricism also sprang, yet its main concern was that facts should not be accepted as the sole reality. On the other hand, in Green's eyes, idealism too, despite moving from a viewpoint antithetical to that of empiricism, flowed into a passive acceptance of facts. In Green's analysis, Puritanism was a useful tool which could remedy the defects both of empiricism and idealism. Empiricism needed to be freed from its tendency to be the prisoner of facts, while idealism needed to be emancipated from its inclination to sanctify facts. Facts formed the focus of Green's position, but both extreme views, empiricism and idealism, should be avoided and Puritanism was to contribute to this end. Accordingly, that anti-formalist view from which the saints drew their inspiration during the Commonwealth, could be very helpful.[17] Because Puritanism attached more importance to substance than to forms, it could help preserve the best of both empiricism and idealism. Indeed, Green particularly appreciated the Puritan rejection of formality because it meant that institutions should not be treated as absolute: the invisible church always comes first.[18]

Nevertheless, Green was well aware that a revived Puritanism had to be of a very different kind from that of the seventeenth-century. According to him, the Independents or Congregationalists, the leading sect in the seventeenth cen-

---

[16] Recollections, in I. Biography, b) Recollection of Green, Green Papers; printed in Herbert M. Schueller and Robert L. Peters, ed., *The Letters of John Addington Symonds. Volume III: 1885–1893* (Detroit, 1969), p. 176.

[17] Green surely admired the Puritans whenever they fought for unity within formal diversity. "If unity were to be preserved – and it was generally agreed that anything less would be catastrophic – there were only two approaches: to insist on uniformity, by persuasion and coercion, or, alternatively, to minimise formal differences and stress unity of substance." J.C. Davis, 'Against Formality: One Aspect of the English Revolution', *Transactions of the Royal Historical Society*, Sixth Series, 3 (1993), p. 279.

[18] See Davis, 'Against Formality: One Aspect of the English Revolution', pp. 269–71.

tury revolution, could be remembered as champions of toleration and their example could inspire the policy of those who in
the nineteenth century were still fighting for religious liberty.
Yet the Independents had not managed to be tolerant in their
own age. In the same way, the Levellers' ideas were intrinsically democratic but the Levellers themselves were bound by
the conditions of their own times and did not always think or
act democratically. Both the Independents and the Levellers
were unable to put their ideals into practice, Green judged,
because they lacked a proper philosophy. The Puritan philosophy was condemned to give rise to nondemocratic governments: it sanctioned the supremacy of both an elite and a
dictator. In Green's view, therefore, the accomplishment of the
Puritan revolution required that toleration and democracy be
embodied in a new philosophy.

Already in his undergraduate essays, Green seemed to offer
the teaching of Hume in a new form. Empiricism resulted in
scepticism and, for Green, that could have caused the collapse
of the young English democracy. Nonetheless, the common
sense that lay at the basis of Hume's position had to be preserved. According to Green, it was a matter of marrying
empiricism with the urge for improvement which came from a
genuine religious belief. At the same time Green had to turn
idealism into a vehicle of the Puritan anti-formalist attitude. I
aim to prove that for Green, Puritanism could be regarded as
an instrument which could avoid what he considered a risk:
the excessive abstractness of German idealism. As Maurice
Mandelbaum suggested in *Man, History and Reason*, Green
found important those aspects of Fichte's philosophy showing
the impossibility of conceiving a self independently of the
empirical world.[19] But, as Nettleship reported, Green read
more of Fichte only in his later years.[20] On the other hand,
Green knew that abstractness was indicative of an anti-democratic attitude. I intend to show how Green avoided that by
turning to F. C. Baur. Green said that Baur was nearly the most

---

[19] M. Mandelbaum, *History, Man, and Reason: A Study in Nineteenth-Century
   Thought* (Baltimore & London, 1971), pp.221–3.
[20] R.L. Nettleship, *Memoir* in Nettleship, ed., *Works of Thomas Hill Green: Vol. III.
   Miscellanies and Memoir* (London, 1888), reprinted in *Collected Works of T.H.
   Green*, edited and introduced by P. Nicholson, 5 vols (Bristol, 1997), III, p. cxxv.
   In 1906 the *Memoir* was published separately (London, 1906; reprinted Bristol,
   1993). All citations from Green's *Works* are drawn from Nicholson's edition .

instructive writer he ever met with.[21] It was Baur who accused Hegel of having separated "matter" and "form": the idea was not prior to history, history was prior to the idea.

Green did not doubt that German idealism stemmed from the Lutheran Reformation, and he took it for granted that an idealism engendered by the Puritan revolution would be of a very different kind. Hegel deployed his position along lines laid down by Luther, so it had been adapted to a tradition which originated in another context. Almost from its beginning the Lutheran Reformation did not distinguish between church and state, seen as two faces of the same spiritual organism. Both Luther and Calvin claimed the primacy of the *Ecclesia Invisibilis*, but the former was unable to defend his viewpoint. Indeed Green was convinced that the reality of neither church nor state could correspond to the idea and that, despite its permeating strength, German thought was destined to reveal itself as a powerless tool. By contrast, the popular feeling out of which the Reformation arose in England was one of rebellion against any institutional interference in religion. The English Reformation was based on Calvin's doctrine, which was more akin than Luther's to a practical and commercial bent which nourished a sense of personal freedom and independence fully compatible with a republican spirit. That spirit would be fostered by the influence of the Puritan revolution.

Green's interpretation of the relationship between "matter" and "form" was thoroughly congruous with a political theology which, by bearing witness to a God who is in the world but not of it, aimed at reaffirming the pre-eminence of the invisible church. It followed that institutions, above all the state, cannot arrogate to themselves a right to prescribe right and wrong in such an abstract and absolute way as to set aside what is going on among ordinary people. Ordinary people are more willing to compromise and less inclined to unreasonable quarrels about speculations. Green knew that both Puritan philosophy and Hegelian idealism were prone to ignore the sufferings of ordinary people.

Nevertheless, like Tocqueville and J.S. Mill, Green was aware of the risk that the advent of a mass democracy might make it acceptable for individuals to be unscrupulous and bend the world to their own satisfaction. For that reason,

[21] Nettleship, *Memoir*, p. xxxvii.

unlike Victorian novelists, he believed that that sociability which flourishes from sharing the same destiny was not only an escape route from evil but also a constitutive element of a personality whose ripening (self-realization) was assured by a spiritual agent (the eternal consciousness).

I examine here Green's position with regard to the theme of exceptional individuality, arguing that he shared with J. S. Mill the viewpoint that the corruption of democracy could be alleviated by an individual able to resist the force of circumstances, whenever this force boosts egoism and lack of respect for others. Circumstances play an important role in the moulding of character, but they are not decisive. Green's support for democracy made him sharply critical of Carlyle's intention of reviving the Puritan past by resorting to the leadership of heroes. To Carlyle's hero, Green opposed his Puritan exceptional individuality, which in the seventeenth century revolution was exemplified above all by the saints: Cromwell and Vane. They were against any dogmatism, persuaded that the invisible church was more important than the institutional one. If Cromwell and Vane were right about dogmatism, Green judged that they were mistaken on another matter: they regarded themselves as uninfluenced by historical circumstances. It followed that Green's exceptional individuality, the philosopher-saint, despite preserving the anti-formalist attitude of the Puritans, would be based on a philosophy that was much more concrete and historical than Puritan philosophy. As an instance, the philosopher-saint, unlike the Puritan saints, did not reject every kind of dogma but only the tendency to see it in a definitive form. Only in this way could the Puritan liberal and democratic ideals be put into practice.

Green's Puritan democracy was deeply imbued with common sense. On Green's interpretation, democracy came from that peculiar religious sense first exported to America by the Pilgrim Fathers and strengthened by the Puritan revolution. Puritanism was so embedded in common sense that it was only through common sense that changes could be effected. For that reason, conscience was viewed as an organ by means of which both common sense and the Divine can reveal themselves; and the people were the medium between these two terms. No abstract plan would have interfered with the expression of common sense. On the other hand, to the extent political power distanced itself from common sense, the basis of its authority would be weakened and, as a consequence, it would have to resort more and more to force rather than consent. At the same time, common sense was not destined to perpetuate itself in the same form but to grow and mature, and political power had to change according to this evolution.

This book aims to demonstrate that democracy, as Green knew it, should be understood only as the latest product of common sense and, for that reason, it could not be regarded as a final form either. Green was well aware of this, and this is probably why he was not particularly interested in the forms of democracy. My work shows how Green's conception of democracy, stemming from a common sense enlivened by a rational will which reflected the Puritan primacy of the spirit, implied at least three principles: a) conscience should not to be interfered with, because it bears witness to the expression of common sense and the Divine; b) every push coming from below should not only be encouraged, but considered a necessary element to develope common sense; c) the people is more likely to be able to express such common sense if it is associated.

Accordingly the structure of the book is as follows. Chapter I shows how Puritanism was a theme underpinning Green's position from its beginnings and influencing its whole development. I establish that the typical anti-formalist attitude which lies at the basis of Puritanism was the main factor which led Green to realize that both idealism and empiricism had to be amended. At the same time, I show how Puritanism grounded Green's effort to mediate between empiricism and idealism. By way of illustration, Green's judgment on India already bore witness to his conviction of the necessity to conciliate idealism and empiricism with an evident religious goal in view. Chapter II deepens the analysis of Green's reception of Puritanism. The chapter starts from Green's elaboration of the concept of exceptional individuality, and is intended to show how Green, through his concept of exceptional individuality, reacted against the risk that egoism was further encouraged by the advent of a mass society which, as novels attested, would have sanctioned the death of the aristocratic hero. Further, exceptional individuality is a Puritan theme bound to be revisited by Green in the light of his new philosophy. In this vein, the key objective of the chapter is to illustrate how Baur was Green's main philosophical point of reference, which led him to a new interpretation of Puritanism. Thanks to Baur Green seemed to be persuaded of the possibility of accomplishing the Puritan revolution. Green's *Four Lectures on the English Revolution* can be regarded, therefore, as a sort of manifesto expounding his political project.

This is complemented by the study of the impact of Green's political project on reality, that is, by the detailed examination of his political activity contained in Chapter III. This chapter uses Green's political biography as a lens through which to view how Green's political ideas came from his new philosophy and how his political activity was influenced by it. In his public speeches Green did not seem to be very interested in arguing about the forms of democracy. I intend to prove here that Green's political activity was mainly concerned with avoiding the risk that conscience, as far as it is a vehicle both of common sense and the Divine, would be interfered with by political power, and to demonstrate that Green thought the progress of common sense would be checked by obstacles which hindered the growth of morality on the part of the most disadvantaged. From this perspective, the chapter identifies the Land and the Liquor Questions as two central problems which had to be tackled in order to avoid the risk that the Divine, which makes common sense ripen, would dry up. In addition, I establish that education was in Green's view the only means by which such a conceived common sense could grow and mature without interfering with conscience. This chapter also sets out to show how, for Green, people are more likely to express common sense if they are associated, and how those who rejected democracy were always bent on preventing them from associating.

Chapter IV compares Green's conception of political obligation with his philosophy, illustrating how in Greens' position there is no interruption between philosophy and practice. J.S. Mill, despite admitting the lack of a general theory on state intervention, thought it was better to refrain from formulating such a theory. Hegel, on the other hand, stated that English backwardness came just from the fact that the English were unable to overcome the level of particularities. I argue that Green saw a third way — which I term the Puritan way — and that accordingly he thought it was possible to find an exit from the impasse which troubled English champions of democracy. This chapter claims that Green's conception of political obligation stemmed from a teleological view like Vane's rather than from Kantian formalism. Green's distinction between positive and negative freedom itself owes much to Vane. In the light of the third Puritan way thought up by Green, this chapter provides an examination of various questions concerning political obligation, and shows that many inconsistencies in Green's position usually identified by commentators are not inconsistencies at all. Green himself did not do enough to explain his unusual viewpoint. Indeed, because it aims to mediate between empiricism and idealism with a religious target in view, Green's political philosophy can be rightly regarded as unprecedented in the English philosophical tradition.

Chapter I

The Influence of Puritanism

1. Cromwell and Aristotle

Thomas Hill Green was born on 7th April 1836 at Birkin, a village in the West Riding of Yorkshire of which his father, Valentine, was rector.[1] His mother's family included many academics.[2] Green's mother, Anna Barbara Vaughan, died in 1837. Thomas was only a year old and had one brother and two sisters.[3] Just in those years, Puritanism became the hobbyhorse of radical reformers, and clubs dedicated to the leaders of the Puritan revolution increased. Intentionally in contrast to the radicals who were praising Puritanism, the Whig John Russell published his *Essay on the History of the English Government and Constitution* (1821), where he lauded the Glorious Revolution. Macaulay on the other hand thought the Puritan revolution was more important than the Glorious Revolution. More and more people were persuaded that nineteenth century political questions could not be solved simply by appealing to that constitutional continuity claimed by Whigs at the end of the seventeenth century. In nineteenth century England

---

[1] Almost all Green's major writings, except the two introductions to *The Philosophical Works of David Hume*, see 'General Introduction' to *The Philosophical Works of David Hume*, ed. T.H. Green and TH. Grose, 4 vols (London, 1874–1875), I, pp. 1–299, and 'Introduction to the Moral Part of the Treatise', II, pp. 1–71, were published posthumously. The *Prolegomena to Ethics* was first published in 1883, ed. A.C. Bradley (Oxford, 1883). In the same year two of Green's sermons, *The Witness of God* and *Faith*, were published: *The Witness of God and Faith: Two Lay Sermons*, ed. A. Toynbee (London, 1883). The 'Lectures on the Principles of Political Obligation' were first published in 1886, see *The Works of Thomas Hill Green*, ed. R.L. Nettleship, 3 vols (London, 1885–8), II, pp. 335–553.

[2] Richter, *The Politics of Conscience*, pp. 41–3.

[3] Nettleship, *Memoir*, p. xi.

a more serious conflict was going on than that between Crown and Parliament. As Macaulay emphasised, it was a conflict between the majority of the people, on the one side, and Crown and Parliament, on the other.[4]

By chance, the Puritan myth, and particularly the Commonwealth, was almost the main theme of Green's biography. His father Valentine descended from Colonel Sanders, one of Cromwell's officers.[5] It is likely that ever since he was a child, Green was deeply familiar with Cromwell and his entourage. When Green was fourteen, he went to school at Rugby. Never a typical schoolboy, he was rather apathetic except when his imagination was quickened by the memory of the Puritan revolution. This was strikingly shown on the single occasion on which he gained the Prize for Latin prose composition: the passage to be translated was taken from Milton's *Areopagitica*.[6] The young Green wanted to be like Cromwell. At Rugby his school-fellows identified him with the Lord Protector: "even then he seemed to us boys (as in later days to others) to have some of the character of Cromwell about him, his favourite hero."[7]

The comparison with Cromwell stood because of Green's unusual authoritativeness. Though he was the only one of four hundred pupils to drink nothing stronger than tea or coffee, nobody thought this was due to any want of energy. Though he abstained from ill-treating younger boys, Green was not regarded as weak-kneed. His behaviour was seen rather as a sign of inner strength and originality. His school-fellows realized that Green was exempt from any affectation and that his aloofness was not due to any kind of superiority complex. His precocious independence of judgment, which revealed itself for the first time during school debates, and the fact that he showed no intellectual competitive impulse, gave him a peculiar impressiveness to a small number of intimates.[8] Known as

---

[4] T. Lang, *The Victorians and the Stuart Heritage: Interpretations of a Discordant Past* (Cambridge, 1995), pp. 50–1.

[5] Nettleship, *Memoir*, p. xi. Sanders is mentioned as an officer of Cromwell's army with the rank of major: C.H. Firth, *Cromwell's Army* (London, 1962), p. 256. Alternatively, a Saunders is mentioned with the rank of colonel, pp. 38, 367. One cannot doubt that an officer of Cromwell's army was among Green's ancestors.

[6] Nettleship, *Memoir*, pp. xii–xiii.

[7] *Ibid.*, p. xv.

[8] *Ibid.*, pp. xv–xvi.

one of the politicians of the school, he was instinctively adverse to papism and everything associated with it. Thomas Carlyle was one of his favourite authors in this period: in his lectures *On Heroes, Hero-Worship and the Heroic in History*, Carlyle emphasized the importance of Cromwell; and in 1845 Carlyle edited Cromwell's letters and speeches.[9]

Green began reading Aristotle at Rugby and his first metaphysical analysis seemed to be influenced by him. At Rugby Green read many authors, among whom one can mention besides Carlyle, Frederick Denison Maurice and Charles Kingsley, but Aristotle was certainly the most important. In England at that time the teaching of Aristotle was considered an indispensable tool for preparing young men for university. As in the case of subjects connected with the Puritan revolution, Aristotle stimulated Green's interest. Despite his seeming indolence, in 1852 Green was the only one to make out a tough bit of Aristotle set in an examination; and a school-fellow told of Green's attempting to impart some elementary metaphysical conceptions.[10] In *The Nicomachean Ethics* Aristotle wanted to prove that, though everybody might see a thing in many different and sometimes contrasting ways, this thing existed and was objective. For Aristotle, objectiveness stemmed from a variety of conventional perspectives.[11] Likewise Green, referring to a bridge on the Newbold road, probably attempted to show how, though the existence of the bridge was unquestionable, our perception of it was determined by our subjective viewpoint. Green seemed to have assimilated from Aristotle the notion that, though the starting point of an investigation was to be identified with facts, conventions and common sense, philosophy should search for something beyond them.

If Aristotle was Green's main philosophical reference point, Cromwell embodied his human model. In 1854 Green had to look after his brother, who was an alcoholic; he was at Oxford,

[9] T. Carlyle, *On Heroes, Hero-Worship and the Heroic in History: Six Lectures* (London, 1841) ; T. Carlyle, *Oliver Cromwell's Letters and Speeches: with elucidations*, 2 vols (London, 1845).

[10] Nettleship, *Memoir*, pp. xiv–xv.

[11] See for instance Aristotle, *The Nicomachean Ethics*, trans. H. Rackham (Cambridge, Mass., 1956), pp. 3–5.

and there was no one there to help him.[12] That autumn he also had to face the fatal insanity which struck one of his closest Rugby friends.[13] With him, some months earlier, Green had visited Oxford, his future alma mater. Despite the agreeableness of the place, he formed quite unusual views of the University. He thought Oxford was a whited sepulchre where the insides of the colleges were incongruous with the outside: "the finest colleges are the most corrupt, the functionaries from the heads to the servants being wholly given to quiet dishonesty, and the undergraduates to sensual idleness."[14] This severe judgment was similar to that expressed by seventeenth century Puritans about the licentiousness of citizens and courtiers.[15] Like Cromwell, Green countered the corruption of Babel with an exaltation of country life. "He seemed to feel himself at home with [country people] at once, and seized without effort the political and economical features of their life."[16] At Rugby, he liked to spend his Sunday afternoons in the fields by himself and, when he was laughed at about it, replied he could worship God best in that way.[17] Like Cromwell, Green descended from a family that had managed through the hard work of many generations to acquire a landed estate which ensured its members the title of squires.[18]

2. Idealism and Empiricism

In 1855 Green entered Balliol College, Oxford. There his typical independence of judgment, which had revealed itself for the first time at Rugby, became more and more obvious when he showed his comprehensive sympathy towards the sufferings of the poorer classes. Green made clear his conviction the people must get directly involved in politics, allowing them the possibility of forming and expressing their views. Because

---

[12] "It is most important that I should be as much possible with my brother in his present some what unsettled state. His other friends are merely exaggerations of himself, and anything but prudent, so I hope my caution may be useful to him." Letter to David Hanbury, Spring 1854, in I. Biography, a) Green's Correspondence, Green Papers, Balliol College Library.

[13] Letter to David Hanbury, 24 September 1854, Green Papers.

[14] Nettleship, *Memoir*, p. xvi.

[15] See H.R. Trevor-Roper, 'The General Crisis of the Seventeenth Century', *Past and Present*, 16 (1959), pp. 31–64.

[16] Nettleship, *Memoir*, p. xviii.

[17] *Ibid.*, p. xvi.

[18] Richter, *The Politics of Conscience*, p. 40.

his seriousness was relieved by a genial and sympathetic sense of humour, one fellow-student thought Green could be compared with Carlyle. Nevertheless, one could not have ignored an essential difference between them: Green was much more lenient towards ordinary people than was Carlyle.[19] Green had not been at Oxford very long when he complained that F.D. Maurice had not been invited there yet.[20] Like Maurice, Green was eager to offer the working classes the possibility of entering university. On that occasion Green's comment was: "there is a working [Men's] College being agitated here, but it is not yet established."[21]

At least at the beginning Green's academic career was not outstanding. Benjamin Jowett, his tutor at Balliol, soon realized that though Green was a very talented pupil, he needed to be constantly encouraged and stimulated.[22] Consequently Jowett decided to follow his progress with special dedica-

---

[19] Nettleship, *Memoir*, p. xix.

[20] On Frederick Denison Maurice, see B.M.G. Reardon, *From Coleridge to Gore: A Century of Religious Thought in Britain* (London, 1971), pp. 206–13. It is very likely it was his uncle, the Rev. David James Vaughan, who first made Green read Maurice. Vaughan opened a working men's college in Leicester (see Richter, *The Politics of Conscience*, pp. 42–3). In 1854 Green had already read Maurice's *Theological Essays* and *Prophets and Kings of the Old Testament* (Nettleship, *Memoir*, p. xiv). Green, who seemed to share the viewpoints Maurice expressed in his *Theological Essays*, probably was prone, since Rugby times, to believe that dogmas and religious doctrines were not essential. Green, who recommended the *Theological Essays* to a friend of his, thought this book was "truly edifying and interesting" (see Green, letter to David Hanbury, 24 September 1854, Green Papers). Significantly, James Martineau was one of the few who agreed with Green. Martineau founded the Free Christian Union, which aimed to overcome those doctrines and dogmas that hindered a more profitable exchange among Christian Confessions; on the link between Maurice and Martineau, see J.P. Parry, *Democracy and Religion. Gladstone and the Liberal Party, 1867–1875* (Cambridge, 1989), p. 223. Towards the end of the 80s, Martineau's viewpoint was akin to that of F.C. Baur (1792–1860), the German theologian destined to play a crucial role in the forming of Green's mind: see J. Martineau, *A Study of Religion: Its Sources and Contents*, 2 vols (Oxford, 1889), I, pp. xii–xiii. In 1861, Green said he could accept a modified Unitarianism (Nettleship, *Memoir*, p. xxxv). On the theological position of Maurice and its political aspects, see H. Davies, *Worship and Theology in England: From Watts and Wesley to Martineau, 1690–1900* (Cambridge, 1996), pp. 283–315.

[21] Letter to David Hanbury, undated (probably 1855–57), Green Papers.

[22] Nettleship, *Memoir*, p. xvii. On Jowett, see G. Faber, *Jowett: A Portrait with Background* (London, 1957). Hinchliff was persuaded it was Jowett who acquainted Green with Kant, Hegel and F.C. Baur: P. Hinchliff, *Benjamin Jowett and the Christian Religion* (Oxford, 1987), pp. 159–60. On the relationship between Jowett and Green, see pp. 159–68.

tion.[23] At that time Jowett had already paid for his fidelity to his principles.[24] A member of the so-called Broad Church Party, Jowett tended to acknowledge an important role for human judgment. Despite human reason's partiality, Jowett thought it the best tool for investigating theological subjects. By contrast, the High Church Party's members were persuaded that, with reference to Christian belief, it was better to admit that dogmas were far beyond the reach of human reason. Dogmas had to be accepted as absolute truths in virtue of a long tradition.[25] The High Church Party contended that the church should be organized according to a hierarchical conception tending to restrain any kind of dissent. The Broad

---

[23] During his first term at Balliol, Green observed: "My tutor is most kind to me, and I like him exceedingly. I breakfast with him occasionally, when he talks to me freely, and not the commonplaces which such men generally do to their pupils" (Nettleship, *Memoir*, p. xvii).

[24] In 1854, Balliol failed to elect Jowett as Master of the College. Owing to the publication of his commentaries on St. Paul's Epistles (*The Epistles of St.Paul to the Thessalonians, Galatians and Romans*, 2 vols (London, 1855), Jowett was regarded as an adversary by the Church establishment. It is likely that this fact made Green admire Jowett for his courage. Green recorded: "I get awfully bullied by the Dons, all of whom I dislike more or less, except Jowett, who is my tutor and kind to me, and for whose book I have a profound respect." Letter to David Hanbury, undated (probably 1855–57), Green Papers.

[25] The novelist Mary Ward, author of the famous *Robert Elsmere*, one of whose main characters (Professor Grey) was inspired by Green, reported that the difference between High and Broad Church Party could have been summarized with reference to two typical characters: "the character that either knows no doubts or has suppressed them, and the character that fights its stormy way to truth", *A Writer's Recollections* (London, 1918, p. 169). Ward was also aware of the effects produced by these characters. "The Master [Jowett], Green, Toynbee — their minds were full, half a century ago, of the 'condition of the people' question, of temperance, housing, wages, electoral reform; and within the University, and by the help of the weapons of thought and teaching, they regarded themselves as the natural allies of the Liberal party which was striving for these things through politics and Parliament . . . And the significance of it is only to be realised when we turn to the rival group, to Christ Church, and the religious party which that name stood for. Read the lives of Liddon, of Pusey, or - to go further back - of the great Newman himself. Nobody will question the personal goodness and charity of any of the three. But how little the leading ideas of that seething time of social and industrial reform, from the appearance of *Sybil* in 1843 to the Education Bill of 1870, mattered either to Pusey or to Liddon compared with the date of the book of Daniel, or the retention of the Athanasian Creed!" (pp. 133–4). Later, the peculiar inclination of the Broad Church Party was well described by Webb: "To such a generation the new idealist philosophy professed itself able to show that the true object of religious faith and hope was to be sought not *without* but *within* the world", Clement C.J. Webb, *A Study of Religious Thought in England from 1850* (Oxford, 1933), p. 102.

Church Party, on the contrary, supported a church organisation with a more democratic distribution of power. By challenging the viewpoint of those who disparaged human reason, Jowett showed how democracy could spring from liberty of conscience. As at the time of the Puritan revolution, democracy and religious toleration seemed to be strictly intertwined. One can easily imagine how in Green's view the conflict between High and Broad Church Party could be seen as like that between Anglicans and Puritans.[26] Green noted as in Cromwell's time, there had been an ill-fated combination between "a court party and a church party, each using the other for the purpose of silencing the demand for a 'reason why' in politics and religion."[27]

Jowett thought idealism could be very useful for reinforcing his position. But, though he agreed with Kant about the distinction between noumenon and phenomenon, Jowett wanted to prove that human reason could not be confined to the phenomenal world: both realities originated from God and were destined to be complete in God.[28] Probably Jowett intended to keep himself aloof from authors who, like William Hamilton, resorted to Kant's distinction to demonstrate that human reason was unable to inquire into matters of belief.[29] It is likely that for the same reason Green regarded the philosophical structure outlined in the *Critique of Pure Reason* more as a reference point than as a model. In one of his undergraduate essays (they were composed between 1855 and 1859), 'On the Origin of Ideas', Green stated that the a priori conditions were made by mind: mind was the only element which could be considered as innate.[30]

'On the Origin of Ideas' is an essay which can be easily compared with the first section, first part, first book of David Hume's *Treatise On Human Nature* entitled 'Of the Origin of

[26] See J.F.H. New, *Anglicans and Puritans: The Basis of Their Opposition, 1558–1640* (Stanford, 1964).

[27] 'Four Lectures on the English Revolution', *Works*, III, p. 287.

[28] Hinchliff, *Benjamin Jowett and the Christian Religion*, pp. 52–4.

[29] J.S. Mill reacted in the same way: *A System of Logic: Ratiocinative and Inductive*, ed. J.M. Robson, Introduction by R.F. McRae (Toronto, 1978), pp. 59–60; see also Mill, *An Examination of Sir William Hamilton's Philosophy*, ed. J.M. Robson, Introduction by A. Ryan (Toronto, 1979).

[30] 'On the Origin of Ideas', *Works*, V, p. 48.

our Ideas'. [31] Like Hume, Green acknowledged an essential role for memory in the transmission of ideas and, again like Hume, Green argued that notions like space and time were indivisible.[32] For Hume, it was impossible "to conceive either a vacuum and extension without matter, or a time, when there was no succession or change in any real existence."[33] In a similar way, for Green, the notions of space and time were not innate but implied "in our earliest conceptions."[34] At the same time, by reversing Hume's position, Green drew the conclusion that mind existed apart from sensations. Green thought that ideas could be regarded as a result of experience only so far as mind was "unconscious of itself."[35] Fichte's influence revealed itself. His biographer stated that when Green was still a student at Oxford, he probably managed to read some of Fichte's writings translated from German into English.[36] Though Fichte argued that reason was independent of sensations, he maintained it was impossible to conceive the existence of a self apart from the empirical world. Like Fichte, Green was inclined to see historical progress as the progress of a reason whose starting point was to be identified with unconsciousness. Fichte showed how human reason embodied itself in the primeval stages of life. "It is not indeed true", Fichte observed,

> that the *pure Ego* is a product of the *Non-Ego* — (so I denominate everything which is conceived of as existing external to the *Ego*, distinguished from, and opposed to it:) — it is not true, I say, that the *pure Ego* is a product of the *Non-Ego*; — such a doctrine would indicate a transcendental materialism which is entirely opposed to reason; — but it is certainly true, and will be fully proved in its

---

[31] D. Hume, 'A Treatise of Human Nature' in *The Philosophical Works of David Hume*, ed. Green and Grose, I, pp. 311–6.
[32] 'Treatise', I, pp. 317–9 and 385–8; 'On the Origin of Ideas', V, p. 46.
[33] 'Treatise', I, p. 346.
[34] 'On the Origin of Ideas', V, p. 46.
[35] *Ibid.*, V, p. 48.
[36] "The writers from whom he seems at this time to have assimilated the most were Wordsworth, Carlyle, Maurice, and probably Fichte in his lectures on the 'nature' and 'vocation' of 'the scholar' and of 'man'": Nettleship, *Memoir*, p. xxv. See *The Popular Works of J.G. Fichte translated from the German (the Vocation of the Scholar – The Nature of the Scholar – The Vocation of Man – Characteristics of the Present Age – the Way towards the Blessed Life – Outlines of the Doctrine of Knowledge)*, with a memoir of the author by W. Smith (London, 1848–9); see also Fichte, *The Vocation of the Scholar*, trans. from the German by W. Smith (London, 1847).

proper place, that the *Ego* is not, and can never become, conscious of itself, except under its empirical determinations.[37]

But Green did not delve deeply into Fichte's teaching. As again his biographer reported, Green read more of Fichte in his later years.[38]

However, in his 'On the Origin of Ideas' Green clearly expressed his intention of tempering idealism with empiricism. The young Green already aimed to find a way out of the fruitless antithesis between a scepticism that resulted from empiricism and the abstractness of German idealism, and particularly of Hegel. Both scepticism and abstractness could have jeopardized the future of English democracy. Just because of his tendency to move from facts, Green underlined the importance of public opinion which, because it could amend itself, should not be ignored: "often in public opinion itself we may find the refutation of its own more objectionable parts, and the means of raising it to an higher level."[39] In the same way, the utilitarian notion of happiness should not be disparaged. It should not be rejected, rather it should be tempered and improved.[40] In another of his undergraduate essays Green maintained that there was no incompatibility between the categorical imperative and the utilitarian law of pleasure maximization, provided that these notions were not regarded as absolute.[41] From this viewpoint, institutions were unavoidably a product of mediation: they had to be the best not in an absolute way but according to circumstances and situations. His aim of preserving society made Green inclined to compromise. Society was composed of a multiplicity of contrasting elements and each one sought its particular good. The equilibrium of the whole could be preserved on condition that each part renounced any dogmatic claim to its rights: "So long as most men are selfish, universal rapine can only be avoided by the institution of property, and from this institution many apparent immoralities of necessity follow."[42] Consequently, all legislation resulted from choosing the lesser evil.

---

[37]   Fichte, *The Vocation of the Scholar*, pp. 18–19.
[38]   Nettleship, *Memoir*, p. cxxv.
[39]   'On Authority and Private Judgment, or Reason and Faith' in *Works*, V, p. 39.
[40]   *Ibid.*
[41]   'Utility as a Principle in Art and Morality' in *Works*, V, p. 52.
[42]   *Ibid.*, V, p. 53.

> 'Expedient', according to its etymology, implies a way out of diffi-culties, and in politics it is not too much to say that 'whatever is expedient is right'. 'Acting on principle' is the universal pretence of those politicians who oppose all accommodations necessary to meet the actual state of affairs.[43]

Hume had already emphasised how annoying it was to argue with people who insisted on preserving their principles intact: "Disputes with men, pertinaciously obstinate in their principles, are, of all others, the most irksome."[44] Hume was aware of the important role language played with reference to common sense and how it made common sense concrete.[45] In his view, one had to admit that "all political questions are infi-nitely complicated."[46] That is why politicians were not able to make any kind of decision which could be "either purely good, or purely ill."[47] Hume observed that, though justice was neces-sary, "some extraordinary circumstances may happen, in which a man finds his interests to be more promoted by fraud and rapine, than hurt by the breach which his injustice makes in the social union."[48] Hume noted that "in all governments, there is a perpetual intestine struggle, open or secret, between AUTHORITY and LIBERTY; and neither of them can ever absolutely prevail in the contest."[49] Moreover, Hume high-lighted how government could offer that "sense of the general advantage", which was relevant for Green too.[50] The original-ity of Green's philosophy, marked from the beginning by the search for a via media between idealism and empiricism, does not favour one-sided interpretations. In one of his undergrad-uate essays, Green wrote that

> Indeed, simply with a view to intellectual excellence, fiction should never in education be separated from fact, for at best it can give but one aspect of truth and human life at a time, and a man

---

[43] *Ibid.*
[44] 'An Enquiry Concerning the Principles of Morals' in *The Philosophical Works of David Hume*, IV, p. 169.
[45] "As every tongue possesses one set of words which are taken in a good sense, and another in the opposite, the least acquaintance with the idiom suffices, without any reasoning, to direct us in collecting and arranging the estimable or blameable qualities of men", *ibid.*, IV, p. 173.
[46] 'Of the Protestant Succession' in *The Philosophical Works of David Hume,* III, p. 475.
[47] *Ibid.*
[48] Hume, 'Of the Origin of Government' in *ibid.*, III, p. 114.
[49] *Ibid.*, III, p. 116.
[50] Hume, 'Of the First Principles of Government' in *ibid.*, III, p. 110.

ought to have a wide knowledge of facts to qualify his several ideas, and exhibit them in their general bearings. Nor without this can he have that impression of the complexity of life, which tends especially at once to exalt and humble the mind. In short, as in nature "the ideal everywhere underlies the actual", so in education a knowledge of facts should be built upon a training of fiction, that there may neither be high motives without the power of putting them to practical use, nor skill in the business of life without high ideas to ennoble and purify it.[51]

When Green wrote his undergraduate essays, English and particularly Scottish philosophy had been examining Kant for a long time. Kant's most important works had been translated into English: for instance *Essays and Treatises on Moral, Political, and Various Philosophical Subjects* (London, 1798–99), *The Metaphysics of Morals, divided in Metaphysical Elements of Law and of Ethics* (London, 1799), *Prolegomena to Every Future Metaphysics, which can Appear as a Science* (London, 1819), *Metaphysical Works of Emmanuel Kant* (London, 1836), *The Metaphysics of Ethics* (Edinburgh, 1836), *Religion within the Boundary of Pure Reason* (Edinburgh, 1838), and *Critique of Pure Reason* (London, 1838). Furthermore, since in this period Green was not yet able to read German, he probably did not know much of Hegel. In 1855 only a fragment of *The Subjective Logic of Hegel* and a summary of *The Philosophy of Rights* had been published. In 1857 Sibree translated into English Hegel's *Lectures on the Philosophy of History*. In 1856 the Italian A. Vera had published *An Inquiry into Speculative and Experimental Science*. It was another nine years until the famous *The Secret of Hegel* (1865) by J.H. Stirling was published. These facts confirm that Green's position cannot be reduced to an uncritical importation of the philosophy of Hegel. Of the so-called idealist school, R. G. Collingwood observed:

> The philosophical tendencies common to this school were described by its contemporary opponents as Hegelianism. The title was repudiated by the school itself, and rightly. Their philosophy, so far as they had one single philosophy, was a continuation and criticism of the indigenous English and Scottish philosophies of the middle nineteenth century. It is true that, unlike most of their compatriots, they had some knowledge of Hegel and a good deal more of Kant. The fact of their having this knowledge was used by their opponents, more through igno-

---

[51] Green, 'The Comparative Value of Fact and Fiction in Education' (see Appendix).

rance than through deliberate dishonesty, to discredit them in the eyes of a public always contemptuous of foreigners. Green had read Hegel in youth, but rejected him in middle age; the philosophy he was working out when his early death interrupted him is best described, if a brief description is needed, as a reply to Herbert Spencer by a profound student of Hume.[52]

It has to be ascertained how Green managed to reconcile idealism and empiricism. His attempt seemed to be much more absurd due to the fact that utilitarianism, the philosophical current destined to run counter to idealism, sprang from empiricism. It must be remembered that the forming of Green's mind was influenced not only by many personalities, among them J.S. Mill, Carlyle and Mazzini, but also by his peculiar religious background, which favoured the attuning of different and sometimes contrasting viewpoints.[53] As Green's biographer reported, a friend recorded at the time that

> almost all his definite opinions might be endorsed by Bright or Cobden, but neither Bright nor Cobden could understand the process by which Green's opinions are obtained, nor the arguments by which they are defended. An idealist in philosophy, he argues for the most utilitarian of political schools on idealist principles.[54]

At Balliol Green was soon identified with a small group of students who, though not very popular, animated the intellectual life of the College.[55] Then, as in the following years, Green's position was not altogether clear. Green must be regarded as an atypical radical philosopher. He fought against any measures which would make working class conditions worse, as well as for a peace which would allow the most vulnerable sections of society to improve their life.[56] But if Green's deep relationship with Puritanism is left out out of consideration, one can say only that his viewpoint was entirely outside the con-

---

[52] Collingwood, *An Autobiography*, pp. 15–6.
[53] "The fate of Utilitarianism", Lindsay observed, "they would have said, shows how entirely insufficient, because how shallow, is a theory of democracy which seeks to-day to minimise the importance of religion ... And so these liberals went for their philosophical inspiration to some very undemocratic sources, to Plato and to Hegel, as well as to Kant and the seventeenth-century Puritans; but their purpose in so doing was to carry out better and more thoroughly what the Utilitarians had begun": 'Introduction' to *Lectures on the Principles of Political Obligation*, pp. viii–ix.
[54] Nettleship, *Memoir*, p. xx.
[55] Richter, *The Politics of Conscience*, p. 79.
[56] Nettleship, *Memoir*, p. xxi.

text which fed the main reforming currents in nineteenth century England.

3. The Primacy of the Spirit

The influence of Puritan theology becomes plain only through considering how Green referred in an undergraduate essay to Milton and H. T. Buckle.[57] Green compared the doctrines of his own age with those of the Puritan revolution. The essay in question is 'Political Idealism', written in 1858. Here Green noticed how in Victorian England the most important doctrines were prone to regard human society as a sort of machine and how these doctrines, by discouraging individual effort, tended to keep honest people away from politics. Moreover, Green showed the benefits that would have resulted from a wider circulation of ideals which allowed individuals to be more sensitive to duties towards the political community.[58] The young Green seemed to have already assimilated the Puritan anti-formalist teaching. For the Puritan politician and theologian Henry Vane, human socialization stemmed from a divine law which had been infused in the heart of men on creation.[59] In another of his undergraduate essays, Green emphasised that the tendency to form societies revealed how men were intimately conscious that their minds were pervaded with a feeling of life and that this feeling originated from a superior being.[60] By taking up one typical theological expression, Green affirmed that humanity never agreed to confine "the range of the mind within the limits of the fleshly tabernacle" and that, following this inclination, it discovered

[57]   Henry Thomas Buckle (1821–1862) published a *History of Civilization in England*, 2 vols (London, 1857–1861), which was destined to be regarded as a very interesting work both in England and the rest of Europe. Buckle's viewpoint was challanged by Mill in his *System of Logic*, II, pp. 931–6.

[58]   Nettleship, *Memoir*, pp. xxi–ii.

[59]   See G. Sikes, *The Life and Death of Sir Henry Vane* (London, 1662); J. Forster, *Sir Henry Vane the Younger* in J. Forster, *Eminent British Statesmen*, Vol. IV (London, 1838); J.K. Hosmer, *The Life of Young Sir Henry Vane* (London, 1888); F.J.C. Hearnshaw, *The Life of Sir Henry Vane the Younger, Puritan Idealist* (London, 1910). See also M.A. Judson, *The Political Thought of Sir Henry Vane the Younger* (Philadelphia, 1969).

[60]   'Loyalty' in *Works*, V, p. 12. This essay had already been published by P. Harris and J. Morrow in 1986: see T.H. Green, *Lectures on the Principles of Political Obligation and Other Writings*, ed. P. Harris and J. Morrow (Cambridge, 1986), pp. 304–6.

"loyalty", supported by the conviction that the common rational nature of men boasted a divine seal.[61]

For Green, the opposing parties of the Puritan revolution could be classified by resorting to just this principle. At the time of Charles I there were, on the one side, the aristocracy and those who favoured a literal interpretation of the law, on the other, the "loyal men" who fought for a universal law.[62] The "loyal man", more inclined to interpret the law according to its spirit, was disposed to obey only laws which allowed every individual to use his reason. He did not, on the contrary, feel bound by a king or a church which claimed a blind obedience. English law and religion stemmed from the efforts of the "loyal man" and the rational or inner spirit which characterized English institutions changed only with circumstances. As Vane observed, obedience should not be unconditional.[63] In the same way, Green maintained that

> we should indeed be loyal to the king, but only as the symbol of law — and to the Church, but only as the symbol of spiritual government. If the symbol ceases to be such, our loyalty towards it is at an end.[64]

It was violence which made laws break with the divine spirit inspiring them, and if the "loyal man" was instinctively adverse to any kind of despotism, at the same time he was against any kind of selfishness to the detriment of the common good: "the loyal man is bound to his fellow-citizens in the unity of a common object, which gives to the private pursuits of his daily life their value and spiritual meaning."[65] In another of his undergraduate essays Green stated that it was because of selfishness that nations were destined to decline. Disunion and mutual suspicion among private men, and corruption among officials, followed from the habit of putting ourselves first; "and when men have come to regard their own interests

---

[61] 'Loyalty', V, p. 12. Parnham argued that, for Vane, the dialectic between faith and reason was like that between flesh and spirit: see D. Parnham, *Sir Henry Vane, Theologian: A Study in Seventeenth-Century Religious and Political Discourse* (Denver, 1997), p. 21.

[62] 'Loyalty', V, p. 14.

[63] See Parnham, *Sir Henry Vane*, pp. 38–9.

[64] 'Loyalty', V, p. 14.

[65] *Ibid.*

as everything, and those of the state as nothing, the state practically ceases to exist and is the prey of the first-comer."[66]

4. Faith in Progress

Green's faith in progress was strengthened by a long series of events. The 1832 Reform Act added to the representation of land owners that of the middle class which traditionally nourished religious dissent. Green compared the parliament which resulted from the election that followed the 1832 Reform Act with that purged by Colonel Pride in December 1648.[67] By making the abolition of any kind of religious discrimination inevitable, the Reform Act encouraged a wider religious toleration. The Act was itself a product of a hard fought dispute for recognizing more religious liberty. In 1828 the Whigs promoted the abolition of the Test Act and Corporation Act and, in 1829, the emancipation of Roman Catholics. Such discriminations originated from seventeenth century religious dissensions: the Test Act and Corporation Act against Puritans were approved, respectively, in 1661 and 1673; the Parliamentary Test Act against Catholics was passed in 1678.[68] In 1831 an Anglican exponent stated: "I refer our calamities to the repeal of the Test Act; for then the State *virtually* renounced any connection with religion."[69] In the meanwhile members of the Broad Church Party, believing there was a core of truths which were separate from dogmas and therefore were shared by different churches, sought to create a religion able to unite society and consequently the state.[70]

In education too the advent of a more extensive suffrage seemed to revive passions which had been quiescent since the time of the Puritan revolution. In nineteenth century England the argument concerned the Dissenting British and Foreign School Society and the Anglican Church. In such a context, the reform approved by Russell in 1839 was opposed because he

---

[66] ' "Quondam etiam victis redit in praecordia virtus". What is the truth of this, as viewed in the light of history?' (see Appendix).

[67] 'Four Lectures on the English Revolution', III, p. 338.

[68] G.I.T. Machin, *Politics and the Churches in Great Britain, 1832–1868* (Oxford, 1977), pp. 20–1.

[69] W.F. Hook, letter to A.P. Perceval, 25 May 1831, in Machin, *Politics and the Churches in Great Britain, 1832–1868*, pp. 21–2.

[70] On the reaction of the High Church Party's members and Tractarianism, see J.R. Moore, ed., *Religion in Victorian England* (Manchester, 1991), pp. 4–12.

aimed to create a national inspectorate charged with the task of opening and managing schools which would serve as models of religious toleration. State funding would be allowed only to these schools, and to those which chose to impart a religious teaching which was neither confessional nor dogmatic. In February 1844 Peel supported an increase of grants to the Irish catholic college of Maynooth. Despite the dissent of the Protestant Association, the law was passed in March 1845.[71] Two years later, Russell wanted to promote better qualifications of school teachers. At the same time, he confirmed that only schools which imparted a religious teaching that could be shared by all confessions, could benefit from state grants. Russell's proposal was approved in 1847.[72] In 1854 Russell and Gladstone managed to allow religious dissenters to enter Oxford University. The Oxford University Reform Act permitted dissenters to obtain bachelors degrees.[73]

Probably influenced by these events Green believed that progress stemmed from the widening of social ties. Green expressed his viewpoint in some of his undergraduate essays, particularly 'The Principle of Honour; its History and Value in Ancient and Modern Times' and 'The Effect of Commerce on the Mind of a Nation'. For Green, honour helped to make the feeling of loyalty in every vassal stronger towards his own Lord and it was mainly honour which humanized life for all, "for instead of every man's hand being against his neighbour, it was turned against some distant baron."[74] But in the Elizabethan age, men became more and more aware of the value of justice and regarded it as incompatible with honour. Significantly, Green underlined that this conflict coincided with the Puritan revolution: "at home, in the time of the rebellion, we find the cause of justice ranged in actual opposition to the cause of chivalry, and since then the former seems to have been steadily advancing while the latter retreats."[75] Commerce too played a very important role. Its effects could not be distinguished from those of Christianity. Both testified to the existence of an inclination "to regard men as originally and

---

[71] Machin, *Politics and the Churches in Great Britain, 1832–1868*, p. 170.
[72] *Ibid.*, pp. 184–5.
[73] *Ibid.*, pp. 267–9.
[74] 'The Principle of Honour; its History and Value in Ancient and Modern Times' in *Works*, V, p. 7.
[75] *Ibid.*, V, p. 8.

practically equal."[76] Commerce, which broke down all notions of chivalry and feudal allegiance, favoured the progress of humanity. For Green, commerce not only encouraged every kind of material improvement, but was "an indispensable condition of any national cultivation of the intellect."[77] The young Green maintained that those who defended Church properties were very like those who opposed free-trade: they supported that "conservative party" which came into existence after the Reform Bill.[78] It was a party which showed a strong interest in maintaining its monopoly in religion as in trade. "Happily", Green observed, "there was sufficient theoretical knowledge on the matter to prevent the contest becoming one of simple force, and, as is always the case with conservatism, the doctrine which it so long opposed, has become one of its own recognized principles."[79] Green knew that the most important reform of the first half of the nineteenth century had been achieved by Peel in May 1846. The Anti-Corn Law League persuaded public opinion of the innumerable benefits which would result from free-trade: greater prosperity for industry, cheaper bread, less unemployment, and a more efficient and competitive agriculture; a new era of peace and prosperity would begin, as international trade expanded once it ceased to be endangered by mutual suspicion and distrust. By popularising free-trade, the Anti-Corn Law League revealed that aristocracy could be criticised, not only from a political and economical viewpoint, but also ethically.[80] The progress of western nations, for Green, was "a fact."[81] Progress, according to Green, resulted from the continuous widening of social ties, and this was halted only by war. In war men went back to the principle of honour, for from its nature war "can never admit

---

[76] 'The Effect of Commerce on the Mind of a Nation' in *Works*, V, p. 3. This writing had already been published: see Green, *Lectures on the Principles of Political Obligation and Other Writings*, ed. P. Harris and J. Morrow (Cambridge, 1986), pp. 302–4.

[77] *Ibid.*, V, p. 4.

[78] 'Conservatism' in *Works*, V, p. 30.

[79] *Ibid.*

[80] See, for instance, G. Kitson Clark, *The Making of Victorian England* (London, 1962), pp. 41–2; N. Gash, *Reaction and Reconstruction in English Politics, 1832–1852* (Oxford, 1965), pp. 48–54.

[81] 'Conservatism', V, p. 29.

of any higher code."[82] War was "inconsistent with the moral law, and only to be justified as a necessity arising from our depraved nature."[83] Those who one-sidedly undermined the mutual trust from which social stability sprang had to be considered responsible for war. For that reason, Green argued that in a war fraud and falsehood, if necessary to its success, would be justifiable only according to the justness of the cause for which the war was undertaken.[84]

5. International Politics

The memory of 1848's events probably lodged in Green's mind. In March 1854 the Crimean War broke out. Napoleon III undertook the defence of Catholics, while Nicolas I of Russia patronized the Orthodox Christians subjected to the sovereignty of the Ottoman Empire. The Russians refused to budge from their standpoint and this encouraged the English to intervene. The peace party, inspired by Cobden and Bright, was in a minority, and also Gladstone, who certainly was not inclined to an aggressive foreign policy, recognized that war might be necessary to guarantee respect for international law. It is likely that Green decided to support intervention for reasons similar to those formulated by Gladstone.[85] For Green, interference with another nation could be justified only to prevent that nation from itself interfering with other nations. Russia violated the integrity of both Hungary and the principality of Wallachia. The young Green emphasised that it was legitimate

---

[82] 'The Principle of Honour; its History and Value in Ancient and Modern Times', V, p. 8.

[83] 'Veracity' in *Works*, V, p. 10.

[84] *Ibid.*

[85] It is likely that initially Green agreed with Cobden and Bright: see R. Bellamy, 'T.H. Green and the Morality of Victorian Liberalism' in Bellamy, ed., *Victorian Liberalism: Nineteenth-Century Political Thought and Practice* (London and New York, 1990), p. 146. Harvie, who quotes A.V. Dicey (from Knight, *Memoir of John Nichol*, p. 140), thought there was dissension between Green, who was against the Crimean War, and Dicey and Nichol, who both favoured the intervention: C. Harvie, *The Lights of Liberalism: University Liberals and the Challenge of Democracy, 1860–86* (London, 1976), p. 102. That is why it is possible to presume that Green became a member of 'Old Mortality' only in 1858 because, before, he dissented from Nichol, leader of the Society, and that Green wrote his essay, 'Can Interference with Foreign Nations in any Case be Justifiable?' when he had come to agree with Nichol.

to make this violation a "'casus belli'."[86] He argued that England had to intervene because of the danger this violation might cause.

National integrity was one of the main principles of European international law and from its violation originated every kind of conflict among nations. A dynasty might reduce a group of nations to the same level of a mass of subjects. It might extend its conquests or be forced to do that in order to preserve its power. It was also possible that one of the nations subjected to this dynasty might persuade some other power to intervene, because of the common language, religion or some other kind of tie. Green believed that Russia, which had already annihilated the nations of Poland and Finland, was going to annex Turkey as well. Turkey was weak because it dominated not a nation, but a jig-saw of peoples some of which were Orthodox Christians like the Russians.[87] Consistently with the teaching of Mazzini, Green believed that peace could only spring from the fact that every state was able to become a nation.[88] The Habsburgs were for neutrality and Cavour, aiming to secure Italian independence, formed an alliance with England and France against Russia. For the English, the war was a complete disaster: the government had to resign and Palmerston replaced Aberdeen. At the Congress of Paris (February and March 1856) Napoleon III triumphed. France emerged as the hegemonic power in Europe and Cavour realized that France would have agreed to make Austria less powerful. Passing in silence over the action of the Italian Prime Minister, Green observed only that Lombardy, which was very like France from a cultural and economic viewpoint, was the Achilles heel of Austria.[89]

Meanwhile, Palmerston strengthened his position: the election confirmed the defeat of Bright and Cobden and of Peel' s followers. In January 1858 Orsini made an attempt on Napoleon III's life. As it turned out that this attempt had been prepared in England, the French seized the opportunity to denounce the unreliability of English security measures.

---

[86] 'Can Interference with Foreign Nations in any Case be Justifiable?' in *Works*, V, p. 19.
[87] *Ibid.*, V, p. 17.
[88] See Bellamy, 'T.H. Green and the Morality of Victorian Liberalism', p. 139; Harvie, *The Lights of Liberalism*, p. 104.
[89] 'Can Interference with Foreign Nations in any Case be Justifiable?', V, p. 17.

Palmerston did not reply but proposed legislation which aimed to keep better watch on refugees. This revived popular indignation, allowing those who showed their solidarity with European patriots to prevail against the Prime Minister. Green expressed his antipathy towards Louis Napoleon by labelling him a "successful brigand."[90] Palmerston's defeat gave Green great satisfaction. The possibility that the law against conspiracy might be passed had almost made him lose his appetite. Green thought that the approval of this law would have prevented Belgium, Geneva and Sardinia from emancipating themselves.[91] In 1865, Green was relieved when Palmerston died, "being persuaded that he did about as much harm as it is possible for an individual Englishman to do nowadays."[92]

Since 1858, the year during which the temporary Palmerstonian debacle took place, Green had been a member of the Old Mortality Society, a student association of republican inspiration. No aristocrat was a member of the Old Mortality Society and its founder was John Nichol, a Scottish student who apart from personally knowing J. S. Mill and Carlyle, was a close friend of Kossuth and Mazzini. From a political viewpoint, Green was the most sensitive member of the Old Mortality. In 1858, the bulletin of the Old Mortality, "Undergraduate Papers", announced Green's speech at the Oxford Union. Green intended to contest the law against refugees. Green visited London to participate in meetings called by radicals, and he organized a trip to Birmingham with the sole aim of hearing Bright.[93] Green's precocity in showing his solidarity with disadvantaged classes shocked Dicey. Green was convinced of the necessity of making the moral and material welfare of these classes the main object of politics.[94] In one of his essays, 'National Life', composed for the Old Mortality Society in 1858, Green asserted: "Let the flag of England be dragged through the dirt rather than sixpence be added to the taxes which weigh on the poor."[95] Green's radicalism made itself more evident when at the Oxford Union he supported a motion in favour of Bright. The Union, launching pad for

[90] Nettleship, *Memoir*, p. xxiii.
[91] *Ibid*.
[92] *Ibid*., pp. xxiii–iv.
[93] Richter, *The Politics of Conscience*, p. 94.
[94] Dicey, Letter to Mrs. Green, 17 September 1882, in I. Biography, b) Recollections of T.H. Green, Green Papers.
[95] Nettleship, *Memoir*, pp. xx–xxi.

future politicians, many of whom were Conservative, rejected Green's motion. Green's comment was: "I am almost ashamed to belong to a university which is in such a state of darkness."[96] In 1858 Green had been particularly impressed by some of Bright's speeches: one about India in the House of Commons on the 24th of June, and those on reforms and foreign policy, given at Birmingham, on the 27th and 29th of October.[97]

At the Old Mortality Society it was possible to breathe an air which was deeply impregnated by Mazzinian suggestions. Bryce intended to join Garibaldi's expedition, though he abandoned the idea.[98] Swinburne hung a portrait of Mazzini in his room and, in Green's presence, used to declaim revolutionary verses in honour of Mazzini and Orsini.[99] Mazzini stayed in London from 1837 to 1848 and, thanks to his strenuous activism, became the most famous political exile in England. Between 1840 and 1845 Mazzini used to spend his time with the Carlyles. In 1840, commenting on the publication of Carlyle's work, *The French Revolution*, Mazzini accused Carlyle of being unable to recognize that Humanity played a more important role than individuals. Though appreciating Carlyle's criticism of utilitarianism, Mazzini did not agree with Carlyle's exaltation of the hero: he regarded that as entirely inconsistent with democracy. Mazzini believed that the democratic movement sprang from a religious inspiration. In the first article of his *Thoughts upon Democracy in Europe*, published on the 29th of August 1846, Mazzini maintained that democracy originated from Christianity.[100]

6. A Judgment on India

If democracy derived from Christianity, from Green's viewpoint, the supremacy of England, which aimed to become a democratic country, should be affirmed because it could bear witness to Christian principles. In one of his undergraduate essays, Green maintained that the mutiny of the army of Bengal, which broke out in May 1857, resulted from the fact that

[96] *Ibid.*, p. xxiv.
[97] See R. Barry O'Brien, *John Bright* (London, 1910), pp. 215–27; G.M. Trevelyan, *The Life of John Bright* (London, 1993), pp. 268–76.
[98] Harvie, *The Lights of Liberalism*, pp. 102–3.
[99] Richter, *The Politics of Conscience*, p. 81.
[100] S. Mastellone, *Mazzini and Marx: Thoughts Upon Democracy in Europe* (London, 2003), pp. 160–1.

British rule in India was lacking in Christian sense. For Green, the right to colonize India derived from the capacity to put Christian principles into practice. According to Green, the British made a big mistake: they allowed only natives belonging to the highest caste to be enlisted in the colonial army. It was this group of privileged people who, appealing to the prerogatives of their own status, stirred up the revolt. But British rule was above all equivocal.

> We have indeed been playing a double game. In our treatment of the Sepoys — first in raising them from the highest caste, and allowing them (as well as the Zemindars) to ill-treat and oppress the people of lower caste, second in cherishing their idolatry — we have governed like heathens, while in abolishing the burning of widows, and allowing converts to inherit property, we have governed like Europeans, and have even sometimes let in a little Christianity by the back door.[101]

Green was persuaded that if the British had carried out more decisively that renovation of Indian society, for which as Christian rulers they were responsible, the natives would have had before their eyes the best proof to them of the truth of Christian principles.[102]

In his undergraduate essays Green was already convinced of the superiority of those societies in which the equality of personal rights revealed itself as "a self-evident proposition."[103] An experiential approach like Hume's seemed to play an important role: custom helped to extend moral principles. "As experience grows, so our notions of what is necessary to a good state of society grow."[104] At the same time, Green argued that his empirical approach was fully compatible with metaphysics. In a very similar way to Hegel, Green observed:

> A Greek limited his notions of society to his own countrymen, and hence thought it right to make slaves of barbarians. We have learnt that all the world is kin, and hence hold ... the equality of personal rights among all men . . . [105]

"The Orientals", Hegel wrote,

---

[101] 'British Rule and Policy in India' in *Works*, V, p. 24.
[102] *Ibid.* See also A.T. Embree, 'Christianity and the state in Victorian India: confrontation and collaboration' in R.W. Davis and R.J. Helmstadter, ed., *Religion and Irreligion in Victorian Society* (London and New York, 1992), p. 152; A. Mayhew, *Christianity and the Government of India* (London, 1929).
[103] 'How far Moral Principles are Probable or Conventional' in *Works*, V, p. 37.
[104] *Ibid.*
[105] *Ibid.*

have not attained the knowledge that spirit — Man *as such* — is free; and because they do not know this, they are not free. They only know that *one is free*. But on this very account, the freedom of that one is only caprice; ferocity — brutal recklessness of passion, or a mildness and tameness of the desires, which is itself only an accident of Nature — mere caprice like the former. — That *one* is therefore only a Despot; not a *free man*. The consciousness of Freedom first arose among the Greeks, and therefore they were free; but they, and the Romans likewise, knew only that *some* are free — not man as such. Even Plato and Aristotle did not know this. The Greeks, therefore, had slaves; and their whole life and the maintenance of their splendid liberty, was implicated with the institution of slavery: a fact moreover, which made that liberty on the one hand only an accidental, transient and limited growth; on the other hand, constituted it a rigorous thraldom of our common nature — of the Human.[106]

Hegel thought that the self-consciousness of liberty, which sprang from religion, the innermost part of human spirit, was destined to confirm the infinite value of the subject.

Despite agreeing with Hegel about the infinite value of the subject, Green did not echo the Hegelian tendency to state in a very abstract way that the inferiority of the Orientals derived from their incapacity to attain the knowledge that spirit is free. Consistently with his aim of tempering idealism with empiricism, Green argued that liberty was embodied in custom and that custom testified to the progress of liberty. Because of this mingling, Green accepted that those societies whose custom was not based on equality of personal rights were inferior. That is why, though he recognized that there had been many injustices, Green stated that progress in India came from "the action of civilization on barbarism."[107] India, which was founded on a caste system and a myriad of religious groups perpetually fighting each other, could be regarded as a nation only with difficulty.[108] Religious toleration and equality of personal rights were to be translated into a more cooperative social order. J.S. Mill — who in a note in *On Liberty* had already considered as idiotic the doctrine that religious toleration

---

[106] G.W.F. Hegel, *The Philosophy of History*, With Prefaces by C. Hegel and the Translator, J. Sibree, and a New Introduction by Professor C. J. Friedrich (New York, 1956), p. 18.

[107] 'British Rule and Policy in India', V, p. 22.

[108] 'Can Interference with Foreign Nations in any Case be justifiable?', V, p. 16.

should be applied only to Christians[109] — identified coopera-
tion as one of the most meaningful signs of the civilization of a
people:

> It is only civilized beings who can combine. All combination is
> compromise: it is the sacrifice of some portion of individual will,
> for a common purpose.[110]

Green agreed with Mill. Progress was always due to compromise and principles must not be regarded as absolute: truth
sprang from a slow process of accumulation deeply rooted in
common sense. According to this view, the inferiority of India,
which was divided into many different sects and castes each
aiming to assert its own principles, stemmed from its incapacity to compromise and cooperate.

---

[109] J.S. Mill, *On Liberty*, in *Essays in Politics and Society by J.S. Mill*, ed. J.M. Robson
(Toronto, Buffalo and London, 1977), pp. 240–1, n.
[110] J.S. Mill, 'Civilization' in *ibid.*, p. 122.

Chapter II

Victorian Puritanism and Green's Conception of Politics

1. Green's Exceptional Individuality

In the nineteenth century a complex and prolonged historiographical argument focused on the Puritan revolution. Tory historians, who were inspired by David Hume's *History of England* (1795-6), were attacked by radical historians prone to emphasize the Puritan past because of its republicanism. Among them one can mention, besides C. Macaulay and J. Millar, William Godwin with his *History of the Commonwealth* (1824-8). Though radical historians regarded the 'Independents' as the champions of religious liberty, they were inclined to blame Cromwell for the failure of the Commonwealth. When later (1830-40) the religious dissenters began to claim their rights, such historians as the Congregationalist Robert Vaughan or the Unitarian John Forster, as well as Thomas Babington Macaulay, issued a series of studies with the sole aim of highlighting how the Puritans shared in the cause of civil and religious liberty. By publishing his biographies on Eliot, Strafford, Pym, Hampden, Vane, Marten and Cromwell, Forster wanted to promote a further extension of suffrage. Despite his admiration for Vane, Forster insisted on judging Cromwell as a tyrant. In 1841 it was Carlyle in his lectures *On Heroes, Hero-Worship and the Heroic in History* who first favoured the rehabilitation of Cromwell.[1] The Puritan revolution was also praised by working-class radicals who applauded Cromwell too. "To earlier republicans, who stood in the Whig and patriot tradition, [Cromwell] had been the vile

---

[1] See Lang, *The Victorians and the Stuart Heritage*, pp. 1-22, 55.

apostate of their cause. Now that republicanism viewed the Crown less as an enemy to parliamentary liberties than as the head of a system of aristocratic oppression, it was able to make common cause with Chartism and socialism."[2]

Green, who probably followed this debate and was aware of its political implications, realized the necessity of reconciling his Puritan background with his democratic bias. By showing that "loyalty" could live only in "higher and more religious minds than are commonly found among men", Green affirmed the importance of a special personal election: that of an exceptional individuality, which, in his view, in the seventeenth century was exemplified both by Cromwell and Vane.[3] In Green's eyes, both shared the same ideals and, though their positions were at variance concerning the future of the Commonwealth, both were destined to fail despite their good intentions. On the contrary, in 1841 Carlyle, underlining how relevant hero-worship could be in Victorian England, clearly elevated Cromwell at the expense of Vane. In order to make Cromwell a hero, Carlyle needed to supplant the Whig heroes of the Puritan revolution.[4] Green probably thought Carlyle created an image of Cromwell to match his own political attitudes. Carlyle maintained that a strong religiously inspired leadership of Cromwell's type would have offset the inadequacies of Parliament and relieved the people's sufferings.[5] Green probably considered that, by holding Parliament in contempt, Carlyle's position would unavoidably flow into dictatorship. For that reason, in 'Loyalty' Green noted that a tendency to prostrate oneself at either a king's and a Pope's feet could easily turn hero-worship into "idol-worship".[6] From the beginning, Green countered the figure of Carlyle's hero with that of his exceptional individual. In another of his undergraduate essays, 'The Influence of Civilisation on Genius', Green clearly intended to distance himself from Carlyle. In his view, Carlyle looked back nostalgically on a

---

[2]   B. Worden, *Roundhead Reputations: The English Civil Wars and the Passions of Posterity* (London, 2001), p. 248.

[3]   'Loyalty', V, p. 13.

[4]   Worden, *Roundhead Reputations*, p. 272.

[5]   See J. Morrow, 'Heroes and Constitutionalists: The Ideological Significance of Thomas Carlyle's Treatment of the English Revolution', *History of Political Thought*, 14 (1993), p. 215.

[6]   'Loyalty', V, p. 13.

community led by heroes.[7] Aware that any idealization of the past might hinder progress, Green did not hesitate to compare the political activism of Milton with the passivity of nineteenth century poets. He drew the conclusion that if the author of the *Paradise Lost* had lived in an age which like Victoria's was deeply impregnated with false literary and philosophical conceptions, he probably would have adopted an attitude very like that of nineteenth century poets.[8] Unlike Carlyle's hero, Green's exceptional individual did not triumph over circumstances.

Significantly, Green agreed with Mazzini. In one of his essays, 'On the Genius and Tendency of Carlyle', written in 1843 during his stay in England, Mazzini saw the main limit of Carlyle's position in his inclination to isolate individuals from the context in which they lived. For Carlyle, who played down collective intellect, "the nationality of Italy in his eyes is the glory of having produced Dante and Christopher Columbus; the nationality of Germany that of having given birth to Luther, to Goethe and to others."[9] Mazzini on the contrary believed that it was impossible to turn history into the biographies of great men: genius could be compared to a flower "which draws one half of its life from the moisture that circulates in the earth, and inhales the other half from the atmosphere."[10] For Mazzini, Carlyle, convinced that only God and heroes ruled the world, was much mistaken in thinking individuals could be entirely independent of any outside influence. Mazzini observed:

---

[7]   Though as Morrow has argued, "although Carlyle won applause for standing up for the Protestant cause, his attitude towards the Puritans perplexed his more liberal-minded contemporaries who found it hard to believe that he was seriously proposing a return to the doctrines adhered to by his seventeenth-century heroes. Carlyle's veneration of the Puritans makes this observation understandable, but there is a sense in which it misses the point. Carlyle was not urging his contemporaries to adopt Puritanism in its seventeenth-century form, and, in more guarded moments he allowed that this doctrine was not a complete guide to human conduct because it lacked the forms in which human thought and conduct had necessarily to be clothed." Morrow, 'Heroes and Constitutionalists: The Ideological Significance of Thomas Carlyle's Treatment of the English Revolution', p. 211.

[8]   'The Influence of Civilisation on Genius', *Works*, III, pp. 18–9.

[9]   G. Mazzini, 'On the Genius and Tendency of the Writings of Thomas Carlyle', *British and Foreign Review*, 1843, reprinted in *Life and Writings of Joseph Mazzini: Vol. IV, Critical and Literary* (London, 1891), p. 77.

[10] *Ibid.*, p. 78.

> Mr. Carlyle comprehends only the *individual*; the true sense of the
> unity of the human race escapes him. He sympathizes with all
> men, but it is with the life of each, and not with their collective
> life.[11]

For Mazzini, genius was a tool of a collective humanity, of that
universal mind which embodied itself in every single ordinary
man.[12] Almost echoing Mazzini's words, Green held that iso-
lation implied the death of genius. Genius, he argued, "goes
hand in hand with sympathy, for it is when we see it manifested in the common affections of men that we most lovingly
and reverently apprehend the divine idea."[13] J.S. Mill too
debated the role of exceptional individuals. In his 'On Genius'
(1832), he made genius coincident with the inclination to avoid
dogmatism. Referring to Jesus, who was regarded as a model
of genius, Mill observed that, later, unfortunately, "the words
of him whose speech was in figures and parables were
iron-bound and petrified into inanimate and inflexible *formu-
lae.*"[14] In *On Liberty* Mill explained that, by praising the role of
the exceptional individual, he did not aim to imitate the des-
potic aptitude of Carlyle, but only to show that genius was able
to point out the right way. In his essay, 'Civilization' (1836),
Mill confirmed the incompatibility between genius and dogmatism.[15]

Mill's and Mazzini's views, unlike Carlyle's, were consistent with the Puritan background of Green. The Unitarian historian John Forster, certainly read by Green,[16] noted that Vane,
embodying the purest ideal of Christian liberty, avoided the
risk of identifying the spiritual life with institutions which
diminished it. As Forster argued, Vane could do that because
he favoured spirit rather than forms. That is why Vane's
behaviour was regarded as extremely controversial, so that it
became a sort of target for everyone.[17] The behaviour of
Green's exceptional individual was not to be analysed merely
on the basis of political principles. The rival parties might

---

[11] *Ibid.*, p. 75.
[12] *Ibid.*, pp. 73–4.
[13] 'The Influence of Civilisation on Genius', III, p. 18.
[14] 'On Genius' in *Autobiography and Literary Essays*, ed. J.M. Robson and
      J. Stillinger (Toronto, Buffalo and London, 1981), p. 337.
[15] 'Civilization' in *Essays on Politics and Society*, p. 144.
[16] 'Four Lectures on the English Revolution', III, p. 297, notes.
[17] J. Forster, *Sir Henry Vane the Younger*, p. 19, quoting Sikes, *Life and Death of Sir
      Henry Vane, Knight.*

encourage his action or reject it, according to expediency and circumstances. This revealed how Green's exceptional individual was realising something that they did not understand, a work which, as Green observed, "has many points of contact with the political and social movements of the day, but which is yet distinct from them both in origin and end."[18] His mysticism made Green's exceptional individual very different from Hegel's hero as well. Green's exceptional individual, unlike Caesar or Alexander the Great, knew he had to fight to free historical progress from its tendency to harden itself in rigid dogmas and institutions.[19] For Green, who was inspired by the Puritan theological vision, the exceptional individual was a man who, bearing witness to the pre-eminence of the *ecclesia invisibilis*, professed himself absolutely independent of every kind of authority, both civilian and religious. The idea of an invisible church contrasted with that of a visible or institutional one was first introduced by Luther, who saw the invisible church as the only one which could legitimately be regarded as divine. The 'Independent' or 'Congregational' ecclesiastical conception not only confirmed that, but stressed the equalitarian character implied in the Lutheran Reformation.

Green's debt to Puritanism made itself obvious in another of his undergraduate essays. He stated that if faith was reduced to trusting submission, it disposed the mind to accept an authority that rejected reason; whereas for him, faith coincided with an evocation of that divine witness which, inhabiting the inner life, revealed itself as "a belief in the unseen."[20] Green knew that this kind of belief had at all times been used by individuals to justify rebellion against the church. Hence not only had the sanction of religion been withdrawn from political regulation, but religious laws themselves, being spiritual, were incapable of being stereotyped and fixed. So long as religious laws preserved their spiritual character, they might be modified by the private judgment of the individual and

---

[18] 'The Force of Circumstances', *Works*, III, p. 10.
[19] "Such individuals [as Caesar or Alexander] had no consciousness of the general Idea they were unfolding, while prosecuting those aims of theirs; on the contrary, they were practical, political men. But at the same time they were thinking men, who had an insight into the requirements of the time – *what was ripe for development*": Hegel, *The Philosophy of History*, p. 30.
[20] 'On Authority and Private Judgment, or Reason and Faith', *Works*, V, p. 40.

never act on him as a purely external authority.[21] "The age of persecution has passed away, but", Green argued, "there are still men who, placing the state above the individual, would prescribe limits to the activities both of genius and religion . . ."[22]

Institutions which denied liberty of conscience became life-less mechanisms, carried along the path of necessity merely by the force of circumstances. Only the spiritual liberty of the few could bring any freedom from the bondage of circumstances. As Green observed:

> Once or twice in a century there arises some great reformer, liter-ary or religious, who seems placed above the earth and born of heaven alone, and who thus exercises an independent influence on the circumstances and destiny of mankind. Such a man can scarcely conform to the ordinary manners of man, or to the 'status quo' of society. Often he exercises rather freely the privileges of Christian liberty.[23]

Green's exceptional individual was the only one who could regenerate the state. For that reason, if the state did not limit its intervention giving legal effect to the moral tone of society, the exceptional individual would unavoidably become "an offender against state-morality."[24]

The state, for Green, was but society gathered into one unit by certain common laws and institutions. It operated through three organs: the civil government, the national church, and custom. Green emphasised the importance of a balanced rela-tionship between them. "None of these powers — neither the government by legislative enactments, nor the church by excommunication, nor society by conventional exclusion — should restrain the freedom of the individual's inner life, or interfere with family authority, nor should any of them tres-pass on the ground properly occupied by the other."[25] In the repression of morality, the civil government should confine itself to the punishment of acts which proved of themselves the guilt of the person who committed them, leaving other offences to the reprobation of society. In the promotion of

---

[21] *Ibid.*
[22] 'Legislative Interference in Moral Matters', *Works*, V, p. 33. This essay was published in Green, *Lectures on the Principles of Political Obligation and Other Essays*, ed. Harris and Morrow, pp. 306–9.
[23] 'Legislative Interference in Moral Matters', V, p. 33.
[24] *Ibid.*
[25] *Ibid.*, V, p. 34.

morality, it should only remove obstacles which hindered the free action of the church or other religious bodies.[26] For Green, the state should not be assimilated to a policeman on a grand scale whose sole aim was "the protection of life and property against force and fraud. No state has ever been found to confine itself to these ends."[27]

The influence of Puritanism was obvious. Green did not doubt that the salvation of society resulted from a faith in the invisible church. Green's exceptional individual was a man who, through his belief in the unseen, could have "insight into that divine idea of which the outer world and the opinion of men are but feeble expressions."[28]

2. The Force of Circumstances:
J.S. Mill and the Victorian Novel

In 'The Force of Circumstances', another of Green's undergraduate essays, he emphasised how the expression "force of circumstances" was unintelligible to a child. Green added that when the man, maturing, became aware that nature was inconsistent with his will and desires, he began to speculate on the relationship between himself and the world.[29] The hiatus between inner life and outer world could be bridged only by a man able, as Aristotle observed, to judge unerringly and act "really, though not apparently, in the same way under all circumstances."[30] Always in search of a mediation between idealism and empiricism, Green explained how such a man could not distinguish good from evil "by the abstract method of general laws (much less by general consequences) but brings to bear on each particular action the critical faculty within him, called 'conscience' and other names, which determines the character of the action according to the attendant circumstances."[31]

When Green expressed his view better, his aim of using idealism to mitigate empiricism, without neglecting the teaching of Hume, made itself more obvious. Nobody could question the existence of conscience, whether it was regarded as a sum

[26] *Ibid.*
[27] *Ibid.*, V, p. 33.
[28] 'The Influence of Civilization on Genius', III, p. 12.
[29] 'The Force of Circumstances', III, p. 4.
[30] 'How far Moral Principles are Probable or Conventional', V, p. 36.
[31] *Ibid.*

of desires and affections, or as a rational principle organizing these desires with reference to the chief good, or as the result of external training and custom. There were two reasons. "First", Green argued, "we have the evidence of consciousness, which we cannot call in question without falling into scepticism even as to our own existence; secondly, we have the evidence written on the whole framework of society and in universal language, which is similar to that on which we believe all external facts."[32] Thus, in Green's conception, the division between inner life and outer world was overcome and the outer became regarded as an integral part of the first. "We are conscious of a law within ourselves, and we see also that without some primary law society could never have been held together, or such words as 'ought' and 'right' have arisen."[33] Custom corroborated the validity of moral principles, even if the individual was prone to ignore them. As an example, Green referred to the principle 'thou shalt not steal': "our assurance of the truth of this is derived", he observed, "partly from our consciousness of benevolence and the like, but mainly from the universal assent of mankind, which proves that it is necessary to society."[34]

For Green, Aristotle's man, who could behave rightly really, though not apparently, in the same way under all circumstances, was a man inspired by a faith in the unseen. By bearing witness to a God who is in the world but not of it, such a man could go beyond facts, conventions and common sense without needing to believe that evil could be definitely defeated by means of a synthesis which would have sanctioned the ethical supremacy of church or state. Green's religious faith was further confirmed by his stating the necessity of a theological point of reference. It was God who offered to man a suitable object.[35] At the same time, Green admitted that towards circumstances "we seem no longer masters but slaves, unable to free ourselves from the chains of cause and effect with which the sins of our fathers and our own past actions bind our present life."[36]

---

[32] *Ibid.*, V, p. 37.
[33] *Ibid.*
[34] *Ibid.*
[35] 'The Force of Circumstances', III, p. 5.
[36] *Ibid.*

Green's position had a significant antecedent in Fichte's. Fichte had already noticed that conscience, developing itself from an instinctive stage to a conscious one, testified to the ripening of rights and duties. Fichte also admitted the existence of a law of cause and effect: he thought man was part of a chain of phenomena in which every link resulted from the previous. "I enter", he argued, "within an unbroken chain of phenomena, in which every link is determined by that which has preceded it, and in its turn determines the next."[37] Fichte maintained that passivity implied a principle of activity and identified this principle with an inclination to promote good instead of evil. This tendency gave place to a society based on fairness and equality: "the impulse", as Fichte observed, "leads to *reciprocal* activity, to *mutual* influence, *mutual* giving and receiving, *mutual* suffering and doing, — not to mere causality — not to mere activity, of which others are only the passive objects."[38] But, unlike Green, Fichte did not need any theological support. He moved from a conviction that man's conscience was animated by an uncontrollable impulse of liberty.

Even if Green's view can be regarded as at least to a certain extent like Fichte's, his criticism was probably intended mainly to amend J. S. Mill's philosophy as presented in the second chapter of the sixth book of his *System of Logic*, 'Of Liberty and Necessity'. Published in 1843, 'Of Liberty and Necessity' was the culmination of Mill's attempt to emancipate himself from those deterministic doctrines which he inherited from Hume, who had given the title 'Of Liberty and Necessity' to the first section, third part, of the second book of his *Treatise On Human Nature*. In his turn, Hume revisited an argument which stemmed from seventeenth century thinkers of the type of Hobbes, who by reducing liberty to a merely rationalist and mechanistic question, thoroughly discredited theology. Almost two hundred years before Mill, Hobbes wrote his *Of Liberty and Necessity* (1646), first published in 1654.

Mill's aspiration to reform his father's and Bentham's determinism, which sprang from his psychological and spiritual crisis of Autumn 1826, induced him to look for a compromise between those theories that sanctioned the absolute necessity of human behaviour and those which, by contrast, praised lib-

---

[37] *The Vocation of Man*, p. 7.
[38] *The Vocation of the Scholar*, trans. by W. Smith (London, 1847), p. 33.

erty independently of conditions and circumstances. Mill rejected any position which, like Robert Owen's, denied individual responsibility, and he disagreed with Carlyle's exaltation of the hero who can set circumstances aside. For Mill, Owen's misunderstanding came from his conviction that man's character was "formed *for* him, and not *by* him."[39] In confutation of Owen, Mill stated:

> this is a grand error. He has, to a certain extent, a power to alter his character. Its being, in the ultimate resort, formed for him, is not inconsistent with its being, in part, formed *by* him as one of the intermediate agents. His character is formed by his circumstances (including among these his particular organization); but his own desire to mould it in a particular way, is one of those circumstances, and by no means one of the least influential.[40]

Likewise, Green accepted that the relationship between cause and effect could be extended to human phenomena. At the same time, unlike Mill, he thought that it was urgent to reintroduce that theological support which was already out of consideration for Hobbes. With the aim of finding a firmer justification for human liberty than the desire to form one's own character, Green wanted to show how, by resorting to the chain of cause and effect, humanity could be linked to heaven instead of earth. The force of circumstances could not be escaped. But it could be turned into a force of good instead of evil.[41] A certain combination of circumstances produced a given effect on a mind, but it did not imply a negation of liberty. One could resist circumstances, instead of being subjected by them.

> The same craving of sensual appetite will move one man to a surrender of the mind to the body, another to humility and self-abasement. The effect in both cases might be known beforehand, if we knew the secret state of the two minds.[42]

In the same way, Mill had argued: "if we knew the person thoroughly, and knew all the inducements which are acting upon him, we could foretell his conduct with as much certainty as we can predict any physical event."[43]

---

[39] 'Of Liberty and Necessity' in Mill, *A System of Logic*, II, p. 840.
[40] *Ibid.*
[41] 'The Force of Circumstances', III, pp. 6–7.
[42] *Ibid.*, III, p. 6.
[43] 'Of Liberty and Necessity', p. 837.

Mill, eager to prove that there was no incompatibility between the existence of general laws and the role played by exceptional individuals,[44] noted that in his *History of Civilization of England* Henry Thomas Buckle intended "no more than to affirm emphatically that the greatest men cannot effect great changes in human affairs unless the general mind has been in some considerable degree prepared for them."[45] Mill did not share the view of those who, maintaining that social progress stemmed from invariable laws, claimed that it could not be influenced by the exertions of the individual person. "Though", Mill argued, "the varieties of character among ordinary individuals neutralize one another on any large scale, exceptional individuals in important positions do not in any given age neutralize one another."[46] Mill seemed to think that an individual, even in yielding to temptations, knew that he could have resisted. By affirming that "none but a person of confirmed virtue is completely free", Mill anticipated Green's intuition about the role of the so-called "good man."[47] It is clear how Green, though he disagreed with Mill on his tendency to think of the progress of history apart from God, would have felt inclined to accept his philosophical and political inheritance.

The impact of the force of circumstances on human character is undeniably one of the main themes of the Victorian Age. If nineteenth century England, being marked by an continual instability and search for new balances, showed the existence of enormous possibilities, at the same time it revealed how the ripening of these possibilities and of character itself could be

---

[44] As Mark Francis and John Morrow argue, "Mill's concern here was to combat one of the features of Whig historiography. In particular, he objected to Macaulay's opinion that great men were absolutely inoperative in history". *A History of Political Thought in the Nineteenth Century* (London, 1994), p. 145.

[45] Mill, 'Additional Elucidations of the Science of History,' Ch. XI, Bk VI, of *A System of Logic*, p. 936. An historian inclined to emphasise the role of exceptional individuals was George Grote (1794–1871). Green probably read his *History of Greece* (1846–56) in twelve volumes and his later *Plato and Other Companions of Sokrates* published in 1865 in three volumes. Mill, who regarded Grote as an intimate friend, cited him for supporting his thesis in his *System of Logic* (*ibid.*, p. 942). Thomas Babington Macaulay, another historian whose works Green certainly knew, was also cited by Mill. Mill thought Macaulay was wrong in minimising the importance of exceptional individuals (*ibid.*, p. 937).

[46] *A System of Logic*, p. 937.

[47] 'Of Liberty and Necessity', *ibid.* p. 841; 'The Force of Circumstances', III, p. 6.

influenced by circumstances.[48] Significantly, one of Green's first undergraduate essays dealt with William Makepeace Thackeray; and in 1862, Green was awarded the Chancellor's Prize right for an essay on the novel.[49] Green believed that, though the novel sprang from the mingling of an external element due to case and circumstances and an internal one made of character and passion, it undoubtedly showed the prevalence of the first.[50] Green was attracted by those novelists who, like Thackeray, were able to show how humanity was subjected to circumstances: Thackeray "fixes our thoughts on the fleeting incidents of social life which he describes, but it is because they are life-like, not because they are 'thrilling'; he brings out even his unimportant characters in the most distinct individuality, but it is their manners, not their minds that he paints."[51] In Victorian England it was impossible to dissociate character from circumstances. With regard to the evolution of poetry, Green observed:

> The antagonism between the two worlds in which man lives — the transient world of sin and sorrow, and the eternal world of righteousness and peace, — which Christianity has made one of the chief elements of modern poetry, has no place in the ancient. "The obstinate questionings of sense and outward things" had not then arisen. Men regarded themselves as parts of the great mechanism of natural existence, able sometimes to reflect the whole in their own minds, but unable to separate themselves from it, or rise above it. And thus, though their copy of external nature might be more correct than ours, they were less able to exercise upon it that modifying and combining power of the imagination, which places the little on a level with the great, and reads *even in the apparent confusion of human life the mercy of a beneficent God.*[52]

---

[48] See S. Collini, 'The Idea of "Character" in Victorian Political Thought', *Transactions of the Royal Historical Society*, XXXV (1985), pp. 29–50; Bellamy, 'T.H. Green and the Morality of Victorian Liberalism', pp. 131–51; S. Collini, *Public Moralists: Political Thought and Intellectual Life in Britain, 1850–1930* (Oxford, 1991), pp. 93–4.

[49] Nettleship, *Memoir*, p. xxx. The latter essay was republished in 1911, edited by F. Newton Scott: *T.H. Green: An Estimate of the Value and Influence of Works of Fiction in Modern Times, With Introduction and Notes* (Ann Arbor, 1911). The former is printed below for the first time (see Appendix).

[50] 'An Estimate of the Value and Influence of Works of Fiction in Modern Times', III, p. 28.

[51] 'On Thackeray's Novels' (see Appendix).

[52] 'The Spirit of Poetry' (italics mine) (see Appendix).

Green believed, against Carlyle's and Hegel's undemocratic inclination to exalt heroes, that the novel foreshadowed the advent of a more democratic society. By showing how morality varied according to circumstances,[53] the novel proved the death of that aristocratic hero who claimed to subdue the world. Thackeray, Fielding, Defoe, Austen, portrayed ordinary people:

> The view of man, therefore, which we attain through them, can only be that which is attainable by observation of outward actions.... Observation shows us man not as self-determined, but as the creature of circumstances, as a phenomenon among other phenomena.[54]

In 1847 Thackeray subtitled *Vanity Fair*, one of his most popular novels, *A Novel Without a Hero*. Green wrote:

> There is as much vanity displayed in a church as in a ball-room, the poor man who cringes before a noble-man has as mercenary a spirit as the rich man who sells his daughter to improve his mercantile connection. Every one has his stall in Vanity-fair, and if through favourable circumstances my trade is an honester one than my neighbour's, yet I cannot tell what I might have become, if I had been tried by his difficulties.[55]

Nor were the characters portrayed by George Eliot exceptional individuals.[56] The novelists told the stories of those ordinary people at the core of Green's political reflection. It is worth remembering what Green said of Samuel Johnson:

> He knew that it was with the stubborn facts of life that he had to deal, — with a body full of hypochondrical humours, with a garret at eighteen pence a week, with his own yearning for indolence, and with the miseries of the afflicted whom he took under his care. And if, with a heroic feeling of the importance of his practical

---

[53] See G. Levine, *Darwin and the Novelists* (Cambridge, 1988), p. 17.
[54] 'An Estimate of the Value and Influence of Works of Fiction in Modern Times', III, p. 32.
[55] 'On Thackeray's Novels' (see Appendix).
[56] Green quoted Eliot in his *Prolegomena to Ethics*, which he wrote between 1879–80. The Eliot passage, drawn from the epilogue to *Romola*, sounds similar: "we can only have the highest happiness, such as goes along with being a great man, by having wide thoughts, and much feeling for the rest of the world as well as ourselves; and this sort of happiness often brings so much pain with it, that we can only tell it from pain by its being what we would choose before everything else, because our souls see it is good": *Prolegomena to Ethics*, sect. 362, *Works*, IV, p. 404.

duties, he had a constant dread of falling into a world of ideas and abstractions, we can only admire his stern temper.[57]

In Green's eyes, Johnson was a man able to resist the force of circumstances without taking refuge in abstractions. For that reason, "the outspoken sincerity of his nature" was more impressive than his opinions; on the other hand, by requiring in himself and others an entire "though unloving submission to 'the powers that be'" because of his "contempt for the folly of men", he reminded Green of Carlyle.[58] For Carlyle, Johnson's heroism stemmed from his stoic nature which led him to subdue circumstances and reject democracy.[59] For Green, by contrast, Johnson's capacity to resist circumstances derived from his social and thereby democratic impulse. Green observed that

> in whatever society he was living, whether he was talking to his king, to Highland Lairds, or to men "who lived in London and hung loose upon society", he could speak as a man to man, with his social impulse unchecked by the accidents of temporary circumstances.[60]

One of Green's favourite poets was William Wordsworth. In many of his works, such as 'Peter Bell' and 'Idiot Boy', Wordsworth meant to show that no one could arrogate a moral consciousness to oneself. For Green, by stating the importance of moral consciousness, Wordsworth rescued literature from the bonds of a deterministic philosophy which, by assimilating man to an aggregate of passions, made ethics artificial.[61] In his 'Ode to Duty', Wordsworth underlined how the levelling down of life conditions had led to the growth of a social consciousness made by anonymous acts which made history without being remembered as historical.[62] Consistently with Wordsworth's view, Green noted that one might affirm that politics was no longer interesting because ideas and power were disseminated among the mass, and reason was no longer regarded as the exclusive domain of an elite or a privileged

---

[57] 'The Character and Opinions of Samuel Johnson' (see Appendix).
[58] *Ibid.*
[59] Reviewing James Boswell's *The Life of Samuel Johnson* (London, 1831), Carlyle described Johnson as a hero: 'Boswell's Life of Johnson' (1832) in *Critical and Miscellaneous Essays in Five Volumes*, vol. III (London, n.d.), pp. 89–92.
[60] 'The Character and Opinions of Samuel Johnson' (see Appendix).
[61] See 'Popular Philosophy in Its Relation to Life', *Works*, III, p. 118.
[62] 'Ode to Duty' in *Poems of Wordsworth*, ed. by M. Arnold (New York, 1880), pp. 193–4.

class. One might think that an aristocrat unable to govern lost his nobility, and that a democratic government was equivalent to no-government.[63] However, Green knew, in a similar way to Mill's philosophy, that novelists created an impression that God did not exist: "this view of the common weakness of men has no doubt its true side, but if it be separated from hope, from the consideration of the good that is wrought out of evil and of the final perfection to which all things are tending, it reduces life to an aimless existence."[64] Though the novel could counter antidemocratic bents, and poetry evidenced the existence of a deep spiritual need which could not be ignored, neither was sufficient. A new philosophy was needed. It had to make a deep spirituality consistent with a deep democratic belief.

At the same time, like Tocqueville and Mill, Green was aware of the risk that a mass democracy might make it acceptable for individuals to be unscrupulous and bend the world to their own satisfaction.[65] Again like Tocqueville and Mill, Green also realized that masses were much more likely than individuals to behave irrationally and that, by increasing their power, the influence of the force of circumstances could become much greater. "The combined motions of a mass of minds, working and counter-working, form a complex external power, which is", Green argued, "by no means analogous to any one of its component parts, and is carried along the path of necessity, to which past crimes or old usage bind it, by a sort of inherent compulsion."[66] Similarly Mill, citing Comte, had stated: "the longer our species lasts, and the more civilised it becomes, the more, as Comte remarks, does the influence of past generations over the present, and of mankind *en masse* over every individual in it, predominate over other forces."[67]

Nevertheless, Green like Mill hoped that the education of the masses would favour the emergence of a more advanced human type. But, unlike Mill, Green did not propose any kind of institutional remedy for checking the tyranny of the majority. Consistently with his Puritan background, he thought that

[63] 'An Estimate of the Value and Influence of Works of Fiction in Modern Times', III, p. 45.
[64] 'On Thackeray's Novels' (see Appendix).
[65] 'An Estimate of the Value and Influence of Works of Fiction in Modern Times', III, p. 22.
[66] 'The Force of Circumstances', III, p. 9.
[67] 'Additional Elucidations of the Science of History', *A System of Logic*, p. 942.

individuals could be "free creative spirits" only by recognizing in circumstances the revelation "of a supreme creative spirit."[68] Green's belief in the invisible church pushed him to state that the political constitutions of European nations were different because of the action of those exceptional individuals able to raise themselves beyond them.[69] Green maintained that in the abolition of slavery, the reconciliation of nations, and the general recognition of personal equality, Christianity had been a decisive element. Christianity, as external influence, enlightened the earthly burden of multitudes which were unaware of their inner strength.[70] Only those who experienced the emancipating power of Christianity were apt to exert "a negative influence in removing the most oppressive evils from the outward circumstances of life."[71] The reformers of the past had been identified too much with the spirit of their own age. As Green argued:

> The world is ever claiming as its own those who have indeed been in it but not of it. The very essence of a true reformer consists in his being the corrector and not the exponent of the common feeling of his day.[72]

Green's exceptional individual was the unique person who could put into practice the social impulse which characterized human conscience. By asserting the divine origin of conscience, Green turned it into a substantial entity.[73] In an undergraduate essay Green observed:

> The different branches of science are sometimes compared to mines of inexhaustible treasure, to fathom any single one of which might well demand the labours of a whole life, and this is true, but the precious ore we may extract will be a little service to us unless we gain light to discern its qualities from the open atmosphere of general knowledge, and from the same source form/ obtain some notion of/insight into the chain by which each treasure of human thought and Divine operation is linked to every other.[74]

---

[68] 'The Force of Circumstances', III, p. 7.
[69] *Ibid.*, III, p. 9.
[70] *Ibid.*, III, pp. 9–10.
[71] *Ibid.*, III, p. 10.
[72] *Ibid.*
[73] 'On the Origin of Ideas', V, p. 49.
[74] 'The Advantages and Disadvantages of Diffusive Reading' (see Appendix).

Kant, who reduced substance to a mental category, was assimilated to the empiricists. Space, time, matter, motion, force, could not exist without consciousness.[75]

3. After Balliol: Green's Radicalism

When in 1859 Green finished his studies at Balliol, he had already laid the bases of his future political philosophy. In 1859, stirred up by Piedmont, the second War of Italian Independence broke out. Earlier, in 1856, Green had expected that the conflicting interests of France and Austria in Italy, "being the interests of rogues", would have led to a quarrel, which popular discontent would have embittered, and had hoped that the war would at least teach the English to trust free national governments and not to support despots.[76]

Then Green became a fellow of Balliol and Jowett offered him the opportunity to teach Greek history for the *literae humaniores* School and English history and early European history for the School of Law and Modern History.[77] Evidently history was a subject that Green knew well. It is likely he considered history as an integral part of his philosophical view.

At the end of 1861 Green was elected president of the Oxford Union, which had never shared his progressive positions in favour of the working classes or Italian liberty. In February he gave a speech at the Union with the aim of pleading for Mazzini. In 1860, confirming that his view was thoroughly like Mazzini's, Green was worried by the disappointing outcome of the expedition of "the Thousand" led by Garibaldi. He realized that the realistic approach of Cavour was going to prevail. Garibaldi did not seem strong enough to have the situation within his grasp. For that reason, Green was afraid that the federal programme supported by Mazzini would not be put into practice:

> I can't think that a Piedmontese king of all Italy, without federal limitations, would ever be trustworthy, or that Italy can ever be permanently safe with Rome and Venetia in the hands of foreign-

---

[75] 'Fragment of An Address on the Text 'The Word is Nigh Thee', *Works*, III, p. 228.

[76] Nettleship, *Memoir*, p. xxiv.

[77] *Ibid.*, p. xxxiii.

ers. But of course there is no good in attempting plans which there is not enough national spirit to carry out.[78]

At the same time, he was relieved by the abolition of the tax on the press (1860): "it is", Green argued, "just what is wanted to secure the position of the penny papers and destroy the despotism of the *Times*."[79]

Green was probably infuriated by the antidemocratic bias of the most important English paper. When the American Civil War (1861–5) broke out, the *Times* promoted a vigorous journalistic campaign for the South. Green urged his sister to pay no attention to the nonsense it published about "the most important struggle that the world has seen since the French Revolution."[80] In the meantime, some English people seemed to be happy for the American democratic experiment to fail.[81] For Green, on the contrary, the American Civil War was the prelude to the birth of a more democratic nation. Persuaded that the North would win, Green was frightened by the possibility that English public opinion, encouraged by the *Times*, might aid the states fighting against the abolition of slavery. "I trust a good deal", he wrote, "to the religious public to keep us out of war; the leading dissenters I see are preaching peace vigorously."[82] Lancashire's economy was seriously damaged by the war. Many firms, which imported cotton from American southern plantations, had to close and unemployment notably increased. With the aim of helping the Lancashire workers who lost their jobs yet continued to support the North, a sum amounting to five thousands pounds was collected in Oxford, of which four hundred pounds came from Balliol.[83] At the Oxford Union in March 1863 Green managed to persuade some of his hearers that the North was right. To those who blamed the North for having attacked the South, Green replied that "it is not a republic that is answerable for this war, but a slave-holding, slave-breeding, and slave-burning oligarchy, on whom the curse of God and humanity rests."[84] Aware of the importance of what was at stake, Green overcame his instinc-

---

[78] *Ibid.*, p. xlii.
[79] *Ibid.*, p. xliv.
[80] *Ibid.*, p. xliii.
[81] *Ibid.*, p. xliv.
[82] *Ibid.*, p. xliii.
[83] *Ibid.*
[84] *Ibid.*

tive hostility towards war. Lincoln's murder was a hard blow for Green. He described it as "the greatest political crime of modern times."[85] Green hoped that this crime was not stirred up by the invective the English press threw at Lincoln, defining him a "bloodthirsty tyrant."[86]

As his radicalism made itself more obvious, it is likely that Green realized he needed to express and justify his position better. In 1861 he began to learn German and chose many of his friends of this period among the Scots who attended Balliol.[87]

4. Anglicanism and Germany

In 1860 at Oxford one could become a Bachelor of Arts independently of his religious belief. But it was still impossible for a religious dissenter to become a Master of Arts, or to hold a fellowship without subscribing to the Thirty-nine Articles of the Anglican church. Green subscribed to them. Probably, as Dicey observed, Green regarded it as just a way of stating that he belonged to the Anglican church.[88] In another of his undergraduate essays, Green argued that, though his belief in the unseen led him to maintain that the spiritual principle might be inconsistent with positive law and that it could live only in the inner life, he thought that a man was not justified "in rejecting everything which does not commend itself to his private reason."[89] Inward experience, not the critical faculty, was the test of religious truth, and "the experience of an individual, placed perhaps in peculiar circumstances, is not to be set against that of ages and generations."[90] Green knew that in some cases the function of private judgment was merely to emancipate ideas from mistakes which had been inherited from the past. For that reason, Green showed his own solidarity with the leaders of religious dissent, but he did not like the tone and spirit of their following.[91] Green looked coldly on a proposal in 1861 to petition Parliament in favour of abolishing

[85] *Ibid.*, p. xliv.
[86] *Ibid.*
[87] See the Recollection of J.A. Symonds, Green Papers; printed in H.M. Schueller and R.L. Peters, eds, *The Letters of John Addington Symonds. Volume II: 1869–1884* (Detroit, 1968), p. 774.
[88] Richter, *The Politics of Conscience*, p. 86.
[89] 'On Authority and Private Judgment, or Reason and Faith', V, p. 41.
[90] *Ibid.*
[91] Nettleship, *Memoir*, p. xxxvi.

clerical subscription. "There are few men who could say that they desired more religious freedom *as christians*, and to petition for it as a sort of intellectual luxury would be simply", Green argued, "to frighten the religious public and make them think that by opening the church door wider they would be letting in general scepticism."[92] Green maintained that it was better to turn the religious problem into a political one, making it obvious that the opening of the universities was mainly "a matter of justice",[93] not only towards dissenters but also the poorer classes. Green's inclination to mediate between idealism and empiricism was reinforced by his reformism which, without neglecting the importance of the past, tended to show how religious toleration would come only with democracy.

Significantly, though Green admired some individual clergymen, such as his uncle David James Vaughan, he never overcame his antipathy to the Anglican hierarchy. His congregational and Puritan background which exalted the importance of the link between democracy and religious toleration, was further exhibited in Green's comment in 1863, when there was a prospect that A. P. Stanley might be made archbishop of Dublin: "The dead may bury their dead. Saving souls is one thing; making a fuss about an institution and a creed quite another."[94]

When Stanley decided to exchange his professorship at Oxford for the deanery of Westminster, Green observed: "he gives up a position in which he was doing great good, and was likely to do more, for one which may do him harm but in which he can scarcely do much good."[95] It is clear, then, that Green's refusal to take orders was not due to any kind of moral or intellectual paralysis. Green probably thought that he could better promote democratic reform of English church and society without taking orders. As a friend of his noted, Green

> advanced naturally from one point to another with no loss, by the way, of strength or of necessary equipment. His steadiness of mind was, in so a speculative a man, quite remarkable; he knew nothing of mental cataclysms, and had none of the qualities which make interesting converts.[96]

---

[92] *Ibid.*
[93] *Ibid.*
[94] *Ibid.*
[95] *Ibid.*
[96] *Ibid.*, pp. xxxvi–xxxvii.

Green's two submissions (1860 and 1861) for the Ellerton
Theological Essay Prize confirmed that his political and philosophical reflection grew from theology. Green was not
awarded any prize on either occasion.[97] However, in these
essays, and particularly in the first, Green made his debt
towards Vane's doctrine more and more obvious. The rationality of man originated from that of a superior being, and it
was from man's reason that personal rights and morality
resulted.[98] As the reason of man progressed, so God was
revealed as a moral being.[99] When human beings were
unaware of themselves and of their originating from a superior being, it was the force of circumstances which prevailed.
"Before this force", Green argued,

> man sinks into nothing. He has no rights, no moral being, no con-
> sciousness of independent existence. Humanity is worthless;
> slavery, even cannibalism, is no wrong. The spirit, which is
> crushed by the dread of supernatural force, affords no resistance
> even to the violence of man.[100]

For Green, those who were unable to conceive of the existence
of a law superior to their own intentions, were equally unable
to conceive of any kind of political link.[101] Consistently with
Vane's position, for Green, the fact that political community
derived from God contributed to guarantee a greater liberty of
conscience.

In April 1862, when Green realized that his efforts to reclaim
his older brother from drinking were going to end unsuccess-
fully, he stated that he wanted to concentrate his own attention
upon writing a book.[102] He visited Germany for the first time
during the summer of 1862. He reported a very favourable
impression of his stay in Dresden:

> I am very well here, and like the place and the people. Indeed if I
> had my choice and knew the language, I should be disposed to
> settle in Germany in preference to England. The social equality,
> and the apparent absence of vice and distress, relieve one's soul

---

[97] *Ibid.*, p. xxxii. See 'Life and Immortality brought to light by the Gospel'
(Ellerton Theological Essay, 1860), *Works*, V, pp. 57–81 and 'The State of Religious Belief among the Jews at the time of the Coming of Christ' (Ellerton
Theological Essay, 1861), *Works*, V, pp. 83–104.
[98] 'Life and Immortality brought to light by the Gospel', V, p. 62.
[99] *Ibid.*,V, p. 68.
[100] *Ibid.*, V, p. 60.
[101] *bid.*, V, p. 61.
[102] Nettleship, *Memoir*, p. xxxvii.

from many burdens, and personally I don't much mind about the stagnation.[103]

Between 1860 and 1864 Green was restless. The teaching at Oxford no longer seemed satisfying. With the aim of discovering a more congenial atmosphere he thought of seeking employment at the Owens College, Manchester.[104] In January 1863 Green wrote:

I still hang on at Oxford, but I don't think my life is a very profitable one . . . Possibly I may establish myself in Germany for some time.[105]

Planning on leaving again for Germany, Green noted:

if I could get up the steam to write something that should be worth reading, I should be at better peace with myself. According to my experience, the only satisfaction to the inward man which lasts longer than a week arises from getting something adequate written.[106]

In May 1863, though he did not disdain academic life, Green continued to think that he would benefit from leaving Oxford. That summer he went to Heidelberg. Green made no secret of the fact that he was worried about the future of Germany, where Bismarck's ordinance against the press had "shorn the liberal papers of leading articles."[107] At the same time, he did not conceal his confidence in the future of Prussia, "for the soldiers can all read, and the artisans (who are strong at Berlin, though I fear not elsewhere) seem to be free from the worse forms of socialism, and under the guidance of Schulze-Delitsch to be developing schemes of co-operation and self-help."[108] Green's stay at Heidelberg dispelled all doubts. As soon as he was back, he confided to J.A. Symonds

that what he wanted was "a stump" − to preach his doctrine to the world from. And the stump to wh[ich] he then inclined was a Nonconformist pulpit . . . The topics wh[ich] he would have wished to expound were philosophical Christianity & philosoph-

---

[103] *Ibid.*, p. xlii.
[104] *Ibid.*, p. xxxiv.
[105] Letter to David Hanbury, 26 January 1863, Green Papers.
[106] Nettleship, *Memoir*, p. xxxvii.
[107] *Ibid.*, p. xlii.
[108] *Ibid.*

ical Democracy — his strong religious instincts & sympathy with the people, refined & fortified by reflection.[109]

Green was persuaded of the necessity "to saturate the English with German ideas — to hold fast the essential solid qualities of the English mind in politics and piety, but to give these a new vigour & intensity, adapt them to a Begriffs-philosophie."[110] For Green, German character was prone "to abstract his mind from external considerations, and push his opinions to their furthest consequences."[111] By contrast, English character stood out for its practical and commercial spirit, which, refined by Puritanism, made English people inclined to favour experience rather than any kind of abstract and sometimes dangerous speculations: when an Englishman, Green argued, "is writing or studying, he has always public opinion, and generally the public good, before his eyes, and hence he promulgates far fewer extravagances of opinion, than a German."[112]

By the end of 1863 Green had begun two pieces of literary work: one was a translation of F.C. Baur's *Geschichte der christlichen Kirche*,[113] the other was an edition of the *Nicomachean Ethics* of Aristotle. Now that Green realized he had a vocation for teaching and writing, the dissatisfaction which had been weighing upon him gradually passed. In preparing his lectures, he said he accumulated "a good deal of

---

[109] 1863. Recollections of J. A. Symonds, Green Papers; printed in Schueller and Peters, *Letters of John Addington Symonds*, II, pp 775–6.

[110] *Ibid.*; Schueller and Peters, II, p. 776.

[111] 'The English National Character Compared with that of the Germans' (see Appendix).

[112] *Ibid.*

[113] Ferdinand Christian Baur (1792–1860), professor of theology at the University of Tübingen, was one of the most controversial scholars of his time. Acknowledged as one of the founders of the so-called critical-historical theology, initially he drew on Schelling and Schleiermacher: see Baur, *Symbolik und Mythologie, oder die Naturreligion des Alterthums* (Stuttgart, 1824–5). Only later did he go into the teaching of Hegel thoroughly. Moreover, he aimed to overcome the views of both Scheiermacher and Hegel, which he maintained were too one-sided. The *Geschichte der christlichen Kirche* has five volumes: I. *Das Christenthum und die christliche Kirche der drei ersten Jahrhunderte* (Tübingen, 1853); II. *Die christliche Kirche vom Anfang des vierten bis zum Ende des sechsten Jaharhunderts in den Hauptmomenten ihrer Entwicklung* (Tübingen, 1859); III. *Die christliche Kirche des Mittelalters in den Hauptmomenten ihrer Entwicklung*, ed. F. F. Baur (Tübingen, 1861); IV. *Kirchengeschichte der neueren Zeit, von der Reformation bis zum Ende des achtzehnten Jahrhunderts*, ed. F.F. Baur (Tübingen, 1863); V. *Kirchengeschichte des neunzehnten Jahrhunderts*, ed. E. Zeller (Tübingen, 1862).

material for a possible book *in futuro*."[114] Stimulated by such intentions, in 1864 Green competed for the chair of moral philosophy in the University of St. Andrews. A year later, in 1865, Mill became the chancellor of St. Andrews. However, Green was not successful.[115] The studies which suggested to him a translation of Baur — whom Green described as "nearly the most instructive writer I ever met with" — were condensed into an 'Essay on Christian Dogma'.[116] In this essay, Green followed in Baur's footsteps.[117] He observed how the consciousness of God in man was able to attain its ideal form of the philosophical Christ only by passing beyond its intuitive form, that of the historical Christ.[118] As R.L. Nettleship explained, during this process "the primitive historical 'fact' does not

[114] Nettleship, *Memoir*, p. xxxvii.

[115] *Ibid.*, p. xli.

[116] Nettleship, *Memoir*, pp. xxxvii–viii. James Bryce reported that Green began the translation of *Geschichte der christlichen Kirche. Erster Band: Dritte Ausgabe. Kirchengeschichte der drei ersten Jahhunderte* during his stay in Germany in the summer of 1863. Green used the third edition (Tübingen, 1863): *Works*, V, p. 432, n. 50. However, it is likely that Green was first introduced to Baur through Benjamin Jowett's edition of the Epistles of Paul (1855): Nettleship, *Memoir*, p. xxxvii. But probably it was only in the sixties that Green realized the role Baur could play in his philosophy.

[117] In his introductory lectures on the history of dogma, Baur stated that as Christianity was a series of historical manifestations, it could be studied only through history. In the same way, Christianity as historical manifestation was part of the history of the Christian church. In its turn, this history could be interpreted as a history of 'forms'. Each 'form' accorded with a certain stage of doctrine's or dogma's evolution: see P.C. Hodgson, *The Formation of Historical Theology* (New York, 1966), pp. 237–41. Baur published many studies on the problem of Christian Dogma, see *Die christliche Lehre von der Dreieinigkeit und Menschwerdung Gottes in ihrer geschichtlichen Entwicklung*, in three volumes: I. *Das Dogma der alten Kirche bis zur Synode von Calchedon* (Tübingen, 1841); II. *Das Dogma des Mittelalters* (Tübingen, 1842); III. *Die neuere Geschichte des Dogma, von der Reformation bis in die neueste Zeit* (Tubingen, 1843). In 1847 he published his *Lehrbuch der christlichen Dogmengeschichte* (Stuttgart). Among the works that were published posthumously, see *Vorlesungen uber die christliche Dogmengeschichte*, ed. F.F. Baur in three volumes: I./1 *Das Dogma der alten Kirche von der apostolischen Zeit bis zur Synode in Nicae* (Leipzig, 1865); I/2 *Das Dogma der alten Kirche von der Synode in Nicae bis zum Ende des sechsten Jahrhunderts* (Leipzig, 1866); II. *Das Dogma des Mittelalters* (Leipzig, 1866); III. *Das Dogma der neueren Zeit* (Leipzig, 1867).

[118] Nettleship, *Memoir*, p. xxxviii. Baur noticed that in the age of the primitive church the idea of unity had to be impressed through the dogmatisation of the person of Christ. In the middle age dogmatism corresponded to the affirmation of the hierarchical structure of the church. But, as it contrasted with the genuine evangelical message, the Reformation, by revaluing inner life, was itself an unavoidable stage in the maturing of the church. However Baur thought this maturity of the Christian conscience culminated only in the most

evaporate in the ultimate 'idea', nor is the idea a merely glori-
fied reproduction of the fact; the idea *is* the fact in its full significance."[119] In December 1869 Green had not yet abandoned the
idea of translating Baur's chapter on Gnosticism included in
the *Geschichte der christlichen Kirche*.[120] In that chapter Baur
compared Hegel's philosophy of religion with the Gnosticism
of the second century.[121] Baur saw in Hegel the same split
between the historical Christ and the philosophical Christ
which characterized Gnosticism. For Baur, historical becoming did not result from a simple accidental aggregate of events.
Baur aimed to move from facts, searching for a universal from
which the particular sprang, and thus penetrating the innermost recesses of history. Baur found fault with Hegel's work
because of Hegel's tendency to state that the idea was prior to

---

recent speculative theology: Hodgson, *The Formation of Historical Theology*,
p. 126.

[119] Nettleship, *Memoir*, pp. xxxviii–ix. Probably thanks to Baur, the Christ of St.
Paul exemplified for Green the spiritual faith, independently of any kind of
system both theological and dogmatic (see Green, 'Essay on Christian
Dogma', *Works*, III, p. 161). According to Baur, the evangelists John and St.
Paul embodied two contrasting christological approaches. John's Gospel is
deeply marked by a dualism between light and darkness, and identified
Christ with the logos. John tended to undervalue the historical fact and be too
abstract and rational. On the contrary, Paul saw in history a tool which would
have allowed him to discover the person of Christ on the base of a spiritual
intuition. See Baur, *Die christliche Lehre von der Dreienigkeit und Menschwerdung
Gottes in ihrer geschichtlichen Entwicklung*, III, p. 969.

[120] Significantly, in 1869 Green still aimed to translate Baur: his English version
covered only one third of the first volume. In December 1869 Green wrote: "I
have not yet been able to make any definite scheme for the translation of
Baur's book. Several men, to whom I have spoken about it, talk as if they
would be glad to take part in a translation, but how far they can be trusted to
take the trouble, when finally put to the proof is not certain. I have no prospect
of being able to attend to it for another 9 months. I will promise then, however,
to assail the chapter on Gnosticism" (Letter to Mrs. Clough, 12 December 1869,
in *Works*, V, p. 432). The first volume of Baur's *Geschichte der christlichen Kirche*
was translated into English some ten years later as *The Church History of the
First Three Centuries* by the Rev. Allan Menzies (London and Edinburgh,
1878–9).

[121] Probably Baur went into Hegel's *Vorlesungen uber die Philosophie der Religion*
thoroughly only in 1835, that is to say, to coincide with the publication of his
*Die christliche Gnosis, oder die christliche Religions-Philosophie in ihrer
geschichtlichen Entwiklung* (Tübingen, 1835). Gnosticism was certainly one of
Baur's main themes. Baur was negatively impressed by that typical Gnostic
tendency to counter spirit to matter, ideal to real, liberty to authority. On the
contrary, for Baur, the opposition between authority and liberty, between
Peter's and Paul's conception, could be overcome only by means of historical
development.

history; for Baur, on the contrary, history was prior to the idea. That is why Baur accused Hegel of having separated "form" and "matter". Baur thought that "form" and "matter" were intrinsically connected. In Baur's view, Hegel was eager to impose on history an abstract rationality which cut his philosophy off from real life.[122]

5. The Role of the Philosopher

In one of his undergraduate essays, Green emphasised how Christianity contributed to highlight the difference between inner life and outer world.[123] By the light of Baur's position, Green maintained that this contrast, like that between liberty and authority, could be overcome by the philosopher alone. While the Puritan saint, embodied by Cromwell and Vane, regarded himself as unbound by historical circumstances and therefore was inclined to privilege the invisible church and to reject any kind of institutional approach, the philosopher, representing Green's exceptional individuality, managed to make his Puritan belief in the unseen consistent with a reforming process which sprang from custom and common sense. "The true philosopher", Green observed, "can find room for the saint."[124] By promoting a gradual extension of the evangelical message to an ever wider sphere of persons, the philosopher was the only one able to preserve the dogma "in its essence and to account for its form."[125] In the same way, Baur maintained that the only absolute content of the church intended as a "form" was to be identified with that feeling of unity between God and man destined to express itself in the progress of humanity.[126]

Significantly, too, the text Green initially wrote as an introduction to the *Nicomachean Ethics* turned on a dualism between "form" and "matter".[127] Green addressed to Aristotle the same

---

[122] Baur, *Die christliche Gnosis*, p. 720.

[123] 'Legislative Interference in Moral Matters', V, p. 32.

[124] 'Essay on Christian Dogma', *Works*, III, p. 184.

[125] *Ibid.*

[126] *Die Epochen der kirchlichen Geschichtsschreibung* (Tübingen, 1852), p. 251.

[127] The edition of the *Nicomachean Ethics* that Green intended to produce with Edward Caird was not published because the arrangement with the Oxford University Press fell through. What Green wrote on that occasion was later partly modified and published in the *North British Review* in September 1866. It was simply entitled 'The Philosophy of Aristotle'. Green probably decided to

criticisms Baur addressed to Hegel. Aristotle made a mistake: he saw in God a mere first cause, not a "*causa immanens*" and, by opposing God to the world, Aristotle turned them into two antithetical entities.[128] It was the same antithesis which characterized what Green called "popular philosophy". Despite its tendency to generalize from experience, "popular philosophy" did not question the origin of experience.[129] In this case, Green's target was Mill's *System of Logic*. By making his research area bounded by experience, Mill had deliberately excluded metaphysics. Mill's aspiration was to transform logic into "common ground on which the partisans of Hartley and of Reid, of Locke and of Kant, may meet and join hands."[130] Nevertheless, for Green, the price paid for this reconciliation was too high. Mill did not overcome that antithesis between experience and reason which characterized those ontological-intuitionist doctrines that he aimed to fight. Mill was wrong when, separating the real from the ideal, he believed that a thing could be "more real than its properties."[131] In a similar way, Plato had affirmed the existence of an unknown substratum of attributes.[132]

For Green, the inadequacy of Aristotelian logic stemmed not from "its being too 'idealistic', but from its not being idealistic enough."[133] "By the identification of the universal with a class", Green argued, "the true view of it is lost as soon as it is gained."[134] Green thought a more exact dialectic needed to be elaborated.[135] This assumed that the sensible becomes real

---

publish it as soon as he knew in 1866 that Alexander Grant had published a new edition of the *Ethics*: Nettleship, *Memoir*, pp. xxxix–xl. On the influence of Greek culture on Victorianism, see R. Jenkins, *The Victorians and Ancient Greece* (Oxford, 1980) and F.M. Turner, *The Greek Heritage in Victorian Britain* (London, 1981).

[128] 'The Philosophy of Aristotle', *Works*, III, p. 88.
[129] *Ibid.*, III, p. 48.
[130] 'Introduction' to *A System of Logic*, p. 14.
[131] 'The Philosophy of Aristotle', III, pp. 67–8.
[132] *Ibid.*, III, p. 68.
[133] *Ibid.*, III, p. 61.
[134] *Ibid.*, III, p. 57.
[135] *Ibid.*, III, p. 60. The dialectic elaborated by Green has usually been seen as a sort of transposition of Hegel's: see for instance Milne, *The Social Philosophy of English Idealism*, pp. 15 and 100–1. By contrast Seth, following Balfour ('Green's Metaphysics of Knowledge'), though not noticing the influence of Baur, realized the atypical nature of Green's dialectic. "Accordingly", Seth observed, "as Mr Balfour pointed out in a criticism of Green's metaphysics, published in 'Mind' a few years ago, if we speak of activity at all, 'we must allow that it is as

only in relation to the thinking self: relation constitutes a universal or common element able to connect the self with all other things. For Green, such realism was no enemy "either to common sense or to scientific investigation."[136] Green stated that "the individual thing is real", but its reality, in distinction from the scholastic or Aristotelian, was not bounded by the limits of a class. It was a unity relative to a multiplicity and, like the thinking self, was capable of infinite determination.[137]

In the light of Green's new dialectic, a new interpretation of the relationship between "form" and "matter" was necessary. For that reason, it was important to start from those treatises such as the *Metaphysics* and particularly *De Anima*,[138] in which Aristotle identified with the notion of "matter", not only the *prius*, but also the *posterius* of the process of knowledge. From this viewpoint, "matter" no longer corresponded to a mere sensible perception from which reason, abstracting its attributes and combining them, reached the definition of a "form" or a universal. "Matter" became itself "a relative term."[139] Thus, the Aristotelian notion of "matter" had a new meaning: it was "the less completely formed or known in contrast with the more completely."[140] If the Kantian synthetic unity of apperception was the condition of any kind of sensible experience, for Green the thinking self was present even in the germs of experience. Following a position which was more like Fichte's than Kant's, Green also kept himself aloof from Hume who affirmed the total inactivity of reason. Meanwhile Kant was accused of having accepted the same dichotomy between sensation and its object, which stemmed from Aristotle.[141] According to Green's dialectic, the process of thought was one not of abstraction but of concretion. It progressed, not towards the most abstract universal, but from it. It integrated just so far

---

correct to say that nature makes mind as that mind makes nature; that the World created God as that God created the World'": Seth, *Hegelianism and Personality*, p. 26. Seth realized that Green's position was not to be simply identified either with Kant's, or with Hegel's. "The self or unifying principle has then, according to Green, no nature of its own apart from what it does in relation to the manifold world": *ibid.*, pp. 27–8.

[136] 'The Philosophy of Aristotle', III, p. 60.
[137] *Ibid.*
[138] Significantly, before thinking of a new edition of the *Nicomachean Ethics*, Green had planned a new edition of the *De Anima* (Nettleship, *Memoir*, pp. xxxix–xl).
[139] 'The Philosophy of Aristotle', III, p. 62.
[140] *Ibid.*
[141] *Ibid*, III, p. 71.

as it differentiated. Beginning with an assertion of being or identity with self, A is A, it went on to bring A into relation to some other object. This relation gave a contrast and difference. Green argued:

> A is not B. But as not B it is something more than mere A. The difference has not taken something from it, but added something to it. It has not become a fraction of what it was before, but a fuller integer. It is no longer a bare unit, but a unity of differences, a centre of manifold relations, a subject of properties. It is not an 'abstract universal', but it has an element of universality in virtue of which it can be brought into relation to all things else. Its universality is the condition of its particularisation.[142]

Aiming to avoid any separation between immanent and transcendent, Green counter-poses to dead matter "a 'principle of motion'" and to mere substance "a creative subject."[143]

For Hegel too, "form" and "matter" were strictly intertwined. The German philosopher knew that the Spirit, perpetually renewing itself, did not bring itself back to the old "form". "Matter", Hegel argued,

> has its essence out of itself; Spirit is *self-contained existence* (Bei-sich-selbst-seyn). Now this is Freedom, exactly. For if I am dependent, my being is referred to something else which I am not; I cannot exist independently of something external. I am free, on the contrary, when my existence depends upon myself. This self-contained existence of Spirit is none other than self-consciousness — consciousness of one's own being.[144]

Since for Hegel the idea was *prior* to history, and consequently history was destined to accomplish itself in the idea, through the idea even evil could be overcome: "the ill", as Hegel observed, "that is found in the World may be comprehended, and the thinking Spirit reconciled with the fact of the existence of evil."[145] From this viewpoint, philosophy was more than a mere comfort, it reconciled real and ideal, unjust and just, irrational and rational. By acting through the universal man was able to separate himself from his instincts: the ideal, the rational, would restrain man from putting into practice his more egoistic impulses.

By contrast, Green thought that man was not able to separate himself so clearly from his instincts. Against Hegel's

[142] *Ibid*, III, p. 63.
[143] *Ibid.*, III, p. 80.
[144] *The Philosophy of History*, p. 17.
[145] *Ibid.*, p. 15.

abstractness, Green seemed to think the teaching of Hume should be retained. For Hume, it was impossible "that the distinction betwixt moral good and evil, can be made by reason; since that distinction has an influence upon our actions, of which reason alone is incapable."[146] The relationship between "matter" and "form" did not overcome evil. The universal, implied in the most simple and primitive perceptions, could not be known apart from the particular, and man had to recognize that his knowledge is partial. The self knows only through the senses, "yet, as acting through them, it is subject to a necessary delusion, the continued removal of which, never ending, still beginning, gives an essential character to human knowledge as at once imperfect, and, through its imperfection, progressive."[147]

Moreover, this interpretation of the relationship between "form" and "matter" was perfectly congruous with a political theology which, by bearing witness to a God "who is in the world but not of it", aimed to confirm the pre-eminence of the invisible church.[148] Green was aware that the unresolved Aristotelian dualism between immanence and transcendence could be reconciled only by a more advanced philosophy.[149] Despite its tendency to emphasise the importance of practical life, this philosophy allowed the philosopher, who shared this privilege with the poet and the saint, a foretaste of the spirituality of the world.

> As the poet, traversing the world of sense, which he spiritualises by the aid of forms of beauty, finds himself ever at home, yet never in the same place, so the philosopher, while he ascends the courts of the intelligible world, is conscious of a presence which is always his own, yet always fresh, always lightened with the smile of a divine and eternal youth.[150]

Green's philosopher was in some ways like Fichte's scholar — in charge of stimulating the progress of humanity. The true vocation of the scholar was "*the most widely extended survey of the actual advancement of the human race in general, and the stead-*

---

[146] *A Treatise of Human Nature*, II, p. 239.
[147] 'The Philosophy of Aristotle', III, p. 73.
[148] *Ibid.*, III, p. 87. It is worth emphasising that the distinction between visible and invisible church represented the clue to Baur's theological position: Hodgson, *The Formation of Historical Theology*, pp. 51–2.
[149] 'The Philosophy of Aristotle', III, p. 66.
[150] *Ibid.*, III, p. 90.

fast promotion of that advancement."[151] Likewise the philosopher, who knew the best way to follow, was the teacher of the
human race. For that reason, he had to be ethically the best:
"the *Guide* of the human race."[152] Like Fichte,[153] Green
believed that moral example was highly useful. Nevertheless,
while Fichte's scholar founded his acts on the idea of freedom,
Green's philosopher bore witness to the fact that history
stemmed from the divine.

As soon as he had returned from Heidelberg (1863), Green
demonstrated his philosophical maturity. Twenty years after
Mill had published his *System of Logic* (1843), Green elaborated
a new dialectic which allowed him at once to complete the
political and cultural inheritance of the author of *On Liberty*
and to move beyond it. Green's polemical target was not solely
the ontological inclinations of those authors like Whewell and
Hamilton who, for Mill, embodied the national support for the
old social order; his target was also that determinism from
which Mill thought he had freed himself. Thus, while Mill was
prone to regard German philosophy as an enemy, Green was
convinced that idealism, besides being a useful tool against
determinism, could be made consistent with Mill's radicalism.

6. Assistant to the School Commission

In December 1864 a royal commission was appointed to
enquire into the education given in those schools in England
and Wales which were not comprised within the two former
commissions of 1858 and 1861, that is, practically, "the schools
attended by the children of such of the gentry, clergy, professional and commercial men as are of limited means, and of
farmers and tradesmen."[154] The commissioners conducted
their enquiry partly by examining witnesses, partly by send-
ing circulars of questions to the schools, and partly by appoint-
ing assistant commissioners to inspect personally certain
districts of England and Wales. Dr. Temple, who was one of
the commissioners, obtained Green an assistant commission-
ership. However, Green's appointment caused some alarm to
other members of the commission. The young Oxford scholar
was known as "'an extreme man, an ultra-radical in politics, an

[151] Fichte, *The Vocation of the Scholar*, p. 54.
[152] *Ibid.*, p. 58.
[153] *Ibid.*, pp. 57–8.
[154] Quoted in Nettleship, *Memoir*, p. xlv.

ultra-liberal in religious opinion'."[155] The selected districts which fell to his lot were Warwickshire and Staffordshire; and when the commissioners resolved to extend the enquiry to all endowed grammar schools in England and Wales, Green's share of this supplementary work was the counties of Buckingham, Leicester, and Northampton. He was occupied during the last three quarters of 1865 and from April to June 1866. Green regarded himself as totally unfit for this charge. Nevertheless, he was paid adequately and it could be considered "a good opportunity for acquiring practical habits."[156] In addition Green had to make a special report on King Edward's School at Birmingham, one of the eight endowments selected by the commission for their size and importance to serve as examples. In his report Green observed that fewer than a hundred of the boys of the grammar schools of Staffordshire and Warwickshire (not including Birmingham) could make out for themselves an ordinary passage of Cicero and Virgil. Of these not more than thirty could be expected to rise considerably beyond their present standard of attainment, and of these thirty again, not more than half would be likely to go to university.[157]

The remedy lay neither in a radical change of the subjects of instruction nor in new methods of teaching. Green identified the great check on aspiration towards university at present as the prevalent notion that education should be an easy and agreeable process, which would qualify the recipient for making money as soon as possible. "The real difficulties which have to be met on the part of the taught", Green argued, "are an absence of intellectual interest, an incapacity for intellectual effort, and an obtuseness for distinctions of thought."[158] Moreover, the smaller grammar schools, in attempting to satisfy the special educational requirements of both the professional and the commercial class, generally failed to satisfy either. The plan of having separate commercial and classical departments reinforced a separation that was social more than educational. "I never met with a school", Green noted, "where a system of transfer from the commercial department to the classical was effectively worked."[159] The education of the commercial man

---

[155] *Ibid.*
[156] Letter to David Hanbury, 20 April 1865, Green Papers.
[157] Nettleship, *Memoir*, p. xlvii.
[158] *Ibid.*, p. xlviii.
[159] *Ibid.*, p. l.

usually stopped at the age of fifteen, while that of the professional man continued from three to eight years longer. This situation clearly resulted from the difference of educational impulse which the parents applied to their children:

> In the one case there are no books (except a few with gilt leaves, only moved to be dusted), no intellectual traditions, small opportunities of study at home. The father probably spends the evening with his friends at some place of social resort; the mother is tired with household cares, and if she had the will, has not often sufficient elementary knowledge to overlook even the studies of a small boy . . . the son of a professional man, on the other hand . . . is early accustomed to the sight and use of books. There are those about him at home, who, if they like, can see that he does at home what his master sets him, and as he grows older, familiar example may accustom him to the notion of knowledge as a source of utility and estimation.[160]

According to Green, a new system of education was necessary. Such a system would at once meet the aspiration of the few and raise that of the many. It would catch the boys who wanted a commercial education and having caught them, would at the same time keep for the higher learning all who were fit for it. By avoiding the risk that the prospect of an intellectual career was discarded when a boy was too young to decide, this system would gain the favour of the poorer clergy, the dissenting ministers and the better sort of private and government schoolmasters who, though few in number, were "the salt of their class."[161] For that reason, it would have got rid of the notion, ingrained in the commercial class, that high education was the perquisite of the clergy and gentry. Green expressed his own solidarity with those members of the middle class "whose heart is with their few books, or in the Lord's house, while they are behind the counter or at the clerk's desk."[162] Educational endowments would encourage the practice of "'the career open to the talents'."[163] Consistently with his new dialectic, which regarded every separation of theory from practice as politically dangerous, Green's proposal was intended to overcome any tendency to segregate commercial from high education. They should be integrated in order to facilitate a more democratic selection based on merit.

---

[160] *Ibid.*, p. li.
[161] *Ibid.*, p. liii.
[162] *Ibid.*, p. lvi.
[163] *Ibid.*, p. lvii.

7. The Puritan Revolution

A brother-fellow who was in constant communication with Green between 1866 and 1870 described him as "drawn to plain people, to people of the middle and lower class rather than of the upper, to the puritans of the past and the nonconformists of the present, to Germans, to all that is sober-suited and steady-going."[164] In the spring of 1866 Green was invited to lecture before the Edinburgh Philosophical Institution. The subject, 'Cromwell and the English Commonwealth', was, as Green said, "an old love of mine."[165] In January 1867 he went to Edinburgh, where he gave four lectures.

Green observed that Puritanism was characterized by conflicting tendencies to freedom and bondage. It was the temporary triumph of the first that made the commonwealth a possibility, and the interference of the other that stopped its expansion.[166] That was why the Puritan revolution should not be interpreted in terms of ideological categories and interests. Both those republicans who accused Cromwell of having caused the failure of the commonwealth and those who, like Carlyle, exalted Cromwell as a hero, simply ignored that the Puritans had to pay the reckoning of having anticipated history.[167] Green was probably under the impression that Carlyle used the figure of Cromwell to justify his idea of leadership. Indeed, in a very similar way to Carlyle,[168] Green's account of the English Revolution aimed to identify those principles which could serve to illumine the main political questions of nineteenth-century England.

In speaking of the short life of English republicanism, Green endeavoured to treat it as the last act in a conflict beginning with the Reformation. Thus, Green situated the Puritan revolution in the context of the dialectic described by Baur. In the light of Baur's dialectic, Green could easily show how the Puritan revolution was deeply different from lutheranism.[169] Also the Reformation brought the Germans not peace but war.

[164] *Ibid.*, p. lxii.
[165] *Ibid.*, p. lviii.
[166] 'Four Lectures on the English Revolution', III, p. 286.
[167] *Ibid.*, III, p. 278.
[168] See Morrow, 'Heroes and Constitutionalists: The Ideological Significance of Thomas Carlyle's Treatment of the English Revolution', pp. 210-1.
[169] Andrew Vincent has already identified Baur's dialectic as the main key used by Green for his analysis of the Puritan revolution. "The significance of the English Revolution, within the broader sweep of the Reformation", as Vincent

However, their religious wars were rather caused by crowned violence and the ambition of the House of Habsburg than the result of any strife of principles involved in lutheranism itself. This circumstance prevented "the antagonism of the secular and the religious from developing itself in the lutheran countries."[170] A conclusion could be easily drawn: the German, with his speculative grasp, was very inclined to regard church and state as two sides of the same spiritual organism. "How little", Green argued, "the reality of either church or state may correspond to the idea, how powerless in action may be the permeating strength of German thought, an Englishman needs not to be told."[171] All that the English associated with the term sectarian was unknown in Germany. Consequently, if the conflict between reason and authority had not indeed ceased among the Germans, its arena had been "the study and the lecture-room, not the market-place or the congregation."[172] On the contrary, in England, when Elizabeth sought to restore state religion, she had to deal with a different system, namely, "the full articulation of that voice of conscience, of the inner self-asserting spirit which the Reformation evoked."[173] The result was that those who listened to that voice broke with the old religion, and established a new and independent religion: they were "the predestined people of God."[174] Green quoted the exhortation that John Robinson, the founder of the Independents, addressed to the pilgrim fathers. In it, Green saw, "breathes a higher spirit of christian freedom than anything that had been heard since christianity fixed itself in creeds and

---

observed, "is to introduce a new subject or individual, that may be called a radically free subject, or a Christian citizen. The underpinning for this subject and his interpretation of the English Revolution, lies in [Green's] theological views. These theological views owe a great deal to his studies in German theology, specifically of the Hegelian doyen of the Tübingen school of theology, Friedrich Christian Baur." A. Vincent, 'T.H. Green and the Religion of Citizenship' in Vincent, ed., *The Philosophy of T.H. Green* (Aldershot, 1986), p. 53. More recently the importance of the Puritan revolution for Green's political philosophy has been confirmed: see D. Kelly, 'Idealism and Revolution: T.H. Green's Lectures on the English Commonwealth' (paper for the International Conference on Anglo-American Idealism, 20–25 August 2003, Pyrgos, Greece) and D.P. Leighton, *The Greenian Moment: T.H. Green and Political Argument in Victorian Britain* (Exeter, 2004), pp. 172–6.

[170] 'Four Lectures on the English Revolution', III, p. 284.
[171] *Ibid.*
[172] *Ibid.*
[173] *Ibid.*, III, p. 285.
[174] *Ibid.*

churches."[175] Robinson insisted on not transforming his ministry into a dogmatic teaching. Robinson knew that, as Green underlined:

> It is one of the distinguishing features of fanaticism that, while it begins with a genuine love for some high principle it ends with a love for the party or cause which represents the principle, and is itself unconscious of the change.[176]

Robinson's disavowal of any theological finality embodied itself in a system of church government leaving room for a liberty of conscience which the rule of bishops or a presbytery denied. It was based on the doctrine of the absolute autonomy of the individual congregation, and the rejection of a special order of priests or presbyters. Each congregation was to elect or depose its own officers and no congregation or sum of congregations was to have any control in regard to doctrine or discipline over another.[177] As Green argued:

> The progress of the Reformation in the two nations illustrates another feature of diversity in their characters. In Germany the religious opinions of the reformed attained a much greater completeness than in England, but the people and their different governments remained very widely divided in religious matters, and no permanent ecclesiastical system was established. But we have to turn to Germany, if we would study the religious theories of the reformation, while England produced hardly any purely doctrinal writers, though many on ecclesiastical matters. With us the reformation, as soon as it began to prevail extensively among individuals, effected a corresponding work on the state and the government. This arose partly from the fact that the English government and church were, from their position, less open to external influences, but also from the compromising tendency of the English mind.[178]

Green believed that English philosophy had to revalue, through idealism, that Puritan inclination to privilege reform and liberty of conscience implied in the pre-eminence of the invisible church. At the same time, it should not neglect that typical bent for compromise which made the English wiser than the Germans. For that reason, Green preferred Baur's dialectic to Hegel's.

---

[175] *Ibid.*, III, p. 289. Robinson's exhortation is printed as the epigraph to this book.
[176] 'The Character of Mahomet' (see Appendix).
[177] 'Four Lectures on the English Revolution', III, p. 289.
[178] 'The English National Character Compared with that of the Germans' (see Appendix).

Vane studied at Leyden, where Robinson, driven from England by episcopal persecution, formed a congregation. Vane, imitating the pilgrim fathers, moved from Leyden to Massachussets. There in 1635, as governor of Massachussets, Vane had to deal with the matter of Anne Hutchinson. This originated, as Green observed, in the same strife between the inner life and the force of circumstances, which later formed the tragedy of the commonwealth.[179] For Vane, history developed itself through three stages: the natural, legal, and evangelical conscience. The natural conscience was the source of ordinary right and obligation. It was, Green argued, "at once the source and the limit of the authority of the magistrate."[180] From the legal conscience stemmed the ordinances and dogmas of the christian. It embodied the stage in which the christian clings to rule, letter and privilege. At the same time, it belonged to the champions of the covenant of grace as much as to their adversaries. For that reason, it had to be overcome by the evangelical conscience. Only through it was human spirit able to hold intercourse "'high, intuitive and comprehensive' with the divine."[181] Vane's analysis of dogma was fully consistent with Baur's: in his 'Four Lectures on the English Revolution' Green quoted a long passage drawn from his 'Essay on Christian Dogma' inspired by Baur.[182]

Green claimed that the doctrine of natural right and government by consent first appeared in Vane's writings. This doctrine resulted from "his recognition of the 'rule of Christ in the natural conscience'."[183] From the same idea followed the principle of universal toleration, the exclusion of the magistrate's power alike from the maintainance and restraint of any kind of opinion. Green emphasised that

> this principle did not with Vane and the independents rest, as in modern times, on the slippery foundation of a supposed indifference of all religious beliefs, but on the conviction of the sacredness of the reason, however deluded, in every man, which may be constrained by nothing less divine than itself.[184]

---

[179] 'Four Lectures on the English Revolution', III, p. 294.
[180] *Ibid.*, III, p. 295.
[181] *Ibid.*
[182] Compare the 'Essay on Christian Dogma', III, pp. 178–9 with 'Four Lectures on the English Revolution', III, p. 280.
[183] 'Four Lectures on the English Revolution', III, p. 296.
[184] *Ibid.*, III, pp. 296–7.

According to Vane, the rule of the magistracy should content itself with the outward man, and intermeddle with the relationships among men only "'upon the grounds of natural justice and right in things appertaining to this life'."[185] This system had to be supported by a belief in the "spiritual church."[186] Before the Puritan revolution (1642–1649) broke out, Vane was the only member sitting in parliament to realize how close Anglicanism and Presbyterianism were in their tendency to claim absolute truth. That is why both of them were eager to look for strong institutional support.[187] For Green, Cromwell's action on the contrary was inspired by his belief in the invisible church. His *Heads of Proposals* would have given England at once a genuine parliamentary government and a free national church. Had Charles I accepted it, he would have prevented "two centuries of government by borough-mongering and corruption, of church-statesmanship and state-churchmanship."[188] In the meanwhile, Green judged the reforms the Levellers demanded as so in advance of the times, that for the most part they waited "for nearly two hundred years, till they began to be carried out by the 'purged parliament' of 1832."[189]

However, the commonwealth was the culmination of a parabola stirred up by men who lived "in the stage of the 'unbodied thought'."[190] For that reason, that "*jus divinum* of individual persuasion", which expressed itself in their action, was unable to govern.[191] Elicited by the antagonism of two equally absolute systems, Anglicanism and presbyterianism, both stemming from a mixture between church and state, this *jus* made itself obvious as "a spirit without a body, a force with no lasting means of action on the world around it."[192] Green perceived in Milton's writings on the one hand a deep contempt for the high ranks of the court, and on the other a detachment towards a people that was victim of a sensual degradation which estranged them from a government

---

[185] *Ibid.*. III, p. 297.
[186] *Ibid.*
[187] *Ibid.*, III, p. 299.
[188] *Ibid.*, III, p. 346.
[189] *Ibid.*, III, p. 338.
[190] *Ibid.*, III, p. 332.
[191] *Ibid.*, III, p. 327.
[192] *Ibid.*

founded on reason conceived in such an elitist way.[193] By ignoring that the *jus divinum* of individual persuasion had to be made consistent with custom, the revolutionaries created "a democracy without a *demos*."[194] Cromwell's failure made the limits of "the puritan philosophy" obvious.[195] It revealed itself unable to put into practice that "wider comprehension" which resulted from his action.[196] Cromwell was unaware that there were wars destined to be won "not in days but in centuries, and by the energy not of feeling but of thought."[197] In one of his undergraduate essays, Green had already stressed how the enthusiast was prone to form an ideal of the world which was inconsistent with reality:

> He has a passion for reforming the world, but the world will not listen to him, and sooner or later he discovers his mistake. He falls out with mankind and they with him, and he is thrown back even more than before to brood on his own consciousness. He shuts himself out from all the good influences current in the world, quarrelling with religion because it does not make men better, and even with morality because it shackles the free exercise of his own high impulses.[198]

Green quoted the words pronounced by Vane on the scaffold. Vane said that the people of England had been long asleep and Green added: "they have slept, we may say, another two hundred years."[199] Green asserted that the people could still be nourished by Vane's ideas, now clarified and ripened by a new philosophy. The enthusiasm, however, which animated Cromwell and Vane was not Puritan or English merely. "It belonged", Green observed, "to the universal spiritual force which as ecstasy, mysticism, quietism, philosophy, is in permanent collision with the carnal interests of the world, and which, if it conquers them for a moment, yet again sinks under them, that it may transmute them more thoroughly to its service."[200] Baur's dialectic, which pivoted on the dualism between "form" and "matter", offered Green a new interpretive key. It allowed him to mitigate idealism and empiricism

---

[193] *Ibid.*, III, p. 329.
[194] *Ibid.*, III, p. 330.
[195] *Ibid.*, III, p. 352.
[196] *Ibid.*
[197] *Ibid.*, III, p. 354.
[198] 'Enthusiasm' (see Appendix).
[199] 'Four Lectures on the English Revolution', III, p. 364.
[200] *Ibid.*

and, above all, gave him the possibility of preventing the risk that the reforming impulse, which had been embodied by the Puritans, would continue to be useless.

Chapter III

Political Activity

1. The Importance of Facts

This chapter examines Green's political activity in some detail. This opening section introduces some central themes which are elaborated and illustrated at length in the rest of the chapter.

Although Green has been unanimously regarded as an activist intellectual, it has not been generally understood that his political commitment was an integral part of his philosophy. Founded on the interplay of "matter" and "form", his philosophy had an empirical basis and his positions were constantly moulded in the light of the facts. Green's philosophy had to reflect the problems of daily life and, instead of abstracting from reality, had to develop a continuous dialectical interaction with it. It assumed that reality is dynamic: it involved the possibility of a moral growth which tended to free individuals from every burden (political, social or economic) which hindered it. Consequently, every attempt to stop this process was bound to produce set patterns of thought and fossilized institutions which were useful only to justify exploitation (subjection of the working classes) and exclusion (discrimination against the non-conforming churches). It was essential to pay the closest attention to social and political facts in order to avoid perpetuating privileges.

When in the spring of 1866 Green was invited to lecture before the Edinburgh Philosophical Institution on 'Cromwell and the English Commonwealth', Gladstone had just presented a programme for electoral reform supported by Bright, and when Green gave the four lectures in January 1867, Disraeli was about to launch an electoral reform programme which Green judged quite negatively. Green's lectures seem to be strictly linked to the beginning of his political activity — he gave his first public speech in March 1867 — to such an extent that one could consider them as a sort of manifesto in which he made his political position explicit. Green thought Puritanism confirmed the importance of facts, and revealed how privileges were nourished by abstractions. In this sense, Green's dialectic between "matter" and "form" revived the anti-formalist Puritan attitude which denied the primacy both of church and state institutions. Facts and men's sufferings always came first. Green inherited the Puritan wariness of any kind of form — religious as well as political — presenting itself as final and thereby prone to defend its own interests at the expense of others. Political parties and Parliament were no exception to the rule. On the other hand, Green also realized that from an historical viewpoint the crux of the matter was the same as in the Puritan revolution. In nineteenth century England Parliament had become a clique which, fostering the interests of the clergy and landowners, perpetuated public ignorance and apathy. Democratic electoral Reform would bring with it a free Church, free land and free education. The intelligentsia, which supported the oligarchy in power, was produced by an educational system endowed by state subsidy of the established church. Indeed, according to Green, the oligarchy in power deliberately shut its eyes to facts.

At the same time, Green was aware that electoral reform was a lever capable of being used as much for ill as for good. Green did not regard Gladstone's government as blameless. Although, as a consequence of the 1867 electoral Reform, the Irish Church Bill, the Irish Land Bills and the Elementary Education Bill were approved, the Liberals could be accused of indifference to facts as well. Green found the Elementary Education Act disappointing, the condition of English agricultural labourers unimproved and the Permissive Bill entirely useless. It is also worth noting that, in Green's analysis, the 1874 election defeat could be put down precisely to the negligence of the Liberals and their inability to be more sensitive to facts. For instance, William Harcourt, the Liberal candidate in Green's constituency, was insensitive to the pain of many working class families ruined by excessive drinking. In accordance with the teaching of Vane, Green's conception of democracy was founded on the assumption that political obligation, though distinct from moral obligation, was instrumental to it. However, in line with his inclination to reject any kind of abstract position, Green did not turn his teetotalism into an absolute principle but supported Harcourt anyway. In a similar way, despite maintaining that the Church of England should be congregationalized, Green opposed its disestablishment and disendowment. Facts were useful to dismiss any kind of dogmatic viewpoint: whether of those who wanted to resist reforms or of those who were inclined to fight for reforms but ignored ordinary people's attitudes.

Dedication to facts required that new citizens accepted their share of responsibility and became more and more aware of their condition. So from Green's perspective the alliance between the Conservative Party and the brewers was almost a foregone conclusion. Because they knew that awareness of facts was an essential requisite for full citizenship, Conservatives transformed the public-houses into Tory clubs. The awareness of facts naturally flows, for Green, into that sense of solidarity which, according to the Puritan Vane, was of divine origin. Any associated action, which implied some concrete form of devolution of powers (local committees, school boards, and so on), was both a symptom of a certain amount of democracy and the means by which democracy could be improved. Green was constantly taken up with encouraging associated action. Every step forward required more wise associated action. Indeed, only through being associated could the people express that common sense that made it wiser, guarding against any kind of abstract and ideological position. By forcing people to face up to facts, local committees and boards made the expression of common sense easier. From Green's viewpoint, the Liberal Party was right to leave any decision on the choice of candidates to a body which included all potential Liberal voters of every single district.

The Conservatives, by contrast, saw a threat in every impulse rising from below, to such an extent that they used nationalism to deter political participation and the desire for reforms. The Conservatives, who were essentially antidemocratic, wanted to check reform. In Green's eyes, they represented the interests of the landlords, the clergy, the publicans and the armed services. These four interests cemented their union in order to abuse the suffrage. Because they wanted to preserve their monopoly of power, they had to be indifferent to facts. For that reason, while the Conservatives were to be seen as the Party of vested interests, the Liberals were to be considered the Party of the public good, and whereas, in Green's eyes, the Conservatives won elections by resorting to beer and bribery, the Liberals would win only thanks to the hard work of motivated volunteers.

However, facts had to be nurtured, and Green was well aware that among the poorer people on the Liberal side there were many who were tempted by the attractive offers from the Conservatives. Consistently with his inclination to reject absolute and abstract principles, Green proved to be not only tolerant of corruption when Liberals resorted to it, but bent on justifying it whenever circumstances made it the only possible way to defeat an adversary — the Conservative Party — whose strength came precisely from weakening the moral sense of the masses. Green also favoured an anti-corruption law and encouraged the Liberals to emancipate themselves from corrupt practices.

The accomplishment of the Puritan revolution desired by Green was going to face many unexpected difficulties. State intervention was confined to external actions, helping to guarantee liberty of conscience and to allow an individual to develop his inner life without hindrance. At the same time, nineteenth century democracy would reveal how Green's faith in the moral progress of ordinary people would be disappointed: the advent of a mass democracy showed how powerful those forces were which could condition the inner life of an individual. Green's analysis of the electoral defeat of the Liberal Party in 1874 assumed that drunkenness played an important role: it weakened the moral sense of the masses. In the same way, electoral corruption resulted from a moral feebleness and a working class whose rising prosperity rendered it more willing to yield to corruption. For Green, liberalism failed because it did not realize how important the education of the masses was. Significantly, the last public act of Green's life — of which he was particularly proud — was to create the High School for Boys in Oxford. One can argue that it embodied the main objective of all his political commitment. Once again, according to Green, the position of those who opposed any kind of State intervention in education did not square with the facts and, by losing sight of facts, they perpetuated the sufferings of children who would continue to be excluded from having a decent standard of life and, thereby, from realizing themselves. Green's liberalism did not deny reality. Facts represented its starting point — though its goal was to go beyond them. The vitality of Green's liberalism came from its capacity to be nourished by facts without losing faith in the progress of humanity. Green's Puritan citizen, despite remaining a believer, had to be conscious that his faith should never be set against facts.

2. The 1867 Electoral Reform

Green's first public speech came on the 25th of March 1867 when he took part in a meeting organised by the Oxford branch of the Reform League[1] to discuss Disraeli's programme for electoral reform.[2] Addressing an audience consisting mostly of workers, Green was pleasantly surprised by the degree to which he found himself in agreement with his listeners, who were so different from those who usually crowded into the halls of the Oxford Union. As he commented afterwards:

> my speech was very successful. At least I spoke for half an hour amid the great applause of the citizens, and without saying anything that I afterwards regretted. It was very unlike my old experience at the Union, where I used to be always groaned at and interrupted.[3]

Drawing attention to the fact that aristocrats were in the majority in the House of Commons, Green spoke in favour of an agenda which emphasised the importance of continuing the battle for reform.[4] In Green's opinion, the electoral reform programme launched by Disraeli on the 18th March 1867 was

---

[1] The National Reform Union had been founded in 1864 in the Free Trade Hall in Manchester. Previously, the Anti-Corn Law League had used the same venue to plan its campaign: see A. Briggs, *The Age of Improvement, 1783–1867* (London and New York, 1979), pp. 496–7. Green was a member of the National Reform Union: see E.J. Feuchtwanger, *Democracy and Empire: Britain 1865–1914* (London, 1985), p. 29. The Reform League was set up in February 1865 and had a greater working class orientation.

[2] Following the death of Palmerston (18 October 1865), Russell became Prime Minister while Gladstone remained Chancellor of the Exchequer. Both Russell and Gladstone were in favour of the extension of the suffrage: see Feuchtwanger, *Democracy and Empire*, pp. 27–30. In the period immediately after Palmerston's death, the government had to deal with both electoral reform and the Eyre case. Eyre was the governor who had put down a revolt in Jamaica with a degree of severity that many considered excessive. For Green's view on this, see Nettleship, *Memoir*, p. xliii.

[3] Quoted in Nettleship, *Memoir*, p. cx.

[4] *Ibid.*

far from democratic.[5] Green was quick to dismiss it as "fraudulent and delusive."[6] He was convinced of the urgency of removing the Conservative government which was openly trying to strike a deal with those "Moderate Liberals" who had tried to dissuade Gladstone from opposing Disraeli's reform.[7] On the 12th of March 1866 Gladstone had presented a programme for electoral reform supported by Bright, but opposed by many radicals.[8] Gladstone was in favour of an extension of the suffrage to those tenants paying an annual rate of at least seven pounds in the boroughs and fourteen in the counties. In this way, he felt the vote would be given to the more respectable elements of the working class.[9] However, as Green observed, "even if Mr. Gladstone succeeds in carrying such a half-measure as that of last year, the work will be only just begun. The redistribution of seats, and other matters scarcely less important, remain to be dealt with."[10]

The major opponent of Gladstone's proposal was Robert Lowe, whom Green probably had in mind when he referred to those "philosophical Liberals" who, leaving facts aside, con-

---

[5]   The vote in the boroughs was to be allocated according to personal taxation: all homeowners who paid their taxes and had been resident for at least two years in the borough would have the right to vote (household suffrage). Tenants and those who paid their taxes indirectly, through deductions by landlords (compounders), would be excluded. In the counties, the vote would only be given to those who could demonstrate an income equivalent to at least fifteen pounds. In addition, special privileges were granted to those who held a degree and/or fifty pounds in government bonds with the Bank of England or a Savings Bank. Members of the scholarly professions or those who paid the Exchequer one pound per year in direct taxes were also to be rewarded. Citizens satisfying both the relative property requirements and those others mentioned above would be allowed a double vote. See Briggs, *The Age of Improvement*, pp. 507–8.

[6]   'The Reform Bill', 25 March 1867, *Works*, V, p. 230.

[7]   *Ibid.*

[8]   Morley comments: "The chancellor of the exchequer introduced the Reform Bill (March 12) in a speech that, though striking enough, was less impassioned than some of his later performances in the course of this famous contest. He did not forget that 'the limbo of abortive creations was peopled with the skeletons of reform bills'; and it was his cue in a House so constituted as the one before him, to use the language and arguments of moderation and safety". J. Morley, *The Life of William Ewart Gladstone*, 2 vols (London, 1905–6), I, p. 834.

[9]   Feuchtwanger, *Democracy and Empire*, p. 32.

[10] 'The Reform Bill', V, p. 231.

sidered it "absurd to claim representation as a right."[11] Lowe, who had been a staunch supporter of Palmerston, was convinced that any further extension of the vote would result in disaster for the country. He attacked the reform on the grounds that it was necessary to prevent Parliament from being at the mercy of the public mood. Using a line of argument which Carlyle would have appreciated, he maintained that the only way to improve the condition of the working classes was not to bring the right to vote down "to the level of those persons who have no sense of decency or morality", but to keep it as a "privilege of citizenship."[12] Lowe believed that the working classes were interested in the extension of the suffrage solely as a means to ease the transformation to socialism and were largely made up of "impulsive, unreflecting and violent people."[13] For Green, on the other hand, Lowe's view perfectly encapsulated that of what he termed "an oligarchy of wealth, fenced round and protected by a system of law, which makes many poor to make a few rich, and which, as a matter of history, has done its best to keep the mass of the people abject and ignorant, in order to secure the supremacy of a class."[14] The representatives of this oligarchy accused Bright of setting one class against the other.[15] Green challenged this, asking

> in what way do they propose to diminish the power of a class which has too much, unless by setting the rest of the people against it? Is there an instance on record in which a privileged class has passed a self-denying ordinance, and surrendered its power without pressure from outside?[16]

Green recalled how in 1860 the reform programme advocated by Bright had been shelved due to the fact that the public was prosperous and acquiescent.[17] The economic situation had deteriorated noticeably during 1866 and 1867, however.[18]

---

[11] *Ibid.*, V, p. 230. On the other hand, Mill himself argued that the suffrage was a power over others and no such right could exist in a liberal country: see Francis and Morrow, *A History of Political Thought in the Nineteenth Century*, p. 150.

[12] Quoted in Briggs, *The Age of Improvement*, p. 499.

[13] *Ibid.*

[14] 'The Reform Bill', V, pp. 228–9.

[15] *Ibid.*, V, p. 227.

[16] *Ibid.*

[17] *Ibid.*, V, p. 229.

[18] After a disastrous slump on the London stock exchange on the 11th of May 1866, the discount rate had gone up to 10 per cent, resulting in a rise in unemployment. Russell was forced to resign on the 18th of June. In July of the same

The general public's interest in reform also grew thanks to two external factors: the creation of the Reform League coincided both with Garibaldi's visit to England, and with the end of the American Civil War. The civil war in America had been perceived by British workers as a fight for liberty and against slavery.[19] Gladstone was struck by the support the Lancashire cotton workers gave to the Northern cause, even though that was against their economic interests. By imposing a blockade on Southern exports, the American States of the North had in fact helped bring the supply of cotton to Lancashire mills to a standstill. Gladstone said he felt "a shame and a scandal" at the thought that such men continued to be denied the vote.[20]

Green chose instead to focus on the support the ruling class gave to the slave states, commenting that

> there was not a politician or newspaper, claiming to be liberal and enlightened over the whole of Europe that did not know that it was a desperate effort on the part of a privileged class — privileged to hold slaves — to break up a Government, acknowledged to be the most beneficent in the world, because it could no longer work in its own interest. Just for that reason the privileged class in England, with its dependents, took sides with the slaveholders.[21]

Just as in Cromwell's time, an oligarchy had taken control of Parliament. According to Green, Macaulay was right when he asserted that now, as then, the conflict was not between the House of Commons and the Crown, or the House of Lords, but between the people and the House of Commons.[22] Green deemed the House of Commons to be little more than "a House of Lords in disguise."[23] There were 125 titled members such as Baronets, sons and heirs of Peers and so on in the House. In addition, there were numerous Colonels and Captains, the majority of whom belonged to the most important landowning families. Green claimed that "four-fifths of the

---

year, the Hyde Park protest called by the Reform League was banned. Meanwhile, Disraeli and Derby assumed control of the government. The hard line pursued by the Conservatives had the effect of intensifying the League's demands. See Feuchtwanger, *Democracy and Empire*, p. 37.

[19] See Briggs, *The Age of Improvement*, pp. 494–6.
[20] *Ibid.*, p. 558.
[21] 'The Reform Bill', V, p. 229.
[22] *Ibid.*, V, p. 227.
[23] *Ibid.*

members of the lower House are either great landowners or belong to the families of the great landowners."[24]

The Reform League had to equip itself for a long battle in which it needed to encourage public opinion to familiarise itself with the nature of the system by which the holders of power maintained their monopoly.[25] Electoral reform would function as the driving force for all other objectives and a more democratic system would therefore herald an era of major change. Green concluded:

> we know that, the longer our labour, the richer will be our reward: that the slower the harvest in ripening, the fuller it will be when it is ripe; and if the reform of Parliament, for which we wait, brings with it a free Church, free land, and free education, we shall rejoice to have refused all half measures, and shall feel that we have not waited and laboured in vain.[26]

The final agreement of July 1867 was very different from that originally envisaged by Disraeli and Derby. The two year residence requirement was abolished and all distinctions between compounders and householders were annulled. The rules regarding the distribution of seats were also changed. While continuing to privilege the countryside, the Conservatives significantly increased the number of representatives from the cities and highly populated areas.[27]

3. Gladstonian Reformism

Naturally Green was pleased with the outcome of the arduous electoral reform process. He began a speech in February 1869 with a toast in which he said both Conservatives and Liberals alike could join.[28] It was wrong to talk in terms of winners and losers because

> the winner is no party, Whig, Conservative, or Radical. The whole nation wins by a measure which makes us for the first time one people.[29]

Green was aware, however, of the ambivalence of the reform. It supplied "an immense leverage", but was capable of being

---

[24] *Ibid.*
[25] *Ibid.*, V, p. 231.
[26] *Ibid.*, V, p. 232.
[27] See Feuchtwanger, *Democracy and Empire*, pp. 43–4.
[28] 'Parliamentary Reform', 25 February 1868, *Works*, V, p. 232.
[29] *Ibid.*, V, p. 234

used as much for ill as for good.[30] It was clear though that, if in the past the government had not represented the poorer classes, now the situation had radically changed.[31] Green was quick to devise what he felt should be on the agenda of a future Liberal government.

The first major question to be addressed was that of education at all levels right up to university. He asserted that "without opening of the higher education to all classes there is no social unity."[32] The reorganisation of agriculture also needed to be tackled for, as it stood, it nurtured the whole gamut of attitudes underpinning the extravagant luxury of the upper classes, the servility of the middle classes and the poverty and recklessness of the lower ones.[33] Farm workers needed to have a real and permanent interest in the land: "as it is they are absolutely and hopelessly divorced from any prospect of ownership."[34] Their only option in old age was to enter the poorhouse. In times of hardship able-bodied agricultural labourers clogged up the job market in the cities, thus becoming a threat to those workers who were painstakingly struggling to defend themselves through industrial action.[35] The increase in size of that blighted class condemned to living on the margins of urban economies was largely caused by the influx of Irish immigrants who, having been reduced to conditions of slavery, had no option but to leave the land.[36] Green therefore considered land regulation in Ireland to be urgent and essential. By introducing such reforms, the new government would reawaken dwindling public interest in politics; as he emphasised, "these are great questions."[37]

Green was well aware of the risk that without a secret ballot members of the future Parliament might continue to be elected by corrupt municipalities. He thought corrupt men, who could avail themselves of "the long purse and the deep barrel"[38] — of huge economic resources and alcohol's powers

---

[30] *Ibid.*
[31] *Ibid.*
[32] *Ibid.*
[33] *Ibid.*
[34] *Ibid.*
[35] *Ibid.*, V, pp. 234–5.
[36] *Ibid.*, V, p. 235.
[37] *Ibid.*
[38] *Ibid.*

of seduction — constituted the greatest peril. Green hoped for the emergence of men of ability: talented speakers and writers who, most importantly, were not blighted by egoism or attracted by the false trophies of politics.[39] As he commented, "the majority of members of Parliament will doubtless continue to be very much what they have been, but if we can but get a small knot of men of better stuff returned, then the battle of social reform within the Reformed Parliament, though it may be a hard one, will be surely won."[40]

When Disraeli replaced Derby as Prime Minister in February 1868, Gladstone knew he had a reasonable chance of winning the next election. The election campaign focused on the question of the disestablishment of the Church of Ireland. Gladstone, convinced that there was no longer any justification for the dominant position of the Anglican Church in Ireland, quickly won the support of Catholics and members of the nonconformist churches.[41] While not recanting his participation in the ranks of the High Church Party, Gladstone thus became the symbol of a type of politics which sought to create full civil equality between the different denominations.[42]

The composition of Gladstone's government, however, did not fully meet Green's expectations. He had hoped that Bright[43] would have a more powerful role in the coalition and he considered the presence of Lowe harmful. Having opposed the extension of the suffrage, Lowe had also spoken out against the School Inquiry Commission report to which Green himself had contributed.[44] Green dubbed him "the most mischievous politician going."[45] Although the Liberals gained a majority of 110 seats in the election, the results in Lancashire,

---

[39] *Ibid.*

[40] *Ibid.*, V, p. 236.

[41] See Morley, *The Life of William Ewart Gladstone*, II, pp. 237–48.

[42] See Feuchtwanger, *Democracy and Empire*, p. 57. Meanwhile, the Irish independence movement was increasing its number of adherents (*ibid.*, p. 56).

[43] Bright became President of the Board of Trade in the new government formed by the victorious Liberal Party. Green viewed Bright as the man who, keeping "his light burning through the thick darkness of the Palmerston regime", had enabled the new generation to save itself from the kind of political apathy afflicting the rest of the country. Green even cited a few verses from *Paradise Lost* in trying to better convey his image of Bright. See 'The Reform Bill', V, p. 229.

[44] See Nettleship, *Memoir*, p. cxiii.

[45] *Ibid.*

where the Conservatives won twenty-two out of the thirty-three seats, went against the national pattern. This was mainly due to the Conservatives' ploy of exploiting the large presence of Irish immigrants in the area by playing on the anti-Catholic sentiments of the English workers. On the eve of his appointment as prime minister, Gladstone declared his intention to pacify Ireland. He personally pushed for the endorsement of both the Irish Church Bill (the disestablishment of the Anglican Church in Ireland) and the Irish Land Bills.[46] Both were to have major repercussions in Britain as the debate became ever more contentious.[47] Gladstone aimed to address directly the causes of Irish immigration through the Irish Land Bills which were approved in 1870. Green had already expressed his belief that the immigration question could only be solved by tackling the problem at its root.[48] The Irish peasants claimed property rights over the land they worked on, but prevailing British land law condemned them to a condition of endless servitude. Gladstone attempted to rescue them from the perils of evictions and rents which often deprived them of the basic means for survival. Many within the government feared that such legislation might lead to the introduction of similar measures regarding landed property in Britain.[49]

4. The Land Question

In Green's eyes, the land question was a key question. It had to be solved in order to allow common sense as Green conceived it to grow and mature. Facts proved to what extent a dogmatic acceptance of market laws was inadequate. If capitalism was subject to a continuous evolution, and capitalist appropriation was to be traced back to the dialectic between "form" and "matter", then "the increased wealth of one man does not naturally mean the diminished wealth of another."[50] However, the same dynamic did not apply to the case of the appropriation of land: "one man cannot acquire more land without oth-

---

[46] See Morley, *The Life of William Ewart Gladstone*, I, pp. 891–931.
[47] See Feuchtwanger, *Democracy and Empire*, pp. 58–62.
[48] 'Parliamentary Reform', V, p. 235.
[49] See Feuchtwanger, *Democracy and Empire*, pp. 61–2.
[50] 'Lectures on the Principles of Political Obligation', sect. 226, *Works*, II, p. 530.

ers having less."[51] In Green's view, the property of land owners clearly raised the question of those workers who, because they were unable to become possessors of property, were simultaneously deprived of the possibility of developing their moral faculties and, therefore, of realizing themselves. Green admitted that in England at that time great numbers of people could not have property "in that sense in which alone it is of value, viz. as a permanent apparatus for carrying out a plan of life, for expressing ideas of what is beautiful, or giving effect to benevolent wishes."[52] Such people did not have "the chance of providing means for a free moral life, of developing and giving reality or expression to a good will, an interest in social well-being."[53] The question of the land was therefore above all an educational question. Many had so low a standard of living that "if they have the opportunity of saving, they do not use it, and keep bringing children into the world at a rate which perpetuates the evil."[54]

The appropriation of land had been originally effected "not by the expenditure of labour or the results of labour on the land, but by force."[55] So that, when the capitalist created a demand for labour, the supply had come from men

> whose ancestors, if not themselves, were trained in habits of serfdom; men whose life has been one of virtually forced labour, relieved by church-charities or the poor law (which in part took the place of these charities); who were thus in no condition to contract freely for the sale of their labour, and had nothing of that sense of family-responsibility which might have made them insist on having the chance of saving. Landless countrymen, whose ancestors were serfs, are the parents of the proletariate of great towns.[56]

Like Mill, Green was for some form of public control with regard to land. The landlord should be prevented from so using his land as to make it "unserviceble to the wants of men (e.g. by turning fertile land into a forest), and from taking liberties with it incompatible with the conditions of general free-

---

[51] *Ibid.*, sect. 229, II, p. 533.
[52] *Ibid.*, sect. 220, II, p. 525.
[53] *Ibid.*
[54] *Ibid.*, sect. 228, II, p. 532.
[55] *Ibid.*
[56] *Ibid.*, sect. 229, II, p. 532.

dom and health."[57] In England, and still more in Ireland, the landlords not only took no interest in their estates but discouraged their tenants from taking an interest themselves. "Most of them", Mill observed, "by withholding leases altogether, and giving the farmer no guarantee of possession beyond a single harvest, keep the land on a footing little more favourable to improvement than in the time of our barbarous ancestors."[58] Mill maintained that when landed property was no longer expedient, at the same time it became unfair.[59] Like Mill, Green affirmed that the sale of land should be enforced by law when public convenience required it.[60] Once again, like Mill, Green favoured compensation for the land-owner who was compelled to sell his land and, like Mill, he was for the abolition of the right of primogeniture.[61]

Green disagreed, as did Mill, with the idea that the simple application of the laws of supply and demand could improve the condition of the agricultural labourers. However, he did point out the disparity of payment between regions. For example, while the average wage in his native county of Yorkshire varied between sixteen and eighteen pounds, in Dorset it was only eight pounds.[62] Green believed Yorkshire farm workers were better paid because they were able to say to their bosses "if you don't like my terms I can take my labour somewhere else."[63] He felt that the main objective of the National Agricultural Labourers Union should therefore be the establishment of a fund which would enable workers to defend themselves against the abuses of their employers. Green knew that the farmers would never concede anything more than they absolutely had to. The only way to give greater weight to the demands of the agricultural labourers therefore was through combined action. The Union's object was to send men in districts where employment could not be found, to areas where

---

[57] *Ibid.*, sect. 229, II, p. 533.
[58] *Principles of Political Economy, With Some of Their Applications to Social Philosophy*, ed. J.M. Robson, Introduction by V.W. Bladen, 2 vols (Toronto, 1965), bk II, ch. ii, sect. 6, p. 229.
[59] See *ibid.*, bk II, ch. ii, sect. 6, p. 230.
[60] 'Lecture on Liberal Legislation and Freedom of Contract', *Works*, III, p. 377.
[61] *Principles of Political Economy*, bk II, ch. ii, sect. 6, pp. 230–1; 'Lecture on Liberal Legislation and Freedom of Contract', III, p. 377; *Principles of Political Economy*, bk II, ch. ii, sect. 4, pp. 223–6; and 'Lecture on Liberal Legislation and Freedom of Contract', III, p. 378, respectively.
[62] 'To the Agricultural Labourers', V, p. 239.
[63] *Ibid.*

labour was scarce and jobs could be found. For this, Green assured them, "the most rigid economists could not find fault with them."[64]

Both workers and farmers were victims of poor management, which was encouraged by laws such as those regarding the inalienability of the land and poaching. Green noted how even "the most cautious of our public men, who would never speak a word against the sacred privileges of a landlord, admitted that the system was carried too far in this country."[65] Thanks to education, farm workers would be able to be "free, — free to carry their labour to the best market, and free in every way to make the most of the talents which God had given them."[66] In order to remove the monopoly on education in the countryside which allowed the squires and the clergy to oppress the labourers, the employment of school-age children would have to be made illegal.[67] Until such time as the agricultural labourers got the vote, however, there would be no significant improvements to their quality of life. As Green observed, "they knew that five years ago household suffrage was granted to householders in towns, but that the labouring poor in the country were left out."[68] Thanks to the introduction of household suffrage, more measures benefiting urban workers had been approved in the previous five years than in the whole of the previous century.[69]

5. The Liquor Question

While those influences of feudalism and landlordism which tended to throw a shiftless population upon the centres of industry had been left unchecked, nothing was done either to give such a population a chance of bettering itself. "Their health, housing, and schooling were", Green emphasised, "unprovided for."[70] Things were made worse by the liquor traffic, which further undermined human dignity. For that reason, some further restriction of the freedom of contract was unavoidable. "The freedom to do as they like on the part of one

---

[64] *Ibid.*
[65] *Ibid.*, V, p. 240.
[66] *Ibid.*
[67] *Ibid.*, V, pp. 240-1.
[68] *Ibid.*, V, p. 241.
[69] *Ibid.*
[70] 'Lectures on the Principles of Political Obligation', sect. 230, II, p. 534.

set of men may involve", Green argued, "the ultimate disqual-ification of many others, or of a succeeding generation, for the exercise of rights."[71] There was no right to freedom in the pur-chase and sale of a particular commodity, if the general result of allowing such freedom was "to detract from freedom in the higher sense, from the general power of men to make the best of themselves." Green added: "with anyone who looks calmly at the facts, there can be no doubt that the present habits of drinking in England do lay a heavy burden on the free devel-opment of man's powers for social good."[72] However, if the necessity of state intervention was obvious in the case of prop-erty in land, the case of the liquor traffic was much more complicated. Mill's criterion, grounded on interest, was inadequate. Green deprecated the effect of the system then in force, which was to prevent "the drink-shops from coming unpleasantly near the houses of well-to-do people, and to crowd them upon the quarters occupied by the poorer classes, who have practically no power of keeping the nuisance from them."[73] From Green's viewpoint, the drink question had extremely important political implications: it could thwart democracy.

In 1872 Green joined the major British anti-alcohol organisa-tion, the United Kingdom Alliance, which had been founded in 1853.[74] There were few Tories in the movement; indeed, its ability to threaten that it might support the Conservative Party was usually considered a useful means of making the Liberals see reason. When, however, the Alliance stepped up its efforts to have the free sale of alcohol suppressed by law, it was clear that it would come into conflict with those Liberals who believed in the principle of laissez faire.[75]

Rejected by the UK Alliance and opposed by the breweries, Bruce's proposal was withdrawn before it came before the House for a second reading.[76] It was finally approved in 1872

---

[71] *Ibid.*, sect. 210, II, p. 515.

[72] 'Lecture on Liberal Legislation and Freedom of Contract', III, p. 383.

[73] *Ibid.*, III, p. 383.

[74] Nettleship, *Memoir*, pp. cxv–vii.

[75] Feuchtwanger, *Democracy and Empire*, pp. 76–7.

[76] A.E. Dingle, *The Campaign for Prohibition in Victorian England: the United King-dom Alliance, 1872–1895* (London, 1980), pp. 30–3. Bruce had put forward his own proposal in 1871 in an effort to tighten the laws governing the issuing of licences for new pubs. Magistrates would have the power to authorise retail sales of alcoholic beverages although, in such cases, a three-fifths majority of

after having undergone major changes. The new law limited itself to leaving the decision of when public-houses should close to the discretion of the local magistrates responsible for the issuing of licences. This choice, however, was limited to a time between 10 o'clock and midnight. While the UK Alliance organised petitions advocating a 10 o'clock closing time, publicans sought to extend drinking time to midnight. In Oxford, the majority declared itself in favour of setting closing time at midnight while the magistrates opted for half past eleven.[77] This decision inflamed the public. The main streets of the city filled with groups of rioters and for two long weekends, numerous acts of vandalism were committed. The homes of members of the UK Alliance were targeted and heavily damaged.[78]

If nothing else, the entire episode had the merit of highlighting the respective strengths of the opposing sides. The Alliance had to contend not only with the enormous power of those groups with interests linked to the sale of alcohol, but also with a body of public opinion which showed itself unbothered by pleas based on ethics. The Conservative Party now had the opportunity to give vent to that long and undisputed libertarian tradition of 'the simple pleasures of life' which was deeply rooted amongst the working classes.[79] Green decided at this point to declare his teetotalism publicly.[80] He believed that alcoholism impeded the development of moral values and represented a permanent threat to the formation of the kind of social conscience which he considered the pre-requisite for citizenship.

Excessive drinking was one of the key questions of the 1874 election campaign. Green could not but admit his alarm at the fact that the Liberal candidate in his constituency, William

---

ratepayers could limit the number of licences issued and set an earlier closing time. Alcohol retailers presented a united front against Bruce's proposals while the UK Alliance condemned them as not going far enough. The resentment expressed by those interests under threat was thus not counterbalanced by support from the anti-alcohol movement, see Feuchtwanger, *Democracy and Empire*, pp. 97–8.

[77] *Oxford Chronicle*, 31 August 1872, p. 8.
[78] B. Harrison, *Drink and the Victorians: the Temperance Question in England, 1815–1872* (London, 1971), pp. 279–85.
[79] Feuchtwanger, *Democracy and Empire*, p. 78.
[80] See P. Nicholson, 'T.H. Green and State Action: Liquor Legislation', *History of Political Thought*, VI, 1985, pp. 520–1. The same piece also appears in Vincent, ed., *The Philosophy of T. H Green*, pp. 76–103.

Harcourt, seemed indifferent to the problem. According to Green, Harcourt underestimated "the drinking evil altogether and next to run down all legislative attempts to check it on the ground that it is not the business of the state to make people good but to enable every one to do as he likes."[81] The UK Alliance had advised its members not to vote for those candidates who refused to support the revival of Bruce's Permissive Bill. With his customary sense of moderation, Green attempted to put pressure on Harcourt while excluding any prejudicial kind of stance.[82] As he commented, "I never should dream of refusing my vote to a candidate, whom in other respects I thought good."[83] J. S. Mill, cited by Harcourt in his defence,[84] was also opposed to the position taken by the UK Alliance. During the 1868 election campaign, Mill had spoken out against any kind of restriction.[85]

6. The Need for Education

If, in Green's eyes, land and liquor constituted the two greatest hindrances to the expression of that common sense which had to be nourished by every pressure coming from below, education was the means by which the most disadvantaged could realize themselves. Education would emancipate those energies which were oppressed by the force of circumstances. Education must be the vehicle through which a conscience that stemmed from the mingling of common sense and the divine would express itself. Accordingly, despite drawing its inspiration from religion, education should not impose any dogmatic viewpoint. Common sense, as Green conceived it, should not

---

[81] 'Letter to W. Harcourt, January 1873', *Works*, V, p. 450; partially quoted also in Nettleship, *Memoir*, p. cxviii.

[82] See his letter to the Editor, 'Mr. Harcourt and the Licensing Bill', *Oxford Chronicle*, 4 January 1873, *Works*, V, p. 219.

[83] 'Letter to W. Harcourt, January 1873', V, p. 450.

[84] The speech in question was given in Oxford town hall on 30 December 1872 and extensively reported in both *The Times* (31 December 1872) and the *Oxford Chronicle* (4 January 1873). See *Works*, V, p. 218.

[85] In a letter to Dawson Burns published in *The Times* of 7 November 1868, Mill had argued "The use or non use of alcoholic liquors is a subject on which every sane and grown-up person ought to judge for himself under his own responsibility, and . . . interference with that private responsibility from known good motives, and with however much apparent justification is not, in my eyes, made allowable by the fact of its being sanctioned by the vote of the majority" (quoted in Nicholson, 'T.H. Green and State Action: Liquor Legislation', p. 535).

be interfered with. In this way, education was a very difficult instrument to deal with. It is not surprising that of the various legislative measures introduced by the Gladstone government, it was the 1870 Education Act which aroused the greatest dissent.

The Education Aid Societies were founded in Manchester in 1864 and in Birmingham in 1867. In 1869 the Education Aid Society became the National Education League. Amongst the objectives listed in its Charter was the realisation of non-sectarian and free primary schooling with the state or local authorities responsible for ensuring attendance. By using the term "non-sectarian", the League was deliberately avoiding "secular" because it did not harbour any anti-religious prejudice. In fact, the League counted Joseph Chamberlain amongst its members. Chamberlain was the leader of the Unitarians, a group with whom Green felt a particular affinity.[86]

The National Education League considered itself the natural heir of both the Reform League and the Anti-corn Law League. W.E. Forster, who was sympathetic to the ideas of the Broad Church Party and the National Education League, presented his bill on primary education in October 1869. This provided for the subdivision of England and Wales (the bill did not apply to Scotland and Ireland) into school districts. It also contained the provision that *ad hoc* school boards could be put in place should the minister responsible for education judge the existing structures in a particular district to be substandard.

In addition, both town councils and ratepayers, by majority, could request the establishment of a school board. The boards would be composed of between five and fifteen members, according to the size of the district, and would have the power to request local authorities to introduce a tax for the creation of new schools and to guarantee school attendance. The most serious problem to be tackled was that regarding religious education. Forster attempted to resolve this by granting a sort of local option: each board would be able to choose the type of religious education to be taught in the schools under its control, and parents who disagreed with the eventual choice

[86] Feuchtwanger, *Democracy and Empire*, pp. 62–3; Green, letter to Henry Sidgwick, 28 December 1868, *Works*, V, p. 422.

would be able to withdraw their children from these schools.[87] In January 1870, Green expressed his complete confidence in the merits of Forster's proposal.[88] At the same time, however, he advocated an agenda supporting the National Education League's programme which called for a free and compulsory primary school system.[89]

As the reporter from the *Oxford Chronicle* noted, Green reiterated his belief that public funding of the schools and compulsory attendance had to be linked to a non-sectarian form of religious education. Green argued that it was not the state's obligation to continue subsidising the institutional Church which already enjoyed "a great advantage over other denominations in establishing schools."[90] In fact, as Green observed, a large part of these public funds finished up in the hands of those whom he branded as "the richest, the genteelist sect which happened for the present to have the advantage of being established."[91] Green argued that with the advent of a more representative parliament in the wake of the 1867 reform, the citizens of Britain would continue to take on greater responsibilities for themselves.[92] Green also considered compulsory attendance to be the only means of reducing widespread juvenile illiteracy.[93]

Green was very disappointed with the consequences of Forster's law.[94] As he later wrote, its authors "allowed their attention to be concentrated solely on the palpable fact of [the existing system's] insufficiency for providing schools in the less favoured districts, and in their hurry to remedy this evil, did not consider that the plan which should supply schools most quickly might not, in the long run, be the best for the education of the country."[95] Green noted that, after 1870, there were a million and a half children enrolled in government inspected schools. Another million and a half children attended schools in which they had little chance of learning to read and write. Many children in the cities continued hardly to

[87]   See Feuchtwanger, *Democracy and Empire*, pp. 64–5.
[88]   'National Education', 27 January 1870, *Works*, V, p. 238.
[89]   *Ibid.*, V, p. 236.
[90]   *Ibid.*, V, p. 238.
[91]   *Ibid.*
[92]   *Ibid.*, V, pp. 237–8.
[93]   *Ibid.*, V, p. 237.
[94]   Nettleship, *Memoir*, p. cxiv.
[95]   'The Elementary School System of England', *Works*, III, p. 434.

attend school while many village children worked and received no education whatsoever.[96] In Green's opinion, the main flaw of the Education Act was that it failed to extend the system of school boards to the whole country. He hoped to see these boards granted wider-ranging powers. Green himself tried to join the Oxford school board which, after much resistance, was finally enacted in 1871. He did not succeed in doing so until 1874.[97]

In the meantime, Green took over from Edwin Palmer as tutor and Jowett was appointed Master of Balliol.[98] Thanks to legislation by the Gladstone government, Green was probably the first lay person to hold the position of tutor.[99] Green had served on the University entrance examination board since 1866. The following year, he supported a scheme to grant scholarships to candidates who, unable to pay the fees, would otherwise be forced to abandon their studies. In order to supervise his students better, Green decided to move to St. Giles Street where a residence had been provided for them. The new statute of the University of Oxford had permitted enrolment independent of college membership since 1868 and, in the same year, the age-old requirement of participation in religious activities was abolished.[100]

Now that the University allowed students to live outside the colleges and attend University lectures free of charge, Green asked what reason remained to conceive of the University and the city as "two antagonistic bodies?"[101] A Grading of Secondary Schools conference took place in May 1877. On that occasion, Green declared that secondary school should be neither obligatory nor, except for a minority, free. Previously, at the time of the School Inquiry Commission, he had proposed a reform of the education system which, starting with the primary system, would have allowed everyone the possibility of going to University. The differentiated structure of such a sys-

---

[96]   *Ibid.*
[97]   Nettleship, *Memoir*, pp. cxiv–v.
[98]   *Ibid*, p. lxi.
[99]   Nettleship, *Memoir*, p. lxi. In 1871, Gladstone abolished the requirement that tutors in Oxford and Cambridge had to be men of the cloth (see Parry, *Democracy and Religion*, pp. 307–8 and Morley, *The Life of William Ewart Gladstone*, I, pp. 947–8).
[100] Nettleship, *Memoir*, p. cvii.
[101] 'Proposed Oxford High School for Boys', 21 December 1877, *Works*, V, p. 308; 'Candidature for Oxford Town Council', V, p. 280 (for the quotation).

tem would meet the needs of the job market and thus succeed in attracting private financing. It should not be the responsibility of the state to fund scholarships.[102] Green was adamant about the necessity of maintaining fees, saying that "people should not have a present made them of what they can well afford to pay for."[103] An indiscriminate fee-waiver would also have the effect of lowering educational standards.

The key point of Green's proposal challenged the class basis of the existing system. One could say that Green's ambition was to offer the youth of the lower classes the intellectual advantages of the class above them, thus "putting the real scholar in place of the mere gentleman."[104] Green hoped that the situation in England would become like that in Scotland where the proportion of the population with a university education was three or four times that in England.[105] Such an objective implied major changes. Green noted however that there was no longer any "barrier of Church or creed or class in the Universities of the nation."[106] It was essential however that the High Schools modified their traditional curricula and approach. Green asserted that "the sort of education which was needed as preliminary to the highest must be made cheaper and more easily accessible than it had been", while "the benefits of the secondary schools must be open to girls as well as boys."[107]

Green believed that, in order to overcome all kinds of religious, class and sexual discrimination, the number of endowed schools should be increased.[108] The question of education for girls remained essentially a political problem. As with the extension of the vote to the working classes, so in the eventual case of female suffrage it was in the Liberal interest that women be able to exercise their new political rights intelligently. The inadequate education provided for women served

---

[102] The Taunton Commission was much less in favour than Green of providing fee-waivers for deserving students. It was willing to grant three fee reductions for every forty students. On this point, see P. Gordon and J. White, *Philosophers as Educational Reformers: The Influence of Idealism on British Educational Thought and Practice* (London, 1979), pp. 82–5.
[103] 'Lecture on the Grading of Secondary Schools', *Works*, III, p. 412.
[104] *Ibid*, III, p. 390.
[105] 'Education for Girls', 18 June 1878, *Works*, V, p. 323.
[106] *Ibid*.
[107] *Ibid*.
[108] *Ibid.*, V, pp. 323–4.

to exacerbate their subjection greatly.[109] Green envisaged a better quality of education for women which would seek to develop "a character not less manly, but more gentle and sympathetic and religious than they found in our present race of young men."[110] Setting to one side abstract questions "discussed under the head of the rights of women", Green asserted that the progress of a civilisation could be measured by examining the degree to which women were "not merely subservient to the pleasure, but habitual associates of men."[111] Green's decision to join the University Extension movement was also linked to his desire to help effect the surmounting of all kinds of sexual discrimination.[112] Given that women were excluded from university education, Green considered it important that University Extension should at least try to reach them in their homes.[113]

Green also continued to fight for the extension of university education to the working classes. In his role as a governor of King Edward's School in Birmingham, one of the schools he had inspected as an assistant to the Schools Inquiry Commission, he called for the introduction of evening-classes, in the hope that these might become the basis of a local institution of university education.[114] Green believed that a large number of people wished to continue studying and "that among the superior artisans there was a great eagerness for knowledge,

---

[109] *Ibid.,* V, pp. 326–7.
[110] *Ibid.,* V, pp. 326 and 327.
[111] *Ibid.,* V, p. 327.
[112] Green was, along with Jowett, one of the leading members of the so-called University Extension movement. Inspired by the efforts of James Stuart, a lecturer at Cambridge, the movement aimed to bring workers closer to the academic world. During his campaign, Stuart had occasion to meet Green's maternal uncle, David James Vaughan, who had devised a college for workers in Leicester. This collaboration between Vaughan and Stuart quickly turned Leicester into one of the main centres of University Extension. In order to promote University Extension, in an 1874 memorandum for the Royal Commission Jowett budgeted for the allocation of forty thousand pounds by the University of Oxford towards the funding of a series of conferences in locations usually excluded from the academic circuit. When, in 1878, Oxford approved a measure in favour of University Extension for the first time in its history, Green was appointed chairman of the commission authorised to oversee its implementation. See Richter, *The Politics of Conscience,* pp. 360–1; also J.F.C. Harrison, *Learning and Living, 1790–1960: A Study on the History of the Adult Education Movement* (London, 1961), pp. 235–45.
[113] 'University Extension', 25 September 1878, *Works,* V, p. 329.
[114] *Ibid.,* V, p. 330.

especially in certain subjects — such subjects as political economy, history, and some branches of physical science."[115] The
Worker's Education Association was founded in the wake of
the University Extension movement. Along with the Christian
Social Union, the new association worked towards the opening of a college in Bristol.[116] Balliol granted the new college an
annual subsidy of three hundred pounds. In return, the college
undertook to offer reduced fees for adult education.[117] Green
held that the main objective of education should not be that of
helping students

> to become a gentleman at large. It was much more important that
> they should teach the people to respect themselves and to respect
> each other without rising in the world, and to appreciate those
> true pleasures which were not to be bought for money.[118]

It was necessary "to teach them first to read so as to delight in
reading, so as to become what we might call 'freemen of the
Kingdom of books'."[119]

Green gave two lectures in 1878 at the Central School in
Oxford on the English primary school system. He pointed out
that, on its own, the private system could not cope effectively
with the educational needs of a modern democracy and that
the position of the voluntarists "did not square with the
facts."[120] Green also argued that 'voluntarism' produced a
number of undesirable effects with regard to morals. Schools,
often opened under the aegis of religious groups which
stamped a firm denominational character on them, ended up
fuelling the belief that education need not be equal for all: "the
ordinary citizen was thus taught to regard the schooling of his
own and other people's children as a matter which might
properly be left to the zeal of any specially religious people
about him."[121]

---

[115] *Ibid.*, V, p. 329.
[116] See Gordon and White, *Philosophers as Educational Reformers*, pp. 107–8.
[117] When Balliol later decided to renew this commitment for the next five years, at
£250 a year, the money actually came from Jowett and Green personally. Charlotte Symonds was originally from Bristol and the former house of the
Symonds family is now part of the University of Bristol. See Richter, *The Politics of Conscience*, p. 361.
[118] 'The New High School for Boys and Elementary Education in Oxford', 23
December 1879, *Works*, V, p. 359.
[119] *Ibid.*
[120] 'Elementary School System', III, p. 427.
[121] *Ibid.*, III, p. 432.

If, on the one hand, consistently with the dialectic inherited from Baur, Green urged his opponents — and Mill was one of them — to consider more carefully "the conditions" of the maintenance of freedom,[122] on the other, Green's position on the regulation of the liquor traffic revealed a deeper discrepancy from Mill's. The starting point of Green's speculation was not the individual but society. In this sense, Green was more akin, not only to Vane but also to the Italian exile Mazzini, who shared his conception of an educational democracy. While, in Mill's view, liberty should be regarded both as a means and an end, Mazzini, who on this perfectly agreed with Carlyle, identified the end of human liberty not with the highest happiness but *"the highest nobleness possible."*[123] Mazzini considered democracy above all as "an *educational problem.*"[124] He posed the crucial question:

> See before you men, free, emancipated, conscious of their faculties, acquainted with their rights, with God's universe open before them. What use will they make of their liberty?[125]

Thus Mill, Mazzini and Green all highly valued the workers' tendency to form associations, and rejected the theory according to which, as Mill wrote, "the lot of the poor, in all things which affect them collectively, should be regulated *for* them, not *by* them;"[126] Green, like Mazzini, believed that education and self-discipline were preliminaries to a more democratic society in which labourers could become capitalists themselves. As Green noted, "their combination in work gives them every opportunity, if they have the *needful education and self-discipline,* for forming societies for the investment of savings."[127] Green thought that there was nothing in the nature of capitalism to exclude the labourers from that education of the sense of responsibility which depended on the possibility of permanent ownership. Mill's individualistic democracy was rooted in religious dissent: "the principles of the Reformation", Mill stated, "have reached as low down in society as reading and writing, and the poor will not much longer accept

---

[122] 'Lecture on Liberal Legislation and Freedom of Contract', III, p. 367.
[123] Mastellone, *Mazzini and Marx: Thoughts Upon Democracy in Europe*, p. 187.
[124] *Ibid.*, p. 165.
[125] *Ibid.*, p. 166.
[126] *Principles of Political Economy*, bk IV, ch. vii, sect. 1, p. 759.
[127] 'Lectures on the Principles of Political Obligation', sect. 227, II, p. 531 (italics mine).

morals and religion of other people's prescribing."[128] Green's educational democracy, which stemmed from a Puritan conception inclined to view institutions as tools for developing the moral faculties of men, aimed not to deny but to complete Mill's teaching.

7. The 1874 Election Defeat

In Green's analysis, the 1874 Liberal defeat was precisely a consequence of the fact that the Liberals had showed themselves completely uninterested in the problem of the education of the masses. Although the government was working with a vigour never seen before, nothing was being done to train the new voters. The Liberals had disestablished the Anglican Church in Ireland. With the passing of the Irish Land Act, they had tried to solve the Irish land question. With the abolition of the sale of commissions, they had restored the army to the nation. They had even created a national education system which, while not perfect, at least represented a good beginning. Meanwhile, however, as Green remarked,

> the country had been passing through a phase of sudden and unexampled commercial prosperity, and political enthusiasm had been lost in what we might call a general riot of luxury in which nearly all classes had their share. The money and beer flowed freely. Money quickly made was quickly spent, and it seemed as if all classes were disposed, not exactly to rest and be thankful, but at least to take their ease, eat, drink and be merry.[129]

The Liberal candidates in Green's constituency, Cardwell and Harcourt, did not support the Permissive Bill while Hall, the Conservative candidate, was a brewer by trade. Green became chairman of the election committee of the UK Alliance's local section, formed in Oxford ten days before polling.[130] Although the committee advocated a position of electoral abstention, Green was quick to distance himself from this stance.[131] Green was convinced that the political behaviour of the masses was heavily influenced by their dependence on

---

[128] *Principles of Political Economy*, bk IV, ch. vii, sect. 1, p. 762.
[129] 'The New Liberal Hall', 28 September 1876, *Works*, V, p. 270.
[130] See Nicholson, 'T.H. Green and State Action: Liquor Legislation', p. 523.
[131] D.A. Hamer, *The Politics of Electoral Pressure: A Study in the History of Victorian Reform Agitations* (Hassocks, 1977), pp. 190–1, 195, 200.

alcohol.[132] The alliance between the Conservative Party and the brewers was rather predictable therefore.

Like Gladstone, Green identified a clear link between the debacle suffered by the Liberals in 1874 and the inability of the working classes to resist the temptations of drink.[133] As he recalled in a speech in 1879, many British cities "were drawn away from their Liberal allegiance by the seductions of the beer barrel."[134] In Green's assessment, however, the Liberal defeat was primarily the consequence of a more general moral decline which, on the one hand, was the result of greater prosperity and, on the other, was due to the scant enthusiasm displayed by Liberals in their efforts to offer new voters an adequate political and moral training.

The 1874 election thus caught the Liberal Party everywhere unprepared. The constituencies had become sluggish from a political point of view, while those whom Green defined as "the vested interests" were ready for revenge.[135] These interests, identified by Green as the clergy, landowners and publicans, served to create a Parliament which consisted of "more brewers and less brain."[136] Alcohol dependence had played a major role in pushing the masses towards the Conservatives. Green advised farm workers: "Be sober, steady, and self-denying; remember the public-house is your greatest enemy, as the School-house is your greatest friend, and then the victory will certainly be yours."[137] The Liberals had failed to teach the public "that liberalism meant something, and something in which they had a very close interest."[138]

Green frequently heard the counter-argument that those who wanted to regulate trade in alcoholic beverages should be

---

[132] Nettleship, *Memoir*, p. cxviii.
[133] Following the election defeat, Gladstone wrote in a letter dated 6 February 1874: "We have been borne down in a torrent of gin and beer." Morley, *The Life of William Ewart Gladstone*, II, p. 103. For an analysis of the importance of the prohibition question in the 1874 elections, see H.J. Hanham, *Elections and Party Management: Politics in the Time of Disraeli and Gladstone* (London, 1959), pp. 221–7; also Harrison, *Drink and the Victorians*, pp. 279–85.
[134] 'National Loss and Gain under a Conservative Government', 5 December 1879, *Works*, V, p. 348.
[135] *Ibid.*
[136] *Ibid.*
[137] 'To the Agricultural Labourers', 9 December 1874, *Works*, V, p. 250.
[138] 'The New Liberal Hall', V, p. 270.

considered "not the friends of freedom, but its enemies."[139] To those, such as the Bishop of Peterborough, who declared they preferred England free to England sober, Green responded that the sobriety of the English people was a precondition of its liberty.[140] Green argued that it was necessary to understand fully the meaning of the word 'liberty'. As he explained, "if freedom was doing exactly what a person pleased, if he desired to go into a publichouse, and get drunk, and if he thought it was interfering with his liberty for any one to restrain him", then in that case, Green commented, "if that was the sort of freedom they desired they must go back to the naked savage in order to find it."[141]

On the contrary, Green asserted, liberty for the individual implied bringing out the best in oneself, it meant "to turn to the best account all the talents and capabilities God had given him."[142] He added that "only in that sense was freedom worth having."[143] Referring to the 1874 defeat, Green repeated his conviction that the Liberals had been defeated principally by gossip and beer.[144] While the Conservatives had proved capable of transforming "the public-houses into Tory clubs" and of using money and beer to increase their influence, the Liberals had presumed that workers "would be on their side, as they would be if they knew their own interest."[145]

8. The Disraeli Government and Green's Political Activity

The first session of the new Parliament was dedicated to labour laws and, naturally, to the Intoxicating Liquors Bill.[146] The Home Secretary R.A. Cross proposed to extend pub-lic-house opening hours by half an hour and Green felt this was an important signal. At a special conference of the Oxford

[139] 'Temperance and Freedom', 4 March 1875, *Works*, V, p. 255.
[140] 'Temperance and Freedom', V, p. 255. W.C. Magee, an Anglican Bishop and supporter of the Church of England Temperance Society, in fact agreed with the regulation of trade in alcoholic beverages. He felt it entirely arbitrary how-ever that this should be decided by a majority vote. See Nicholson, 'T.H. Green and State Action: Liquor Legislation', pp. 531–2.
[141] 'Temperance and Freedom', V, p. 255.
[142] *Ibid.*
[143] *Ibid.*
[144] 'The Liberal Party and Liberal Policies', 18 March 1875, *Works*, V, p. 256.
[145] *Ibid.*
[146] Feuchtwanger, *Democracy and Empire*, p. 85.

branch of the UK Alliance, called to discuss the Bill, Green commented:

> It was said that half-an-hour made but little difference, but practical men knew differently. It meant the difference on a Saturday night between freshness and drunkenness, between what was bad enough and having so much that they disturbed the peace and probably went home and beat their wives.[147]

If this measure was in the interests of a particular class, which would see its profits rise, it would also clearly have the effect of encouraging immorality and would increase the rates. Furthermore, Cross hoped to abolish the clause providing for the approval of licences by local committees. Green considered this clause extremely important.[148] Green deemed Cross's proposals to be little more than the result "of a tacit understanding between Conservative electioneering wire-pullers and the publicans at the last election."[149] The fact that magistrates and police superintendents from across the whole of England had unanimously come out in favour of the reduction of opening hours made Cross's measures particularly "scandalous" in Green's view.[150]

Green believed it imperative therefore that ratepayers should present a petition against these proposals and he finished his discussion of the subject by advocating support for a motion in which, in view of the clear wishes of public opinion and the unanimous view of magistrates and police authorities nationwide, "this conference expresses its profound regret that Her Majesty's Government have introduced a bill to extend the hours of drinking in gin-shops, spirit-vaults, and public-houses, not only in the metropolis, but also throughout the larger portion of the kingdom."[151] At a rally held in November 1874, Green called for local controls:

> This meeting earnestly calls upon Parliament either to deal directly and efficiently with the cause of these evils, or permit the people in their respective parishes and towns to prevent a nuisance and a curse being thrust upon them or continued in their

---

[147] 'Temperance', 6 May 1874, *Works*, V, p. 243.
[148] *Ibid.*, V, pp. 243–4.
[149] *Ibid.*, V, p. 244.
[150] *Ibid.*, V, p. 243.
[151] *Ibid.*, V, p. 244.

midst, by the action of any licensing authority, or for the profit of a mercenary capitalist.[152]

He also argued that by now the elite of the working classes were in favour of prohibition and that "whatever they asked for loud enough they would be sure to get."[153] Inspired by the presence of General Neal Dow, who had successfully combined the battle for black emancipation with that against the free sale of alcohol, Green observed that the latter was much more difficult to win because the victims of alcohol, unlike those of slavery, were scarcely aware of their condition.[154]

In 1875 Green became treasurer of the Oxford diocese branch of the Church of England Temperance Society and, the following year, was appointed President of the Oxford Band of Hope Temperance Union.[155] Some others, unlike Green, believed that the priority should not be the reduction of alcohol consumption, but rather education and the improvement of living conditions amongst the poor.[156] While not naming Cross, Green was clearly referring to him when he argued that "however useful the various agencies employed for elevating working men were, none of them would be effective until they had broken the back of the drink traffic."[157]

Green disagreed with those Liberals who believed they could simply sit and wait for the Conservatives to make mistakes.[158] He felt it necessary "to enlighten the political darkness" surrounding the masses dependent on alcohol.[159] Green attempted to offer workers an alternative meeting-place to the public-house by opening a coffee-tavern in the St. Clement's

---

[152] 'Temperance', 24 November 1874, *Works*, V, p. 245.
[153] 'Temperance and Freedom', *Works*, V, pp. 255–6.
[154] *Ibid.*, V, p. 255.
[155] Nettleship, *Memoir*, p. cxv.
[156] 'Temperance', V, p. 245.
[157] *Ibid.* In 1875 Cross, while not modifying the Criminal Law Amendment Act which was hated by the unions, launched a measure aimed at improving workers' living conditions. The Artisan Dwellings Act gave Town Councils the power to draw up redevelopment plans for those areas which had been declared insalubrious by the Health Inspector. By 1881, only ten out of eighty-seven cities had made use of the Act. Birmingham, where Joseph Chamberlain, the leader of the National Education League, had been elected Mayor, was one of the few to do so. See Feuchtwanger, *Democracy and Empire*, pp. 88–9.
[158] 'The New Liberal Hall', V, p. 269.
[159] 'The Liberal Party and Liberal Policies', 18 March 1875, *Works*, V, p. 256.

district of Oxford in 1875.[160] While recognising that pub-lic-houses addressed a specific need, Green objected to some of the behaviour they encouraged.[161] He therefore tried to cre-ate a kind of public-house in which there was no consumption of alcohol and where, as a result, other activities might be pur-sued. He hoped the coffee-tavern would be a place where "working men and others might get refreshment of a kind less liable to abuse than that to be obtained at the ordinary pub-lic-house."[162] His intention was to provide people with "a place where men might meet and talk and play harmless quiet games and discuss the questions of the day;" a place where it would be possible to read various newspapers and historical works.[163] He recalled how some immediately made use of the tavern to start an evening-school. There were a lot of illiterate and semiliterate teenagers in Oxford and, as Green com-mented, "that was a very sad state of things, for ... these boys would grow up and then become voters."[164] The St. Clement's coffee-tavern aimed to be completely economically self-sufficient. Green also decided to commit himself to the con-struction of a Liberal Hall which could be rented out at reduced rates.[165]

According to Green, workers needed information and knowledge.[166] Their greatest enemy was the class of people intent on defending their privileges at the expense of the pub-lic good.[167] In his assessment of the two competing parties, "the Tories were the party of vested interests and the Liberals the party of public good."[168] Only a strong movement of public opinion could counteract the power of the aristocrats, who controlled the House of Lords.[169] To highlight Disraeli's sub-servience to the landowners and the Upper House, Green compared the Appellate Jurisdiction law passed by the Con-servatives to the Liberal law abolishing the sale of army com-

---

[160] Nettleship, *Memoir*, p. cxv.
[161] 'Temperance and Recreation', 28 December 1875, *Works*, V, p. 259.
[162] *Ibid.*
[163] *Ibid.*
[164] *Ibid.*, V, p. 260.
[165] Nettleship, *Memoir*, p. cxviii.
[166] 'The Liberal Party and Liberal Policies', V, p. 256.
[167] *Ibid.*
[168] *Ibid.*
[169] *Ibid.*, V, p. 257.

missions.[170] He noted that "everyone admired the pluck with which Mr. Gladstone did this in opposition to the monopolizing house", that is, against the opposition of the House of Lords, which he by-passed by acting by Royal Warrant.[171]

The Education Act approved by the Conservatives ratified compulsory education for children.[172] The law however responded to the fact that many rural districts and cities were without school boards, by entrusting the education of children to the clergy. Thus, if the first task of a future Liberal government would be to extend self-government to the countryside, the second would be to reassert the obligation that schools funded by taxpayers were subject to public control.[173] By passing the 1876 Education Act, the Conservatives aimed to curb the pressures exerted by school boards on private schools. The Conservatives had protected the survival of private schools and those of the High Church Party, and reinforced denominational education.[174]

Green, who had been a member of the Oxford School Board since 1874, took the Wesleyan School in Oxford as his model. He judged it one of the very few schools which gave the student the means by which he could become "a really intelligent citizen."[175] The Wesleyan School was run with "public spirit" and perfectly fulfilled those tasks proper to a publicly-financed school.[176] One of the principal merits of the Wesleyan school, in Green's opinion, was that it gave a non-denominational religious education. In many of the schools run by the Church of England, public money was used to promote the

---

[170] Gladstone attempted a modest modernisation of the army following the outbreak of the Franco-Prussian war. Purchase of commissions had long underpinned the alliance between the upper middle classes and the landed aristocracy. It was Cardwell, Secretary for War in the Gladstone cabinet, who in 1871 promoted the abolition of the sale of commissions (Army Regulation Bill). Although the various provisions were passed in the House of Commons, they were defeated in the Lords. It was the Queen, at Gladstone's urging, who eventually overrode the opposition of many Tories and the Upper House by issuing a royal decree abolishing the purchase of commissions. The Army remained, however, firmly in the hands of the aristocracy: see Morley, *The Life of William Ewart Gladstone*, I, pp. 950–71 and 994–9.
[171] 'The Liberal Party and Liberal Policies', V, p. 257.
[172] *Ibid.*
[173] *Ibid.*
[174] Feuchtwanger, *Democracy and Empire*, p. 90.
[175] 'Oxford Wesleyan Boys' School and Education', 18 December 1874, *Works*, V, p. 251.
[176] *Ibid.*

interest of the Church at the expense of the Nonconformists or, worse, to instil respect for priestly authority through the debasement of the individual.[177] Green considered it important to demonstrate "that it was possible to give children that religious instruction suitable to their tender years without working the school in the interest of Churchmen as against Dissenters, or Dissenters against Churchmen."[178]

At the meeting concerning the building of the New Liberal Hall, Green explained that while England's problems were not resolvable by legislation alone, neither would they be resolved "without legislation."[179] Given the interests it represented, the Conservative Party was incapable of producing such legislation. Green wondered if agricultural workers could "ever hope for local self-government given them by the land-lords?"[180] He also felt that the rampant spread of excessive drinking made stricter controls on the issuing of licences unavoidable and that the introduction of some means of determining the responsibilities of publicans was also necessary. However, Green stressed, "no change of the law in that direction could be given them by the party of which the very breath of life was to be found in the enthusiastic support of the licensed victuallers."[181] The Conservatives had not even kept their modest promises. Green observed that

> we were to have a series of reforms which all sensible men, Liberals as well as Conservatives, could agree upon. They all knew what that came to.[182]

By defending privileges, the Conservatives hindered that maturing of common sense which could not be traced back to ideological or party allegiances and which, as such, should flow into the action of the people in association.

9. The Problem of Mass Political Participation

Green's tendency not to separate theory from practice led him to identify localism as the means by which more meaningful popular political participation could be brought about beyond

[177] *Ibid.*, V, p. 253.
[178] *Ibid.*, V, p. 254.
[179] 'The New Liberal Hall', V, p. 272.
[180] *Ibid.*
[181] *Ibid.*
[182] "The Liberal Faith', 20 September 1876, *Works*, V, p. 264.

the confines of party divisions. Nettleship quotes from Green's speech to his supporters before his election: "he knew that there were many conservatives quite as anxious for the good of the people as he was."[183] Experience had taught him that the common people could dedicate themselves to political and other associations with great ability, realism and devotion.[184] In 1876 Green became the first college tutor to be elected to the Town Council not as one of the representatives of the academic body, but as an ordinary householder in the North Ward. As Nettleship later wrote, this created the base "of the bridge, since carried on by others, which is gradually spanning the gulf between the city and the university of Oxford."[185]

When announcing his candidature to the Town Council, Green wished to dispel any doubts about his presumed 'estrangement' from the city. Although he had lived in a college for many years, he had always followed local politics.[186] Moreover, since his marriage to Charlotte Byron Symonds in 1871, he had become a citizen and ratepayer to all intents and purposes.[187] Not having any private or commercial interests to defend, Green would be able to dedicate himself fully to the construction of a secondary school (High School). This was, in fact, the main consideration which had led him to accept the candidature.[188]

Green was conscious that those who had fought against political power being granted to the working classes were now seeking to deceive them into misusing that power.[189] What was needed was "not more freedom to do as they liked, but more wise, associated action."[190] On Green's analysis, associated action would enforce the expression of common sense. Such common sense was able to promote reforms which, because they were deeply imbued with it, would both be in

[183] Nettleship, *Memoir*, p. cxix. See 'Candidature for Oxford Town Council', 24 October 1876, *Works*, V, p. 274.
[184] 'Liberalism in Oxford and the Country', 7 March 1882, *Works*, V, p. 394.
[185] Nettleship, *Memoir*, p. cxix.
[186] 'Candidature for Oxford Town Council', V, p. 273.
[187] *Ibid.*, V, p. 274.
[188] Robert Buckell, President of the North Ward Liberal Association, had asked him to stand for election specifically to promote the new High School. *Ibid.*, V, p. 275 n. 38.
[189] 'Candidature for Oxford Town Council', V, p. 274.
[190] *Ibid.*

accordance with the real interest of the community and would endure. Associated action was the means by which reformers' proposals could be made consistent with what the people felt, averting the risk that they might result from abstract ideas more familiar to philosophers than ordinary people.

Upon his election to the Town Council, Green urged his fellow Liberals not to sit on their laurels. They had to concentrate more "on the struggle in the future than on past triumphs."[191] The efforts of active and willing men would be required to interest the masses in politics.[192] If the Liberals wanted to have any chance of victory in the next Parliamentary election, they would have to trust in the aid "of such men as these" and such men would only be willing to commit themselves to "a worthy cause" and "a candidate worthy of the cause."[193] He believed they must have a brand of Liberalism capable of engaging the public and "not a washed out and colourless Liberalism."[194] Green's desire to remedy the inadequate rooting of liberalism amongst the general public was manifest during the debate on the selection of new Liberal candidates for Oxford Town Council.[195] He noted that "it was an old complaint that Oxford politics, both municipal and Parliamentary, had been left too much in the hands of cliques, that they were carried on in what was called a hole-and-corner way."[196] Though Green thought the Liberal Party was an important means of political participation, he was aware that, by embodying a form, it was itself prone to become a structure tending to defend its own privileges.

In the wake of the 1874 election defeat, the Liberal Party in Oxford had attempted to organise itself into district associations which would be linked into a political committee responsible for the nomination of candidates. The meeting organised by the North Ward Liberal Association on the 25th of April 1877 marked a turning point in the city's political history.[197] Green observed how at municipal level this meeting represented a step forward, even compared to the way in which his

[191] 'On Being Elected to the Town Council', 7 November 1876, *Works*, V, p. 281.
[192] *Ibid.*, V, pp. 283–4.
[193] *Ibid.*, V, p. 284.
[194] *Ibid.*
[195] A seat had become vacant following the death of Joseph Higgins. See *Works*, V, p. 292 n. 54.
[196] 'Selection of Liberal Candidates', 25 April 1877, *Works*, V, p. 293.
[197] *Ibid.*

own candidature had been decided.[198] Previously, the Liberal Association had delegated the choice of candidates to a smaller committee. Now the committee, while proposing a nominee, left any decision on the matter to a meeting which included not only the members of the Liberal Association, but all potential Liberal voters of the North Ward.[199] Green remarked that "this meeting had not been called together to register any foregone conclusion, but it was convened to deliberate on the situation, and enable them to understand each other."[200]

Green's objective was to encourage the largest possible number of people to get involved in the Liberal Ward Associations and he was particularly anxious to do all he could to extend their influence. He believed that they represented

> the great means which they had to look to for spreading political knowledge and a healthy tone of political sentiment among the masses of the electors, and it was for just that reason that certain people did not like them. They were the growth of this system of electoral organization, and they gave great offence to those who did not wish people to think much on political matters.[201]

Green saw no alternative to putting the selection of candidates in the hands of a representative body other than leaving it in the hands of self-selected cliques.[202]

In an attempt to encourage wider public participation, Green endeavoured to transform the coffee tavern, which he had inaugurated a year earlier in St. Clement's, into a venue capable of satisfying some of the more pressing needs of the working classes. The tavern, in which the consumption of alcoholic beverages was prohibited, now housed a savings bank, a canteen for the poor and a dispensary with sufficient means to pay for a doctor and medicines.[203] Green remained convinced that mass participation in political life, and with it the strength of the democratic process, would depend on the

---

[198] *Ibid.*, V, p. 295.
[199] The nominee in this instance was Robert Buckell (*ibid.*).
[200] *Ibid.*, V, p. 296.
[201] 'Liberal Politics in Oxford; the New High School for Boys', 8 October 1878, *Works*, V, p. 331.
[202] *Ibid.*, V, p. 332.
[203] 'Temperance', 17 January 1877, *Works*, V, p. 289.

resolution of the problem of alcoholism.[204] In March 1879, despite the consensus on Sir Wilfred Lawson's motion in favour of setting local controls, divisions remained regarding the degree of power to be given to ratepayers.[205] Green felt it essential therefore that the citizens organised themselves.[206]

Green hoped that Lawson's proposal would be included within the legislative framework advocated by Bruce.[207] Ratepayers would have a "limited and indirect local option."[208] Should a ruling by magistrates result in the number of public-houses exceeding a set limit relative to the number of rate paying homes, then a fixed number of ratepayers could demand that this increase be put to a vote. Should a three-fifths majority vote against the increase, the new licenses would be revoked.[209] Green continued to urge young people intending to embark on a career in public life to become teetotal in the hope that they would serve as an example to others.[210] He observed that

> it is sometimes falsely said by our opponents that we think we can make men moral by Act of Parliament. Well, we do not think anything of the kind, because we know that morality to be good for anything must be disinterested, and that no law can produce disinterested morality; but we say — I think they are the words of Mr. Gladstone — that is the business of law to make virtue easy, and to make vice difficult.[211]

As if to reaffirm his belief in the importance of finding exceptional individuals, he declared that there existed men of strong character capable of remaining true to a cause, even one which had been discredited and scorned. He stressed however that "they will always be the smallest number, and what we have to do is to lay hold, as far as we can, of the weaker breth-

---

[204] 'Temperance and Democracy', 30 October 1877, *Works*, V, p. 305; see also 'Total Abstinence', 18 February 1878, V, pp. 321–2.

[205] Lawson's proposal in fact supported the principle of local controls without however specifying how these powers would be exercised. See Nicholson, 'T.H. Green and State Action', p. 525.

[206] 'Temperance Work', 18 March 1879, *Works*, V, p. 338.

[207] 'Legislative Remedies for Intemperance', 24 April 1880, *Works*, V, pp. 362–3. On Green's proposal, see Nicholson, 'T.H. Green and State Action', pp. 525–6.

[208] 'Legislative Remedies for Intemperance', V, p. 362.

[209] *Ibid.*

[210] *Ibid.*

[211] 'Temperance Work', V, pp. 337–8.

ren."[212] The dialectic between "matter" and "form" taught
Green that, though perfection must be aimed at, human means
were insufficient to attain it.

10. Electoral Corruption

The Liberals won the 1880 election and Gladstone returned to
power. Contrary to all expectations, the Conservative brewer
Hall won in Green's constituency of Oxford. Harcourt's failure
to secure re-election, despite a seemingly greater reserve of
potential votes than his opponent, immediately aroused the
suspicions of the North Ward Liberal Association. With the
Association's support, Green instigated a petition calling for
an inquiry into the election. The court declared the election
void and Hall not duly elected on account of bribery by his
agents. After this, the Commission of Enquiry, a separate
body, was established. It found however that the Liberals too
had resorted to corrupt electoral practices. The main culprit
was deemed to be Buckell, President of the North Ward Liberal Association.[213]

Buckell resigned from his post following the inquiry. A dis-
mayed Green was quick to speak out in his defence. As an
Oxford Times journalist reported, Green "spoke advisedly,
when he said that but for their Chairman's indefatigable exertions the evidence for the petition would never have been got
up; the petition would not have been successful; Mr. Hall
would not have been unseated; they would not have had the
Commission of Enquiry, and if they had not had that, so far as
human foresight can go, the system of corruption in Oxford
might have gone unchecked for ever."[214]

Green argued that the proposal for an anti-corruption law
could also be traced back to the Enquiry which Buckell himself
had helped bring about. The only criticism which Green felt
should be levelled at the members of the Commission was that
of not having sufficiently emphasised the different nature of
Liberal and Conservative misdemeanours. As he pointed out,
the Conservatives had been employing corrupt practices in
Parliamentary and local elections since 1874.[215] In Buckell's

---

[212] *Ibid.*, V, p. 337.
[213] 'The Corruption Enquiry', 10 May 1881, *Works*, V, p. 370.
[214] *Ibid.*, V, p. 371.
[215] *Ibid.*, V, p. 372.

case, one of the accusations upheld against him was that of having purchased an excessive amount of rosettes. The other was of having employed potential voters in order to influence the outcome of the election.[216] While recognising the illegality of any practice which might lead to an excessive increase in electoral expenditure, Green nonetheless justified Buckell's actions.[217] Green would have preferred to appeal to the working classes in terms of their self-respect, honour and intelligence and thus encourage them to free themselves from the twin temptations of money and drink.[218] However, as he acknowledged,

> if all the electors had been what [the Liberals] wished them to be, there would be no occasion for doing more than that. But unhappily among their poorer brethren on the Liberal side there were many weak ones.[219]

As a result, Green felt that electoral propaganda could fulfil a very important role. It was well known that there were many voters in the North Ward with clear Liberal sympathies who, due to their straitened economic circumstances, were often tempted by attractive offers of temporary work from the Conservatives. Viewed from this perspective, Buckell's actions had been forced upon him.[220]

Green stressed that he did not intend to establish whether "as a matter of abstract principle it would not have been better to refuse employment to those men."[221] Rather, he was merely pointing out that to have denied them employment would have meant accepting defeat in the election.[222] He concluded that nobody else in Buckell's position would have been able to act differently. Indeed, faced with such an elaborate and deep-rooted system of corruption as that developed by the Conservatives, few could have emerged with such minor accusations against them as had Buckell.[223] Following a heartfelt appeal by Green and the acclamation of the North Ward

---

[217] *Ibid.*, V, pp. 373–4.
[218] *Ibid.*
[218] See *ibid.*, V, p. 373.
[219] *Ibid.*
[220] *Ibid.*, V, pp. 373–4.
[221] *Ibid.*, V, p. 374.
[222] *Ibid.*
[223] *Ibid.*

Liberal Association, Buckell withdrew his resignation.[224] In a speech in January 1882, Green called for the approval of the Corrupt Practices Bill. This proposed to establish a ceiling for electoral expenses, thus making access to Parliament less costly. Green argued that so long as Parliament remained "a sort of club of rich men", it should be of no surprise to anyone that it also remained far removed from the interests of the "struggling and suffering classes of society."[225]

Having made clear that he had no intention of standing for election to the House of Commons, Green repeated his belief that it was essential that Parliament contained men of better quality whose presence was not based on their personal wealth. As he asserted, "Parliament ought to be open to every man who was really qualified to serve the country, and who was willing to sacrifice the attractions of private money making for the sake of serving his country."[226] The Oxford Liberals recognised that their party had relied too much in their Parliamentary election campaigns on men who were paid rather than on those who were committed and selfless.[227] Although Green had not had to resort to corruption in his own election campaign for the City Council, he had to admit that the Liberal conscience was not as clear as it should have been.[228] Liberal expenditure had amounted to only half that of the Conservatives in the 1880 elections, nevertheless Green acknowledged that it was still "at least three times as great as under a healthy system it would have been."[229] Green was sure that the Liberals would easily defeat the Conservatives if they could rid politics of the scourge of corruption. In his view, the majority of the middle classes still supported them due to the previous efforts of the party in favour of the causes of free trade and religious equality. In addition, the Liberals could count on the vote of every worker aware of his condition.[230] The party needed to be wary however of those voters who were too ignorant to resist the temptation of bartering their vote for a glass of beer and too poor to withstand the economic rewards offered by rich men. Green believed however that the number of such

[224] *Ibid.*, V, p. 370 n. 91.
[225] 'Liberal Politics in Oxford', 18 January 1882, *Works*, V, p. 382.
[226] *Ibid.*
[227] *Ibid.*
[228] *Ibid.*, V, p. 383.
[229] *Ibid.*
[230] 'The Corruption Enquiry', V, p. 375.

electors would diminish over the years and that the Liberals would thus enjoy increasingly larger margins of victory.[231]

11. Democracy and War

The Conservatives had also threatened the spread of Liberalism among the masses by their foreign policy, which aimed to arouse strong feelings of nationalism. Green believed that the Conservatives would even be prepared to start a war in order to dampen the desire for reform.[232] According to Green, aggressive wars should be seen as the last attempt of oligarchies to preserve their power and postpone the reforms which would undermine their leadership. The Tories' war-like inclinations probably confirmed Green in his view.

Disraeli wanted to occupy the Dardanelles straits and his decision to put to the vote the allocation of a sizeable sum to the military had alarmed the Liberal Party leadership.[233] Green commented that "they now knew for certain that the Government was practically directed by the impatient and reckless vanity of a single man."[234] While he was not for peace at any cost, Green felt it essential that Britain, having failed to conduct a dignified foreign policy in the East, at least avoided opting "for a distinctly bad one."[235] The Oxford Liberal Associations decided therefore to form a kind of watchdog committee to monitor developments in the government's foreign policy.[236] They hoped for the return of Gladstone. Green chaired a public meeting organised by the Liberal Associations in Oxford to present Gladstone with an Address. In welcoming Gladstone, Green said:

> we thank you for having taught us that England has no true interest opposed to the interests of mankind, and that the cause of our country is not to be served by support of a power which denies the simplest personal rights to the greater part of its subjects. The liberation of Bulgaria, we are glad to think, is now nearly accomplished, and while we lament that England cannot claim the glory of having shared in the work of deliverance, we believe it to be

[231] *Ibid.*
[232] 'Current Politics, Domestic and Foreign', V, p. 298.
[233] 'Against Disraeli's Foreign Policy', 26 January 1878, *Works*, V, pp. 313–4.
[234] *Ibid.*, V, p. 315.
[235] *Ibid.*, V, p. 317.
[236] *Ibid.*, V, p. 313.

owing to you principally that we have been spared the shame of hindering it.[237]

Disraeli was still convinced in 1875 that Russian expansion could only be checked by propping up the tottering Ottoman Empire. Green however could not overlook the atrocities committed by the Turks against the Bulgarians.[238] While recognising the need to keep the Russians away from Constantinople, Green wondered whether in this case that very policy, which involved sacrificing all considerations of justice and humanity, might not have the end result of bringing about what it originally sought to prevent. Green asserted that "the honour of England should not again be enlisted in a dishonourable cause."[239] He believed in fact that the indignation provoked by events in Bulgaria might hasten the demise of the Conservative government:

> a few months ago many of them would have said its inglorious existence was likely to be prolonged for another three years, but events of the last three weeks had made a great difference in our expectations. They could not tell how soon this Parliament might be swept away.[240]

Gladstone was the only man capable of saving the nation from the confusion created by "the so-called spirited foreign policy of the Conservatives."[241] Lord Derby's reckless foreign policy represented little other than a blank cheque for the military establishment.[242] The Conservatives had enthusiastically encouraged the Turks to put down the Bulgarian insurrection and, for over a year, had deterred other European powers from intervening to liberate the Christians of the East from oppression. Even if they had wanted to, the Conservatives could not now change their policy. Green believed therefore that "if the people desired it changed, they must have another Government to do it."[243]

The "spirited foreign policy" of the Conservatives had led to an economic deficit thanks to the Zulu war and the campaign

---

[237] 'Presentation of an Address to Mr. Gladstone', 30 January 1878, *Works*, V, p. 319.
[238] 'The Turkish Atrocities in Bulgaria', 12 September 1876, *Works*, V, pp. 261–2.
[239] *Ibid.*, V, p. 262.
[240] 'The Liberal Faith', V, p. 264.
[241] *Ibid.*
[242] *Ibid.*, V, p. 267.
[243] *Ibid.*, V, p. 268.

against the Afghans.[244] As a result, the Conservatives chose to increase taxes in India, imposing levies even on essential commodities such as salt.[245] Green observed that the same government which had made the Queen empress of India "has done more to weaken [the] foundation of our authority there than Russian aggression at a distance . . . ever could have done."[246] They had even introduced a law gagging the press. As Green commented, "discontent of which expression is stifled is only the more dangerous."[247] The reform of the army begun by Lord Cardwell had not been completed.[248] Green wondered "how they justify Beaconsfield's description of the Bulgarian murders as 'Coffee house babble', or his saying that Gladstone, because he brought [the] facts of those murders home to [the] knowledge and conscience of England was a greater enemy of mankind than [the] authors of [the] murders."[249] Green demanded that the Conservative government should explain its role in the negotiation of the Treaty of San Stefano and its position towards the Greeks at the Congress of Berlin where, according to Green, "[the] English Government has betrayed Greece — played false to the very people whom on their showing it was [the] special interest of England to befriend: for it is to [the] Greeks we must look in future to countervail the influence of Russia in the Levant . . . "[250]

In 1879 having been returned unopposed to the Town Council, Green expressed his confidence that Gladstone would be returned to power. Gladstone made the question of foreign policy the keystone of his election campaign.[251] Gladstone listed his famous six principles of foreign policy in a speech in Midlothian on the 27th of November 1879. While the first advocated the importance of good government at home through just legislation, economic growth and the moral wellbeing of the community, the second principle stressed the importance of preserving the spiritual and cultural unity of Christian nations, by force if necessary. The third urged the maintenance

[244] Feuchtwanger, *Democracy and Empire*, pp. 108–9.
[245] 'National Loss and Gain under a Conservative Government', 5 December 1879, *Works*, V, p. 351.
[246] *Ibid.*, V, p. 352.
[247] *Ibid.*
[248] *Ibid.*, V, p. 353.
[249] *Ibid.*
[250] *Ibid.*, V, p. 354.
[251] See Feuchtwanger, *Democracy and Empire*, pp. 110–1.

of European unity and, in order to encourage this, the fourth principle warned against forming alliances which might complicate diplomacy and called for the cultivation of peaceful relations with other states. The fifth recognised the equal rights of all nations, a principle which, in Gladstone's vision of the world, dovetailed with his final one: the love of freedom.[252] The differences between his and Disraeli's approaches to foreign policy could not have been clearer.[253]

Like Kant, Green maintained that war was mainly a consequence of a state which failed in its task of reconciling the rights of its subjects: "the source of war between states lies in their incomplete fulfilment of their function; in the fact that there is some defect in the maintenance or reconciliation of rights among their subjects."[254] It is likely that in Green's view, the Hegelian state was a clear instance of an anti-democratic state. "War", Hegel argued,

> is that condition in which the vanity of temporal things [*Dinge*] and temporal goods — which tends at other times to be merely a pious phrase — takes on a serious significance, and it is accordingly the moment in which the ideality of *the particular attains its right* and becomes actuality. The higher significance of war is that, through its agency (as I have put in another occasion), "the ethical health of nations [*Völker*] is preserved in their indifference towards the permanence of finite determinacies, just as the movement of the winds preserves the sea from that stagnation which a lasting calm would produce — a stagnation which a lasting, not to say perpetual, peace would also produce among nations."[255]

Consistently with the tradition of the reason of state, Hegel also maintained that certain wars were providential just because they were able to avert internal unrest and consolidate

---

[252] See K. Bourne, *The Foreign Policy of Victorian England, 1830–1902* (Oxford, 1970), pp. 420–2.

[253] As Morley recounts (*The Life of William Ewart Gladstone*, II, p. 203), Gladstone "insisted that we should ever 'remember the rights of the savage, as we call him.' 'Remember', he exclaimed, 'that the sanctity of life in the hill villages of Afghanistan, among the winter snows, is as inviolable in the eye of Almighty God as can be your own. Remember that He who has united you as human beings in the same flesh and blood, has bound you by the law of mutual love; that that mutual love is not limited by the shores of this island, is not limited by the boundaries of Christian civilisation; that it passes over the whole surface of the earth, and embraces the meanest along with the greatest in its unmeasured scope.'"

[254] 'Lectures on the Principles of Political Obligation', sect. 167, II, p. 478.

[255] G.W.F. Hegel, *Elements of the Philosophy of Right*, ed. A.W. Wood, trans. H.B. Nisbet (Cambridge, 1991), sect. 324, p. 361.

the power of the state.[256] In his search to reconcile idealism and empiricism, Green adopted a position midway between that of Kant and that of Hegel. "He loses sight neither of the importance of the historical differences between states which Hegel emphasised, nor of the essential community of tradition and interests between states and between men as men which lay at the basis of Kant's political philosophy."[257] In this sense, for Green, it was possible to reconcile the duties of men and of citizens: there was no antagonism between patriotism and humanitarianism.[258]

According to Green, the destruction of life in war was always wrong-doing, whoever be the wrong-doer. In wars defending political freedom the wrong-doing was "only removed from the defenders of political freedom to be transferred elsewhere."[259] Green underlined that if war had to be considered wrong-doing, "it does not cease to be so on account of any good resulting from it in a scheme of providence."[260] The wrong, Green specified, "which results to human society from conflicts between states cannot be condoned on the ground that it is a necessary incident of the existence of states. The wrong cannot be held to be lost in a higher right, which attaches to the maintenance of the state as the institution through which alone the freedom of man is realised."[261] Again, Green thoroughly disagreed with Hegel. In particular, Green's rejection of Hegel's view that civil society has no moral significance until it is brought under the control of the power of the state implies "a reversion to the old English tradition of individualism with its emphasis on the importance of the individual's moral conscience and its mistrust of state authority."[262] For Green, whose view can be rightly contrasted with that of Hegel, the focus is not the state but that wider community which the state can embody to an extent which varies accord-

[256] *Ibid.*, p. 362.
[257] D.A. Routh, 'The Philosophy of International Relations: T.H. Green *versus* Hegel', *Politica*, 3 (1938), p. 233.
[258] See D. Boucher, 'British Idealism, the State, and Inernational Relations', *Journal of the History of Ideas*, vol. 55 (1994), pp. 671–94 and Boucher, 'British Idealist International Theory', *Bulletin of the Hegel Society of Great Britain*, no. 31 (Spring-Summer 1995), pp. 73–89.
[259] 'Lectures on the Principles of Political Obligation', sect. 161, II, p. 471.
[260] *Ibid.*, sect. 163, II, p. 474.
[261] *Ibid.*, sect. 169, II, p. 479.
[262] Routh, 'The Philosophy of International Relations: T.H. Green *versus* Hegel', p. 230.

ing to cases and circumstances. For that reason, in the light of the fact that this wider community progresses, the possibility cannot be denied that the state, regarded as institutional framework, can be improved.[263]

The negative liberty of free trade had not yet affirmed itself within the international sphere. "All restrictions on freedom of wholesome trade", Green observed, "are really based on special class-interests, and must disappear with the realisation of that idea of individual right, founded on the capacity of every man for free contribution to social good."[264] As a consequence of the abatement of national jealousies and the removal of those causes due to the deficient organisation of states, Green believed that an international court with authority resting on the consent of independent states might be realised.[265]

Green was against life imprisonment and the death penalty and thought they could be justified only in case of war, "on the supposition that the war is necessary for the safety of the state and that such punishments are a necessary incident of war."[266] For Green, who rejected any kind of abstract speculation, the true democracy was to be identified with the true state; and though, consistently with his dialectic, the true state was destined to remain an object which no human institution wholly realised, it was obvious that democracy corresponded to the kind of government inclined to make society develop freely. Such a democracy would turn to force only exceptionally. Indeed, the aggressive use of force was to be regarded as a clear sign of regression. "Patriotism, in that special military sense in which it is distinguished from public spirit, is", Green argued, "not the temper of the citizen dealing with fellow-citizens ... but that of the follower of the feudal chief, or of the member of a privileged class conscious of a power, resting ultimately on force, over an inferior population, or of a nation holding empire over other nations."[267]

A reciprocal invasion of right, the invasion of the rights of the state by the church on the one side, and on the other of the

[263] See P. Nicholson, 'Philosophical Idealism and International Politics: A Reply to Dr Savigear', *British Journal of International Studies*, 2 (1976), p. 77.

[264] 'Lectures on the Principles of Political Obligation', sect. 174, II, p. 484.

[265] *Ibid.*, sect. 175, II, p. 485.

[266] *Ibid.*, sect. 205, II, p. 509.

[267] *Ibid.*, sect. 172, II, p. 482.

church by the state, usually caused conflicts in the state and between states. For Green,

> an obvious instance to give of this relation between states would have been that between Russia and Turkey, if Turkey could be considered to have been constituted as a state at all. Perhaps a better instance would be the position of Ireland in the past; its disaffection to England and gravitation, first to France, then to the United States, caused chiefly by Protestant penal laws which in turn were at least provoked by the aggressive attitude of the church towards the English state.[268]

Green believed that those habits and institutions, and modes of feeling, which tended to international conflict were survivals of a past that had not yet managed to emancipate itself from political oppression.[269] In Green's view, the state must guarantee that internal equality and toleration which the Puritans, despite their aims, failed to realize.

12. A Puritan Citizenship

The Congregationalists championed the twin causes of Christian liberty and tolerance, and Green was adamant that these principles needed to take hold in society. Moreover, he argued, nobody should forget that the Congregationalists could count two of the greatest names in English history amongst their members: John Milton and Oliver Cromwell. Indeed, as Green stated, "the service which the early Independents or Congregationalists rendered in the seventeenth century in fighting the battle of freedom had not ceased to the present day."[270] Green referred in particular to the principle which allowed the individual soul to approach God without the mediation of a priest or any involvement of ecclesiastical ordinances.[271] He also expressed the hope that, in the future, the congregation would show itself entirely free of any sectarian elements.[272]

Following the Commonwealth, two hundred and twenty years would pass before Congregationalists were allowed

---

[268] *Ibid.*, sect. 168, II, pp. 478–9.
[269] *Ibid.*, sect. 172, II, p. 482.
[270] 'Congregationalism', 27 May 1880, *Works*, V, p. 367.
[271] *Ibid.*, V, p. 368.
[272] *Ibid.*, V, p. 369. Green is referring to the congregation of the new Congregational Chapel in Oxford: he was speaking at the laying of its foundation stone.

back into the University.[273] Green considered Congregationalism an essential element in nurturing what might be defined
as a higher quality of life in English cities. In his view, the Congregationalists were the only religious group to understand
and appreciate the true nature of political freedom.

> When he talked to members of the Established Church on any
> question that affected the rights and interests of Nonconformists,
> he found that men who on other matters had a keen sense of
> equity seemed entirely to lose it; and in the same manner with ref-
> erence to the Roman Catholics, the Presbyterians were equally
> backward in acknowledging what was due to a fellow-citizen, but
> among Congregationalists he found the questions involving the
> essential principles of political justice were sure to be under-
> stood.[274]

At a National Church Reform Union meeting in December
1881, Green put forward a proposal designed to marry religious and political citizenship. This was perfectly compatible
with Vane's political theology, which aimed at giving substance to a faith in God which is in the world, but not of the
world. This required reviving "*within* what we call 'this world'
that which to the man of the Middle Ages had been on the
whole presented as belonging to 'another world' and manifested in 'this world' only through a supernatural intervention
from that *other*."[275] God had to be made immanent and the
believer's experience had to become more important than dogmas and rituals. In this sense, religious denominations had to
relinquish political power, and religion represented a sort of
substratum embedded in political life. In the words of Harris
and Morrow:

> This doctrine placed the emphasis squarely on men's efforts to
> embark upon the 'new spiritual walk', efforts which depended
> less on the detail and accuracy of the New Testament than on the
> willingness of men to reflect upon their own nature and to strive
> for their own perfection. The desire for reconciliation with God
> lay at the root of the search for perfection in both its practical and
> cognitive forms; it extended beyond the sphere of religion and
> ethics.[276]

---

[273] 'Congregationalism', V, p. 368.
[274] *Ibid*.
[275] Webb, *A Study of Religious Thought in England from 1850*, p. 21.
[276] Harris and Morrow, 'Introduction' to *T. H. Green: Lectures on the Principles of Political Obligation and Other Writings*, p. 4.

As Green observed, "there were many men who would not express a dogmatic agreement with the Church, but who were nevertheless filled with a thorough Christian feeling, and whose work would be thoroughly Christian-like."[277] Due to the exclusion of such men, half of the religious life of the nation took place outside the established church. This resulted in a lot of friction, jealousy, and loss of power and energy wasted both attacking and defending the Church.[278] Referring to the large number of people whose natural vocation would have led them to become Anglican priests, but who instead chose to reject this option, Green said "they are kept out primarily by [the] declaration required, secondarily by repugnance to [the] tone of clerical opinion — in particular to its exclusive and hierarchical tone."[279]

In Green's view, the only solution was "to congregationalize the Church; without disestablishment and disendowment."[280] Community life was practically non-existent because lay people participated neither directly nor indirectly in the appointment of priests. Nor were they involved in the running of religious services, schools or charitable works. At the same time, nothing was being done to encourage active moral participation by men who had developed clear positions on theological and ecclesiastical issues.[281] The movement for disestablishment provoked a strong reaction from married members of the clergy, who perceived it as "a personal wrong."[282] In all probability, disestablishment would have delivered ecclesiastical buildings into the hands of an episcopal sect: that philo-Catholic High Church Party which had long been intent on preventing "any via media between Evangelical religion and current enlightenment."[283] In such circumstances, the priest would become "either a mere Priest or a mere preacher, instead of the leader in useful social work."[284] Green believed that while the Bishops should be responsible for ensuring that only suitable candidates were ordained and for maintaining "an elastic uniformity" with regard to religious worship, it

---

[277] 'Reform of the National Church', 7 December 1881, *Works*, V, p. 376.
[278] *Ibid.*, V, p. 377.
[279] *Ibid.*
[280] *Ibid.*, V, p. 378.
[281] *Ibid.*, V, p. 377.
[282] *Ibid.*, V, p. 378.
[283] *Ibid.*
[284] *Ibid.*

would be better to place control over the appointment of priests, the running of ceremonies and decisions regarding religious rituals in the hands of the congregations.[285] In Green's view, no declaration of faith should be required of those being ordained and nobody should be expelled. Men who had remained true to the aspirations of Christianity and the moral and religious principles at the heart of the Christian life, ought to encounter no difficulties in taking part in the life of the Church.

Green's reaction to the case of Charles Bradlaugh provided further evidence of his distinctive religious outlook. The question was posed: was the oath sworn by an openly atheist parliamentarian such as Bradlaugh valid? The Liberal Party was divided on the issue. Gladstone expressed his preference for freedom of conscience, but his bill to make the oath optional was defeated in the Commons. Naturally, the Conservatives took advantage of the situation by linking the cause of liberalism with that of atheism.[286] Green's view on the matter was unambiguous: "if once the Liberal party lost anything of that religious spirit which had hitherto animated its most vigorous and self-sacrificing members, it would be a bad look out for the party."[287] At the same time, however, Green did not feel that oaths and such like helped the religious cause and he was convinced that "the religious spirit of the House of Commons would not be a jot or tittle less if in the future no oath was required."[288] The affirmation of that *jus divinum* of individual persuasion,[289] proclaimed for the first time during the Puritan revolution, led Green to apply to the world that unity which he felt more and more within himself. Just because of its inclination to overcome the limits implied in the empirical world, idealism was able to revive that Puritan primacy of the inner life, which naturally tended to favour inclusion. As he stated, neither our inability to set out fully the possibilities we are conscious of in ourselves, "nor the appearance of positive inconsistency between much that we observe and any scheme of universal development, can weaken the authority of the idea, which does not rest on the evidence of observation but

[285] *Ibid.*
[286] 'Liberalism in Oxford and the Country', 7 March 1882, *Works*, V, p. 396.
[287] *Ibid.*
[288] *Ibid.*
[289] 'Four Lectures on the English Revolution', III, p. 327.

expresses an inward demand for the recognition of a unity in the world answering to the unity of ourselves."[290] According to this perspective, no discrimination on grounds of religion or class was justified. It was this spirit which informed Green's political ideals. He felt that the main obstacle to the progress of humanity was the dualism between the Church and the world which, in its narrowest sense, had led to a situation in which the masses were judged incapable of developing a sense of religious citizenship.

13. The End of a Life

In Green's view, the spread of Liberalism among the masses would inevitably foster this sense of religious citizenship. However, in this very respect, the policy of the Liberal Party could be considered a complete failure. Gladstone's second premiership (1880-86) was turning out to be less successful than his first and the Conservatives found much to criticise in the government's foreign policy.[291] Only with regard to the Irish Question was it possible to find any kind of continuity with the reformist policies of the previous Liberal administration. Gladstone's aim had long been to pacify Ireland by legislation rather than by force.[292] Many argued however that the Prime Minister's efforts would soon reveal themselves to have been in vain. As Green recounted, "they were told that the Liberal policy in Ireland had been a failure; that nothing yet had been gained by the Land Act."[293] Green opposed this view. He argued that Ulster, home to a third of the population of Ireland, was again loyal to Britain thanks precisely to the Irish Land Act. Moreover, he saw no reason to exclude the possibility that the same could happen in other areas of Ireland.

He held that this success in Ireland was certainly in no way due to the House of Lords.[294] According to Green, in opposing the Irish Land Act the Lords had shown itself for what it was: "a club of great landowners, which unfortunately was invested with coordinate power with the assembly of the peo-

---

[290] *Prolegomena to Ethics*, sect. 186, IV, p. 196.
[291] 'Liberalism in Oxford and the Country', V, pp. 395–6.
[292] *Ibid.*, p. 397.
[293] *Ibid.*, p. 398.
[294] *Ibid.*

ple's representatives in Parliament."[295] Despite this, Green was still in favour of maintaining an Upper House. As he commented, he did not trust much in "the sudden gusts of passion in a democratic assembly."[296] He believed that the representative assembly of the people needed to be flanked by "something else", but that "something else must not be a club of landowners."[297] He did not, however, depict any concrete alternative to the Lords. Green was probably afraid that the common sense which he highly valued could have been easily overcome by a more powerful and unrestrained democratic assembly.

In Green's analysis, the difficulties of Gladstone's second premiership were the result of the major growth in wealth which Britain was experiencing at the time, and he noted that prosperity often tended to diminish Liberal zeal.[298] As he pointed out, "those who looked back to the unfortunate election of 1874, when Mr. Disraeli obtained a majority, would remember that the success of the Tories was largely due to a sort of general political indifference induced by the great tide of commercial prosperity they had enjoyed under a Gladstone administration."[299]

Green was well aware in January 1882 of the problems facing the Liberal Party. In Oxford the Conservatives had won the North Ward municipal elections of the previous November and Buckell, who had been found guilty by the electoral corruption enquiry which he himself had helped to set up, had been defeated.[300] Amongst the Liberal members of Parliament, the prevailing mood was not that of previous times and there was a palpable sense that their power in the constituencies had waned. Green was similarly convinced that the party's strength was dwindling.[301]

It is likely that for Green the failure of the Liberal Party did not imply the failure of his political project. The dialectic between "matter" and "form" allowed him to hope that society would continue to grow and mature independently of the

---

[295] *Ibid.*
[296] *Ibid.*
[297] *Ibid.*
[298] 'Liberal Politics in Oxford', V, p. 381.
[299] *Ibid.*
[300] 'The Corruption Enquiry', V, p. 370 n. 91 and 'Liberal Politics in Oxford', 10 January 1882, *Works*, V, p. 380.
[301] 'Liberal Politics in Oxford', V, p. 380.

fate both of ideologies and political parties. For that reason, one is under the impression that to the end of his life Green never lost his faith in the progress of humanity and that, in his eyes, education remained the only instrument needed. Perhaps it was just because of the political difficulties of this period, that Green could talk with pride about the creation of the High School for Boys in Oxford. This had been the main objective of his involvement in the Town Council. The educational model Green had in mind was based on New England Puritan society.[302] As he commented,

> the ascending scale of schools, with free access from one to the other, for which I plead, has long been part of the settled political framework of the New England States. In 1642, only twenty-two years after the landing of the pilgrim fathers from the 'Mayflower', 'the general court of the colony by a public act enjoined upon the municipal authorities the duty of seeing that every child within their respective jurisdictions should be educated'.[303]

Five years later, a law was passed requiring every district or town with more than fifty householders to appoint a schoolteacher. Furthermore, every district or town with more than one hundred householders or families had to set up a secondary school with teachers capable of preparing pupils for entrance to university. This, as Green pointed out, "was the foundation of the public school system of New England which, though modified by subsequent legislation, has always continued upon the same lines."[304] An enthusiastic Green added that "the possession of high scholarship and science has never in America been a class monopoly."[305]

After having achieved the objective of creating the High School in Oxford, while drafting some notes in praise of the organisational capacity of the Liberal associations in Birmingham, on the evening of the 15th of March 1882, Green was suddenly taken ill.[306] At sunset on the 25th of the same month, he was told that he had only a few hours to live. Having reaf-

---

[302] On the impact of Puritanism on the British educational system, see T. Kelly, *A History of Adult Education in Great Britain* (Liverpool 1992), pp. 32-64.

[303] 'Lecture on the Work to be done by the New Oxford High School for Boys', *Works*, III, p. 463. Green is quoting from James Fraser's report on American education to the Taunton Commission.

[304] *Ibid.*, III, pp. 463-4.

[305] *Ibid.*, III, p. 465.

[306] 'Organisational Lessons from Birmingham Liberalism', 15 March 1882, *Works*, V, pp. 401-4.

firmed his faith in God and life after death, he asked to have the eighth chapter of the Epistle to the Romans read to him. He was not able to listen however. He then expressed his wish to be buried in the Jericho cemetery in the North Ward. As the night drew in, Green became delirious: he talked about the Irish Land Bill and Bulgaria. He died peacefully on the morning of March the 26th at nine o'clock.[307]

One local newspaper later reported that "a more impressive sight has never perhaps been witnessed in Oxford than at the funeral of Professor Green on Wednesday last."[308] The Editor of the *Oxford Chronicle* was particularly struck by the seemingly endless lines of people of all ages and from all social backgrounds including "the Vice-Chancellor with other high officers of the University, and the Mayor and Corporation of the City; the older graduates, and children from the elementary schools; college servants, tradespeople, undergraduates, the masters and scholars of the new High School."[309] As Prest related, "having extolled Green's contribution to the foundation of the Boys School, the *Chronicle* passed on to a summary of his involvement in the temperance movement. Green, the paper said, had agreed with Cobden that the 'Temperance cause lies at the foundation of all social or political reform'."[310] By contrast, the tone of the account in the Conservative *Oxford Times* was different. In reviewing Green's University career "the *Times* made it clear that 'We were opposed almost as much to his Kantean and Hegelian views, as we were to his political opinions'. Turning to his work for the city, it alleged that 'the deceased was a pronounced politician'."[311]

Green believed that the philosopher-saint should be a political activist. He never shirked his own political commitments, careless of his weak health, and this contributed to his early death.

---

[307] Nettleship, *Memoir*, pp. clix–x.

[308] "The Late Professor Green', *Oxford Chronicle*, 1 April 1882, p. 5.

[309] *Ibid.*

[310] J. Prest, 'The Death and Funeral of T. H. Green', *Balliol College Annual Record 1998*, p. 24.

[311] *Ibid.*, p. 25.

Chapter IV

Political Obligation

1. The Puritan Way

In 1878 Green at last managed to obtain the chair of Moral Philosophy in Oxford. Then he could devote himself more methodically to an exposition of his research and, between 1879 and 1880, give his lectures on political obligation.[1] In 1879 Spencer published *The Data of Ethics*. In this work he aimed to show how the transition from a military to an industrial society tended to make state intervention unnecessary.[2] In 1871 a seventh edition of J.S. Mill's *Principles of Political Economy* was published. Mill died in 1873 but his teaching was still the most prominent in the radical world, and those who wanted to argue against Spencer's position still tended to quote Mill. Nevertheless, it is likely that in Green's opinion Mill's view is too ambiguous exactly on state intervention. In Chapter XI, Book Five of his *Principles*, entitled 'Of the Grounds and Limits of the Laisser-Faire or Non-Interference Principle', on the one hand Mill denounced the lack of a general theory able to justify state intervention, but on the other hand he thought it was better that English philosophy continued to refrain from formulating such a theory.[3] Mill considered laisser-faire should be the rule, and state intervention the exception.

---

[1] Nettleship, *Memoir*, p. cxxv.
[2] H. Spencer, 'The Data of Ethics', *The Principles of Ethics*, 2 vols (London, 1892), I, pp. 420–34. In order to refute Spencer's general philosophical viewpoint Green wrote the essays 'Mr. Spencer On the Relation of Subject and Object', *Works*, I, pp. 373–409 and 'Mr. Spencer On the Independence of Matter', *ibid.*, pp. 410–1.
[3] "Without professing entirely to supply this deficiency of a general theory, on a question which does not, as I conceive, admit of any universal solution, I shall attempt", Mill observed, "to afford some little aid towards the resolution of this class of questions as they arise:" *Principles of Political Economy*, bk V, ch. xi, sect. 1, p. 937.

In this way Mill unintentionally endorsed Hegel's bad opinion of the English constitution. Hegel believed that the English constitution was nothing but an "inherently incoherent aggregate of positive determinations" unable to synthetize its particularities: it had not yet undergone that transformation which had been accomplished in the civilized states of the Continent, and which the German territories had enjoyed for a longer or shorter period of time.[4] "England", Hegel noted, "has lagged so conspicuously behind the other civilised states of Europe in institutions based on genuine right, for the simple reason that the power of government lies in the hands of those who possess so many privileges which contradict a rational constitutional law and a genuine legislation."[5] From this stemmed the corruption of the electoral system and the monopoly of the aristocracy which dominated not only the House of Lords but also the Commons. For Hegel, England was unable to follow the German way of gradual democratic reforms adopted and implemented by the executive power, and would in the end follow the French revolutionary way based on dangerous abstractions which could not be reconciled with reality. Because of English political backwardness, the introduction of the Reform Bill would unlock the door to revolution. "That antithesis", Hegel argued, "between *hommes d'état* and *hommes à principes* which at once emerged quite starkly in France at the beginning of the Revolution and which has not yet gained a foothold in England, may well be introduced when a broader route to seats in Parliament is opened."[6]

By contrast, Green thought that Puritanism made the English free both of that antithesis between *hommes d'état* and *hommes à principes*, which characterized the last phase of the life of the Commonwealth,[7] and of those dangerous speculative abstractions which Hegel believed threatened English democracy. Green considered that kind of speculation was not only normal with the Germans, but drove them to ignore the public good. Green wrote:

> An Englishman is in many ways more independent in feeling, and less anxious for sympathy than a German (a difference which

[4]   G.W.F. Hegel, 'On the English Reform Bill', *Political Writings*, ed. L. Dickey and H.B. Nisbet, trans. H.B. Nisbet (Cambridge, 1999), p. 239.
[5]   *Ibid.*
[6]   *Ibid.*, p. 265.
[7]   'Four Lectures on the English Revolution', III, pp. 348–9.

is natural between a wealthy and an oppressed nation), but when he is writing or studying, he has always public opinion, and generally the public good, before his eyes, and hence he promulgates far fewer extravagances of opinion, than a German, who writes under protection of a court with a view merely to his fellow-students, and who is therefore better able to abstract his mind from external considerations, and push his opinions to their furthest consequences.[8]

Furthermore, it was Puritanism which marked the main difference between the English and the German way. Whereas Puritanism avoided any kind of identification between the religious and the political or institutional aspect, from the very beginning the Lutheran Reformation was fostered by political power. It is likely that in Green's view the alliance Luther formed with the Princes was strengthened by the Hegelian inclination to sanction the ethical superiority of the state. "The German", Green argued, "with his speculative grasp, has no difficulty in regarding church and state as two sides of the same spiritual organism."[9] Consistently with the different outcomes which resulted from the Reformation in England and Germany, Green was convinced of the possibility of finding a Puritan way to political obligation. Green wanted to sift German idealism with the aim of formulating that general theory of state intervention of which Mill was afraid. At the same time, such a theory, while not disavowing Mill's doctrine, would have averted both state idolatry and any kind of revolutionary abstract speculation.

2. Inward and Outward Man

For Mill, state intervention was justified only when an individual was unable to be the best judge of his own interests. That was the case with primary education, which could help the individual to strengthen his character. According to the same principle, a restriction of freedom of contract in the case of children (but not women) should be accepted. Mill favoured divorce without reservation and was definitely against any law to restrain the sale of liquors. A merely presumptive injury to others did not allow the state to interfere with individual freedom. "Even", Mill argued, "in those portions of conduct

[8] 'The English National Character Compared with that of the Germans' (see Appendix).

[9] 'Four Lectures on the English Revolution', III, p. 284.

which do affect the interest of others, the onus of making out a case always lies on the defenders of legal prohibitions."[10] Mill acknowledged the necessity of preserving human existence from state interference, but his distinction was not in terms of the domain of the inward man and that of external conduct which, concerning the life of others, might be controlled by the public collectively. Instead, Mill drew his distinction on the grounds of interest. He wrote:

> That there is, or ought to be, some space in human existence ... entrenched around, and sacred from authoritative intrusion, no one who professes the smallest regard to human freedom or dignity will call in question: the point to be determined is, where the limit should be placed; how large a province of human life this reserved territory should include. I apprehend that it ought to include all that part which concerns only the life, *whether inward or outward*, of the individual, and does not affect the interests of others . . . [11]

Though Hegel's viewpoint was based on assumptions which were entirely antithetical to those of Mill, the German philosopher did not conceive any distinction between inward and outward man either. Inwardness and outwardness did not contribute to form that circle around every individual, which no government ought to be permitted to overstep. The action of a state that embodied the highest ethics should not be limited in such a way. The state, Hegel observed, "has its immediate existence (*Existenz*) in *custom* and its mediate existence in the *self-consciousness* of the individual [*des Einzelnen*], in the individual's knowledge and activity, just as self-consciousness, by virtue of its disposition, has its *substantial freedom* in the state as its essence, its end, and the product of its activity."[12]

The very distinction between inwardness and external conduct revealed how Green was indebted to Puritanism and, particularly, to Vane. Though this distinction was similar to the formalism of Kant, it cannot be seen as a consequence of it. Green was harshly critical not only of Hegelian state idolatry but also of Kant's formalism. Indeed, in Green's political philosophy right seems to lose that autonomy it had conquered with Kant. If the state exercised a negative function, at the

[10]   *Principles of Political Economy*, bk V, ch. xi, sect. 2, p. 938.
[11]   *Ibid.* (italics mine).
[12]   Hegel, *Elements of the Philosophy of Right*, sect. 257, p. 275.

same time its removal of obstacles allowed individuals the possibility of realizing themselves and, therefore, the common good.[13] Unlike Kant and in a very similar way to Vane, for Green political obligation was simultaneously distinct from and instrumental to moral obligation.[14]

In *The Retired Man's Meditations*, Vane, while affirming the necessity that government had to limit its intervention "to the outward man, or outward concernes of men, in their bodily converse in this world",[15] stated that the liberty of conscience, which resides in the inward man, favoured the prevalence of the common good. In this sense, the defence of the inward man was preliminary to that of "the whole body of the people; for whose safety and good, government it self is ordained by God, not for the particular benefit of the rulers, as a distinct and private interest of their own."[16] For Vane, the magistrate's task was not "to intrude itself into the office and proper concernes of Christ's inward Government and rule in the conscience ... but is to content it self with the outward man, and to intermeddle with the concernes thereof in reference to the converse which man ought to have with man, upon the grounds of natural just and right, in *things appertaining to this life*."[17] The "natural conscience" marked a boundary which, in order to preserve the common good, should not be overstepped. This showed how far, for Vane, democracy itself stemmed from a liberty of divine origin.[18] Even though the action of the magistrate was limited to the outward man, it had to encourage or discourage certain intentions. In the same way, for Green,

---

[13] See Passerin d'Entrèves, 'Il problema dell'obbligazione politica nel pensiero inglese contemporaneo', p. 32.

[14] "Freedom, for Vane", Parnham observed, "began and ended with God who directed the affairs of humanity. But human lives lived in transit to ends established by God participated in streams of freedom that Vane clearly valued. He valued freedom from covenantal condition, and he valued liberty of conscience, in a way that more conventional disciplinarians never could. But godly discipline was the very rationale of Vane's vaunted freedoms. The 'liberty of the sons of God' is 'a freedom to good only, a liberty to do all things for the Truth'." D. Parnham, 'The Nurturing of Righteousness: Sir Henry Vane on Freedom and Discipline', *Journal of British Studies*, 42 (2003), pp. 31–2, quoting from Vane, *A Pilgrimage into the Land of Promise* (London, 1664), pp. 65, 67.

[15] H. Vane, *The Retired Man's Meditations* (London, 1655), p. 387.

[16] H. Vane, 'A Healing Question propounded and resolved, upon occasion of the late publique call to humiliation, in order to love and union' in *Somers Tracts* (London, 1811), p. 306.

[17] Vane, *The Retired Man's Meditations*, p. 388.

[18] *Ibid.*, pp. 182–3.

though state intervention was inclined to "enforce or prevent ... external action", its function was "to produce or prevent certain intentions, for without intention on the part of someone there is no act."[19] As a moral intention could only come from an inward disposition, the sole aim of state intervention should be that of producing "conditions favourable to action proceeding from that disposition."[20]

Following Vane's inspiration, Green was led to wonder whether the distinction between inwardness and outwardness could be considered as a real guide and, above all, whether this distinction could be applied to special cases. Thus Green drew up a list of laws which checked the development of the moral disposition. "This has been done", Green observed,

> (a) by legal requirements of religious observance and profession of belief, which have tended to vitiate the religious source of morality; (b) by prohibitions and restraints, unnecessary, or which have ceased to be necessary, for maintaining the social conditions of the moral life, and which interfere with the growth of self-reliance, with the formation of a manly conscience and sense of moral dignity, − in short, with the moral autonomy which is the condition of the highest goodness; (c) by legal institutions which take away the occasion for the exercise of certain moral virtues (e.g. the Poor-law which takes away the occasion for the exercise of parental forethought, filial reverence, and neighbourly kindness).[21]

For Green, law had "nothing to do with the motive of the actions or omissions."[22] Nevertheless, state intervention had to ensure the carrying out of those acts which were so necessary to the existence of a society of persons, that it was "better for them to be done or omitted from that unworthy motive which consists in fear or hope of legal consequences than not to be done at all."[23]

For Green, as for Vane, political obligation contributed to the improvement of social life, which was sacred because, in the form of liberty of conscience, it stemmed from the inward man. Liberty of conscience, as Vane argued, "is of high concern to be had and enjoy [sic], as well for the magistrates sake

---

[19] 'Lectures on the Principles of Political Obligation', sect. 12, II, p. 342.
[20] *Ibid.*, sect. 16, II, p. 344.
[21] *Ibid.*, sect. 17, II, p. 345.
[22] *Ibid.*, sect. 13, II, p. 343.
[23] *Ibid.*, sect. 15, II, p. 344.

as for the peoples common good."[24] Hence failure to respect that liberty implied a degeneration of society. But by ensuring respect for liberty of conscience, Vane observed:

> a great part of the outward exercise of antichristian tyranny and bondage will be plucked up by the very roots; which, till some such course be held in it, will be alwayes apt to renew and sprout out afresh, under some new forme or refined appearances.... For since the fall of the bishops and persecuting presbyteries, the same spirit is apt to arise in the next sort of clergy, that can get the ear of the magistrate, and pretend to the keeping and ruling in the conscience of the governours.[25]

Green's elaboration of the dialectic between "form" and "matter", which can be easily interpreted as a dialectic between outwardness and inwardness, can be regarded as an attempt to avoid the risk, already seen by Vane, that progress may be hindered by "forms" bent on denying liberty of conscience.

3. The Problem of Obedience

For the Puritan Vane, obedience was merely a consequence of the rational nature of man and the free consent of the people. It was not "irrational and merely implicit, but rational and voluntary."[26] Vane specified that "for a rational man to give up his reason and will unto the judgment and will of another [man or men] (without which no outward coercive power can be) whose judgment and will is not perfectly and unchangeably good and right is unwise and unsafe, and by the law of nature, forbidden."[27] But Green knew that Vane's inclination to set reason against facts might thwart the reforming process by leading one to believe that individuals were more important than society. For that reason, he held that every right has a double value: it can be regarded not only as an individual claim due to human rationality, but also as something society grants an individual. "We must", Green argued,

> be on our guard against supposing that these distinguishable sides have any really separate existence. It is only a man's consciousness of having an object in common with others, a well-being which is consciously his in being theirs and theirs in

---

[24] Vane, 'A Healing Question', p. 307.
[25] *Ibid.*
[26] Vane, *The Retired Man's Meditations*, p. 385.
[27] Vane, 'The People's Case', quoted in Judson, *The Political Thought of Sir Henry Vane the Younger*, p. 35.

> being his, — only the fact that they are recognised by him and he
> by them as having this object, — that gives him the claim
> described.[28]

Although the mutual recognition drawn by Fichte and already
outlined by the ancients as *isoi kai homoioi* is the main idea operating through the social medium, it cannot be opposed to society: it presupposes the consciousness of a common object.[29]
Consistently with this, Green underlined that "there can be no
right to disobey the law of the state except in the interest of the
state; i.e. for the purpose of making the state in respect of its
actual laws more completely correspond to what it is in tendency or idea."[30]

From that stemmed both the refusal to conform absolutely
to the laws of the state and the notion that the public good
ought always to prevail. "As a general rule, no doubt", Green
observed,

> even bad laws, laws representing the interests of classes or indi-
> viduals as opposed to those of the community, should be obeyed.
> There can be no right to disobey them, even while their repeal is
> urged on the ground that they violate rights, because the public
> interest, on which all rights are founded, is more concerned in the
> general obedience to law than in the exercise of those powers by
> individuals or classes which the objectionable laws unfairly with-
> hold.[31]

Even the duty of befriending the slave may not be paramount
to the duty of obeying the law which forbids his being
befriended. The risk had to be avoided that the violation of law
in the interest of the slave might result in the dissolution of any
form of civil combination. If such a destruction of the state
occurred, it would mean "a general loss of freedom, a general
substitution of force for mutual good-will in men's dealings
with each other, that would outweigh the evil of any slavery
under such limitations and regulations as an organised state
imposes on it."[32] However, sometimes the public interest "not
merely", as Green observed, "according to some remote philosopher's view of it, but according to conceptions which the
people are able to assimilate", is best served by a violation of

---

[28] 'Lectures on the Principles of Political Obligation', sect. 139, II, p. 450.
[29] *Ibid.*
[30] *Ibid.*, sect. 142, II, p. 453.
[31] *Ibid.*, sect. 144, II, p. 456.
[32] *Ibid.*, sect. 147, II, p. 459.

some actual law.[33] In such a case the violation is not only in the interest of the violator but also of the state. Instead of weakening the basis of civil society, it strengthens it and "there is no danger of its making a breach in the law-abiding habits of the people."[34] Hume's influence was evident. Hume maintained that, though on some occasions it might be justifiable, both in sound politics and morality, to resist the supreme power, in the ordinary course of human affairs nothing was more pernicious and criminal, and that such a practice tended directly "to the subversion of all government, and the causing an universal anarchy and confusion among mankind."[35] At the same time, while for Hume the state had to ensure the exercise of the only possible morality, for Green the state had to ensure the conditions which allowed every individual to cultivate the improvement of human character as an end in itself. Green's inclination to combine idealism and empiricism was fully confirmed.[36]

4. Character and State Intervention

Even though, like Kant, Green identified the liberty of the will with the supreme principle of morality, he saw in "a prior morality, founded upon interests which are other than the pure interest in being good, and governed by rules of conduct relative to a standard of goodness other than that which makes

---

[33]   *Ibid.*, sect. 144, II, p. 457.

[34]   *Ibid.*

[35]   D. Hume, *A Treatise of Human Nature*, ed. Green and Grose, II, p. 317.

[36]   With regard to the 'Lectures on the English Revolution', Muirhead observed: "Green was, of course, prepared to recognise the force of circumstances. One of his earliest essays was upon this subject, and the striking *Lectures on the English Revolution* were written with the express object of showing how the greatest concentration and purity of moral purpose may fail when they are dissociated from insight into the actual circumstances of the time. On the other hand, it seemed to follow from the general principles of his philosophy that there could be no ultimate distinction between will and circumstances when taken each in its widest sense" (J.H. Muirhead, *The Service of the State: Four Lectures on the Political Teaching of T.H. Green* (London, 1908), pp. 62–3). Muirhead's view was corroborated by what Nicholson affirmed on Green's state intervention theory. "In short", Nicholson argued, "that Green should take an empirical and pragmatic position on social and political issues is entirely compatible with, and indeed is fuelled by, his Hegelianism. Green's inductivism is undoubtedly an integral part of his political thought, and springs from his basic philosophical assumptions" (*The Political Philosophy of the British Idealists*, p. 192). See also W.H. Walsh, 'Green's Criticism of Hume' in Vincent, ed., *The Philosophy of T.H. Green*, pp. 21–35.

it depend on this interest",[37] the necessary premise preventing goodness from being transformed into an empty ideal. The influence of Hume probably made Green acknowledge the impossibility of an action entirely opposed to egoistic motives, and he consistently diluted the Kantian categorical imperative. As Hume argued,

> 'tis impossible, that the distinction betwixt moral good and evil, can be made by reason; since that distinction has an influence upon our actions, of which reason alone is incapable. Reason and judgment may, indeed, be the mediate cause of an action . . . [38]

Reason, or as Kant called it, "practical reason", was for Green "the capacity in a man of conceiving the perfection of his nature as an object to be attained by action."[39] Although all moral ideas have their origin in reason, Green highlighted that this did not imply that the idea of self-perfection could be stated in "an abstract form".[40] But though, like Hume, Green rejected the abstractness of a reason which thinks itself capable of discerning good from evil too clearly, simultaneously he kept his distance from the Scottish philosopher.[41]

Unlike Hume, Green saw character as an end in itself, and consequently he could not refrain from criticizing that prior morality which, for Hume, was the sole morality. "Those rules of conduct", Green argued, "according to which the terms right and wrong, good and bad, are commonly applied ....

---

[37] 'Lectures on the Principles of Political Obligation', sect. 2, II, p. 336.
[38] *A Treatise of Human Nature*, II, p. 239.
[39] 'Lectures on the Principles of Political Obligation', sect. 6, II, p. 337.
[40] *Ibid.*
[41] As Thomas argues: "Hume rejects talk of the combat of reason and passion or desire because, on his own account, reason and desire, the cognitive and the conative, are strongly heterogeneous in such a way that they are not the kinds of thing which could enter into a 'combat' in any relevant sense. Briefly, reason establishes what is the case: desire relates to what we should like to be the case. No 'conflict' is possible. If a desire arises through some false inference then, agreed, the inference is false: the desire is not 'unreasonable'. Green's repudiation of any conflict between desire and reason rests on a different footing altogether. "For Green the conflict between desire and reason is impossible not because they are so heterogeneous that they cannot conflict, but because no such absolute separation as Hume writes into his account of reason and desire survives critical analysis. .... Hume maintains that reason cannot set the ends of action or supply motivation because of its heterogeneity from desire. Green maintains on the contrary that no such heterogeneity obtains, and that reason can therefore be practical. Both Hume's view of the impotence of reason and his partitional view of mind are here under attack" (*The Moral Philosophy of T.H. Green*, p. 168).

have to be revised according to a method which inquires into their rationale or justification, as conditions of approximation to the highest character."[42] However, as Baur taught, there was no *prius* and no *posterius* either with regard to experience. "Thus", Green observed,

> we only learn to express the idea of self-perfection in that abstract form upon an analysis of an experience of self-improvement which we have ourselves gone through, and which must have been gone through by those with whom we are connected by the possession of language and an organisation of life, however elementary: but the same analysis shows that the same idea must have been at work to make such experience possible.[43]

Green's position sounds very like that of Fichte, who insisted on the impossibility of separating subjectivity and experience. Like Green, Fichte believed that separating them would generate a philosophy consisting of empty formulas.[44] Similarly, Mill maintained that men's actions were "the joint result of the general laws and circumstances of human nature, and of their own particular characters"[45] and that those characters again were the consequence of the natural and artificial circumstances that constituted their education, among which circumstances had to be reckoned their conscious efforts. Even though Green shared Mill's opinion,[46] he emphasised that there was an "intelligent interest" which supervened upon habits disciplined by conformity to conventional morality.[47]

Hume certainly refuted the viewpoint of those who believed that liberty could leave circumstances out of consideration. Significantly, in Green's view, the weakness of Hume's position was not to be identified with its asserting an absolute uniformity of causes and effects, but with its inability to give a sufficiently consistent demonstration of it. Hume failed when asked to explain those irregularities which seemed to cast doubt on the law of cause and effect. Like Mill, the Scottish philosopher ignored that the necessity which links cause and effect implied a rational element that allows an individual to get a higher morality. "It is because Hume de-

---

[42] 'Lectures on the Principles of Political Obligation', sect. 3, II, p. 336.
[43] *Ibid.*, sect. 6, II, p. 338.
[44] Fichte, *The Vocation of the Scholar*, pp. 18–9.
[45] *A System of Logic*, II, p. 932.
[46] *Prolegomena to Ethics*, sect. 106, IV, pp. 109–10.
[47] 'Lectures on the Principles of Political Obligation', sect. 6, p. 338.

rationalizes respectability", Green observed, "that he can find no *rationale*, and therefore no room, for the higher morality."[48]

At the same time, idealism made as serious a mistake, because it was inclined to scorn the respectability inherent in the gradual manifestation of conventional morality. For Green, there is "no other genuine 'enthusiasm of humanity' than one which has travelled the common highway of reason — the life of the good neighbour and honest citizen."[49] The morality of ordinary people and that of the exceptional individuality should be regarded as two stages of the same journey.[50] Hume limited himself to justifying the morality "of the average man in his least exalted moments."[51] Nevertheless, afterwards, there had lived and thought people like "Wesley, Wordsworth, Fichte, Mazzini, and the German theologians."[52] They — and the list does not include Kant or Hegel — provided tools suitable for a better comprehension of religious, political and poetical enthusiasm. "It is now generally agreed", Green noted, "that the saint is not explained by being called a fanatic, that there is a patriotism which is not 'the last refuge of a scoundrel,' and that we know no more about the poet, when we have been told that he seeks the beautiful, and that what is beautiful is pleasant, than we did before."[53]

Green was convinced that conventional morality and practical reason were continuously interacting and that the progress of humanity came from just this interaction. Every man was endowed with what Vane called a "natural conscience", but most men, identifying themselves with a mess of pottage, tended to sell their birthright.[54] The many Esaus, compared to the few Jacobs, were not able to resist the force of circumstances. Even though the self is a factor operating through experience, it can either act according to its rational nature or it can let itself be overwhelmed by circumstances. Green admitted, on the one hand, that when the force of circumstances is too great, the self-consciousness cannot induce the individuals to realize themselves: "healthy houses and food, sound elementary education, the removal of temptations to drink … are

[48]   'Introduction to the Moral Part of Hume's 'Treatise'', *Works*, I, p. 371.
[49]   *Ibid.*
[50]   *Ibid.*
[51]   *Ibid.*, I, p. 370.
[52]   *Ibid.*, I, p. 369.
[53]   *Ibid.*, I, pp. 369–70.
[54]   *Prolegomena to Ethics*, sect. 96, IV, pp. 99–100.

needed in order to supply conditions favourable to good character;"[55] on the other hand, he acknowledged that circumstances themselves were influenced by will and character. The dialectic between "form" and "matter" not only definitely rendered the distinction between hero and common people useless but, as civilization advanced, justified "more and more interference with the liberty of the individual to do as he likes."[56]

If it is because of his moral capacity that the subject conceives his self-realization as "an end desirable in itself", and if rights are the condition of realising it, nevertheless, rights are merely "the negative realisation of this power."[57] Consistently with Vane's doctrine, inwardness cannot be violated and political obligation is instrumental to the moral development of the individual. State intervention must allow an individual the possibility of being treated, as Kant said, as an end in himself. In this sense, institutions should not only ensure the exercise of that prior morality concerning the life of the outward man, but also give individuals the possibility of maturing. Institutions should both make it possible "for a man to be freely determined by the idea of a possible satisfaction of himself", and also enable him "to realise his reason, i.e. his idea of self-perfection, by acting as a member of a social organisation in which each contributes to the better-being of all the rest."[58] So far as institutions do that, they are morally justified and, as Green observed, "may be said to correspond to the 'law of nature', the *jus naturae*, according to the only sense in which that phrase can be intelligibly used."[59]

5. A Teleological Conception of Citizenship

For Green, the Greek philosophers were the first to formulate a teleological conception of citizenship, and Aristotle, who treated man as a political animal and the *polis* as a natural institution based on social rights, was the one who elaborated a true doctrine grounded on natural rights. Green thought that Aristotle regards the state:

---

[55] *Ibid.*, sect. 332, IV, p. 365.
[56] 'Lectures on the Principles of Political Obligation', sect. 18, II, p. 345.
[57] *Ibid.*, sect. 25, II, p. 351.
[58] *Ibid.*, sect. 7, II, pp. 338, 339.
[59] *Ibid.*, sect. 7, II, p. 339.

> as a society of which the life is maintained by what its members do for the sake of maintaining it, by functions consciously fulfilled with reference to that end, and which in that sense imposes duties; and at the same time as a society from which its members derive the ability, through education and protection, to fulfil their several functions, and which in that sense confers rights.[60]

Like Aristotle, for Green, individual rights are first of all social rights. For that reason, in Green's view, the modern doctrine of natural law, which made society originate in a contract, was entirely misleading. Green was afraid that the doctrine of natural law justified the assumption that the individual has "rights against society irrespectively of his fulfilment of any duties to society, that all 'powers that be' are restraints upon his natural freedom which he may rightly defy as far as he safely can."[61] Green responded that nobody could claim a right independently of the social tissue in which he lives. Again in a way similar to Aristotle, Green was convinced that the state presupposes "other forms of community" which are prior to the state.[62] But if the task of the state was to protect pre-existing rights, at the same time these rights were not unchanged but transformed in view of the higher moral end which that wider community, the state, embodied. "Thus", Green argued,

> the citizen's rights, e.g. as a husband or head of a family or a holder of property, though such rights, arising out of other social relations than that of citizen to citizen, existed when as yet there was no state, are yet to the citizen derived from the state, from that more highly developed form of society in which the association of the family and that of possessors who respect each other's possession are included as in a fuller whole . . . [63]

Nevertheless, Green wanted to avoid both the risk that society prevailed over the individual, and the risk that the state prevailed over preceding communities. Indeed, his peculiar dialectic between "form" and "matter" allowed him to admit that an individual, as determined by the idea of a possible satisfaction of himself, cannot very easily identify himself with society, and that the state should not be regarded as a definitive "form", i.e. the Hegelian state able to impose its abstract rules

---

[60]   *Ibid.*, sect. 39, II, p. 363.
[61]   *Ibid.*, sect. 50, II, p. 373.
[62]   *Ibid.*, sect. 134, II, p. 445.
[63]   *Ibid.*, sect. 141, II, p. 452.

on individuals. Unlike Hegel, Green acknowledged that utilitarianism has the merit that it does not seek "the ground of actual rights in a prior natural right, but in an end to which the maintenance of the rights contributes."[64] For Green, the state, instead of wiping out antecedent societies, is "the society of societies:" it only exists as sustaining, securing and completing the rights arising out of prior communities.[65] If the dialectic between "form" and "matter" prevents the whole from overwhelming the parts, at the same time it restrains the parts from crushing the whole.[66] Significantly, Baur's dialectic is fully consistent with Vane's. In the same way, Vane's teleology was based on a triad: the natural, the legal, and the evangelical conscience, which, considering humanity as intrinsically corrupt, tends to avoid any kind of identification between the religious and the institutional aspect.[67]

The Greenian state has constantly to revise its structure with regard to the fact that, though individuals aim to satisfy themselves, they are "what they are in virtue of non-sensible functions, and of certain forms of life determined by relation to more perfect forms which they have the capacity or tendency to become."[68] That is why, even though the civic association should always be preserved, any state which does not allow the citizen to exercise the rights which are the conditions of his moral growth can be viewed as being as much responsible for the lack of public spirit as the citizen himself. The dogmatism that led the supporters of the laisser-faire doctrine to reject state intervention is completely unjustified, and a state whose

---

[64] *Ibid.*, sect. 23, II, p. 349.
[65] *Ibid.*, sect. 141, II, p. 452 and sect. 134, II, p. 445.
[66] "To appreciate", Simhony observed, "the idealist view of society two things are required: the first is that society be regarded as a relational organism and the second is to keep this view of society as a relational organism distinct from the alternative view of society as a holistic organism. The second is particularly important because holistic organicism is criticized by idealists for defending a lopsided view of social relations. At the heart of relational organicism lies a double relation: the mutual interdependence of whole and parts, and the mutual interdependence of the component parts. This presupposes no ontological primacy in either the whole or the parts" (A. Simhony, 'Idealist Organicism: Beyond Holism and Individualism', *History of Political Thought*, 12 (1991), p. 515). See also W.H. Fairbrother, *The Philosophy of Thomas Hill Green* (London, 1896), p. 112; Simhony, 'T.H. Green: The Common Good Society', *History of Political Thought*, 14 (1993), pp. 225–47; and M. Freeden, *Rights* (Milton Keynes, 1991), p. 21.
[67] See Section 10 below.
[68] 'Lectures on the Principles of Political Obligation', sect. 39, II, p. 363.

sole aim is to protect formal liberties cannot expect its citizens to put into practice the patriotic spirit so appreciated by Rousseau. "That active interest in the service of the state, which makes patriotism in the better sense, can hardly arise", Green argued, "while the individual's relation to the state is that of a passive recipient of protection in the exercise of his rights of person and property."[69]

6. Custom and Reason

By conceiving the state of nature and the civil society as separated by "an impassable gulf",[70] contractualism overlooked the fact that institutions orginated from the slow development of custom. Indeed, the way Green criticized contractualism seemed to be very like Hume's.[71] In his 'Introduction to the Moral Part of Hume's *Treatise*', Green credited Hume as the first to state that "rules of justice, as well as our feelings towards them, were not made but grew."[72] Just like Hume, Green considered the covenant a mere fiction:

> If political society is to be supposed to have originated in a pact at all, the difference between it and the preceding state of nature cannot, with any plausibility, be held to have been much more than a difference between a society regulated by written law and officers with defined power and one regulated by customs and tacitly recognised authority.[73]

For instance, no equality of freedom would have been possible except in a society whose members recognised the existence of a common good, and Green argued that such society is "already in principle the same as political society."[74] Hume had contended that "so far . . . our *civil* duties are connected with our *natural*, that the former are invented chiefly for the sake of the latter; and that the principal object of government is to constrain men to observe the laws of nature."[75] Like Green, Hume identified government with a condition which society tends to produce gradually: "tho' it be possible for men to

---

[69] *Ibid.*, sect. 122, II, p. 436.
[70] *Ibid.*, sect. 37, II, p. 362.
[71] Hume dealt with political obligation in Sections VIII–X, Part II, Book III of his *Treatise on Human Nature* (II, pp. 304–28).
[72] 'Introduction to the Moral Part of Hume's 'Treatise'', I, p. 364.
[73] 'Lectures on the Principles of Political Obligation', sect. 52, II, p. 375.
[74] *Ibid.*, sect. 53, II, p. 376.
[75] *A Treatise of Human Nature*, II, p. 308.

maintain a small uncultivated society without government, 'tis impossible", he argued, "they shou'd maintain a society of any kind without justice, and the observance of those three fundamental laws concerning the stability of possession, its translation by consent, and the performance of promises."[76] Like Hume, Green took note of the continuity between social and institutional morality: "To ask why I am to submit to the power of the state, is to ask why I am to allow my life to be regulated by that complex of institutions without which I literally should not have a life to call my own."[77] Submission to its power is owed to the state if such terms as ought and right are to gain a fuller meaning. Nonetheless, Hume had accepted the prevalence of a general scepticism about the possibility of political reforms.

With the sole aim of justifying the *status quo*, Hobbes affirmed that individuals possessed rights in the state of nature. But, Green argued,

> such rights abstracted from social function and recognition could only be powers, or (according to Hobbes's definition) liberties to use powers, which comes to the same; i.e. they would not be rights at all; and from no combination or devolution of them could any right in the proper sense, anything more than a combined power, arise.[78]

Since in the state of nature there are not rights but powers, Green pointed out that Hobbes's prohibition against breaking the covenant could only be conditional, "conditional, in particular, on the way in which the sovereign power is exercised."[79] According to Green, it is not "supreme coercive power, simply as such, but supreme coercive power exercised in a certain way and for certain ends, that makes a state; viz. exercised according to law, written or customary, and for the mainte-

---

[76] *Ibid.*, II, p. 306. Cf. Green, 'Lectures on The Principles of Political Obligation', sect. 55, II, p. 377.

[77] 'Lectures on the Principles of Political Obligation', sect. 114, II, p. 428. Cf. Hume: "The same self-love, therefore, which renders men so incommodious to each other, taking a new and more convenient direction, produces the rules of justice, and it is the *first* motive of their observance. But when men have observ'd, that tho' the rules of justice be sufficient to maintain any society, yet 'tis impossible for them, of themselves, to observe those rules, in large and polish'd societies; they establish government, as a new invention to attain their ends, and preserve the old, or procure new advantages, by a more strict execution of justice" (*A Treatise of Human Nature*, II, p. 308).

[78] 'Lectures on the Principles of Political Obligation', sect. 49, II, pp. 372-3.

[79] *Ibid.*, sect. 47, II, p. 371.

nance of rights."[80] In Green's view, Spinoza was more consistent than Hobbes. Spinoza admitted not only the distinction, later elaborated by Kant, between determination according to law and determination according to the consciousness of law, but also a difference between a higher and lower, a better and worse, state of civil society. Unlike Hobbes, Spinoza acknowledged, Green observed, "the possibility of the course of human affairs being affected by the conception of a final cause."[81] Nevertheless, Spinoza ignored that reason also operates in the more confused and mixed forms of social life. He recognized it solely "in the forms of the philosophic 'amor Dei', or in the wisdom of the exceptional citizen."[82]

Consistently with a viewpoint which tends to make custom and reason interactive, Green affirmed that the state did not set itself in any definitive "form". He held that the primary function of the state was to maintain law in the interest of all equally. It follows that if the state fails in that, it is its fault if the citizen is not even a loyal subject, let alone an intelligent patriot. "It is a sign", Green observed, "that the state is not a true state."[83] In this sense, the Hegelian state is not a true state either. Green did not restrict himself to noting that no government's claim on our obedience can derive from an original covenant. He aimed to show that it resulted from maintaining those "conditions of freedom which are conditions of the moral life."[84] For Green, although right takes root in a prior morality not opposed to egoistic motives, right is "an ideal attribute ('ideal' in the sense of not being sensibly verifiable, not reducible to any perceivable fact or facts)" that exists "so far as in the consciousness of myself and others I have a function relative to this end."[85]

7. An Empirical General Will

Green thought that Rousseau, if he could have freed himself from the presuppositions of natural right, might have admitted that as "the popular vote is by no means necessarily an organ of the general interest, so the decree of a monarch or of

[80] *Ibid.*, sect. 132, II, p. 442.
[81] *Ibid.*, sect. 40, II, p. 364.
[82] *Ibid.*, sect. 41, II, p. 365.
[83] *Ibid.*, sect. 121, II, p. 435.
[84] *Ibid.*, sect. 62, II, p. 384.
[85] *Ibid.*, sect. 38, II, p. 362.

an aristocratic assembly, under certain conditions, might be such an organ."[86] Accordingly, Green wanted to show how Rousseau was compatible with John Austin, who identified the sovereign with a determinate person or persons. In fact, the Austinians were as misleading as Rousseau. Rousseau managed to give merely an abstract definition of sovereignty. Austin, because his formal definition presupposed that coercive power was the sole determinant of the habitual obedience of the people, made as big a mistake. "It is", Green argued, "by no means an unlimited power of compulsion that the superior exercises, but one dependent in the long run, or dependent for the purpose of insuring an *habitual* obedience, upon conformity to certain convictions on the part of the subjects as to what is for their general interest."[87]

Green is obviously attempting to interpret Rousseau's doctrine of sovereignty in the light of Hume's teaching.[88] While in his 'Introduction to the Moral Part of Hume's *Treatise*' Green pointed out that, for Hume, interest and sympathy are the foundations of any kind of moral and civil obligation, in his 'Lectures on the Principles of Political Obligation' Green identified the general will with "that impalpable congeries of the hopes and fears of a people, bound together by common interests and sympathy."[89] Hume underlined the importance of custom with regard to obedience:

> Time alone gives solidity to their [sc. Magistrates'] right; and operating gradually on the minds of men, reconciles them to any authority, and makes it seem just and reasonable. Nothing causes

---

[86] *Ibid.*, sect. 99, II, p. 416.

[87] *Ibid.*, sect. 84, II, p. 402.

[88] With regard to this, Monro's viewpoint is interesting ('Green, Rousseau and the Culture Pattern', p. 347). "There are, I think, three distinct senses in which Rousseau uses the term 'general will'. He means by it, as the nineteenth century idealists used to point out, something very like Kant's 'good will', which all men have in common and which cannot conflict with itself. But he also means, quite as often, the Utilitarian compromise, the mean between divergent interests which takes account of all of them and satisfies as many as possible. And, thirdly, he means something like the 'culture pattern' of the modern anthropologists. I want to show that Green inherits this ambiguity, and that his argument in the *Principles of Political Obligation* is plausible only because he does not distinguish between these three meanings of 'general will'."

[89] 'Introduction to the Moral Part of Hume's *Treatise*', I, pp. 363–4; 'Lectures on the Principles of Political Obligation', sect. 86, II, p. 404.

any sentiment to have a greater influence upon us than custom
. . .[90]

Again Hume noticed how that common interest from which obedience originated, coincided with protection and security.[91] In the same way, for Green, consent itself could be seen as a common desire for certain ends, "specially the 'pax vitaeque securitas' [peace and security of life] — to which the observance of law or established usage contributes."[92]

Hume argued that "even the authority, which confines liberty, can never, and perhaps ought never, in any constitution, to become quite entire and uncontroulable", specifying that there are other principles or prejudices that "frequently resist all the authority of the civil magistrate; whose power, being founded on opinion, can never subvert other opinions, equally rooted with that of his title to dominion."[93] Likewise Green stated that

> when it has been ascertained in regard to any people that there is some determinate person or persons to whom, in the last resort, they pay habitual obedience, we may call this person or persons sovereign if we please, but we must not ascribe to him or them the real power which governs the actions and forbearances of the people, even those actions and forbearances (only a very small part) which are prescribed by the sovereign.[94]

Again in line with Hume's position, Green noted that "the subject people inherits laws, written or unwritten, and maintains them for itself, a certain shelter from violence being afforded by the foreign power."[95] Such was, for Green, the condition of North Italy under Austrian domination.[96] In the same way, the Indian people habitually obeyed the British power "only because the English government presents itself to the people, not merely as a tax-collector, but as the maintainer of a customary law, which, on the whole, is the expression of the general

---

[90] *A Treatise of Human Nature*, II, p. 319.
[91] *Ibid.*, pp. 313–4.
[92] 'Lectures on the Principles of Political Obligation', sect. 84, II, p. 402.
[93] Hume, 'Of the Origin of Government', *Essays Moral, Political and Literary*, ed. Green and Grose, I, p. 116.
[94] 'Lectures on the Principles of Political Obligation', sect. 84, II, pp. 402–3.
[95] *Ibid.*, sect. 89, II, p. 406. Hume writes ('Of the Origin of Government', I, p. 116): "The Sultan is master of the life and fortune of any individual; but will not be permitted to impose new taxes on his subjects: a French monarch can impose taxes at pleasure; but would find it dangerous to attempt the lives and fortunes of individuals."
[96] 'Lectures on the Principles of Political Obligation', sect. 89, II, p. 406.

will."[97] "In principle", Green argued, the same thing was true of states which were despotically governed, e.g. Russia:

> It is not the absolute coercive power of the Czar which determines the habitual obedience of the people . . . The habitual obedience is determined by a system of law, chiefly customary, which the administration controlled by the Czar enforces against individuals, but which corresponds to the general sense of what is equitable and necessary.[98]

Nevertheless, probably with the aim of amending Hume's viewpoint, Green emphasised how the habitual obedience stemmed from the tendency to harmonize will and reason in the character of individuals:

> That which determines this habitual obedience is a power residing in the common will and reason of men, i.e. in the will and reason of men as determined by social relations, as interested in each other, as acting together for common ends. It is a power which this universal rational will exercises over the inclinations of the individual, and which only needs exceptionally to be backed by coercive force.[99]

Using the dialectic drawn from Baur, Green believed that institutions had to reflect the working out of the common good. "The phaenomena of life are not ideal, in the sense in which the ideal is opposed to that which is sensibly verifiable, but they are related to the processes of material change which are their conditions, as ideas or ideal ends which those processes contribute to realise . . . "[100] The conception of an empirically determined ego emerges again, and from it also came the conviction that, if a pure desire for social good cannot be opposed to egoistic motives, egoistic motives themselves do not act without direction from an involuntary reference to the social good.[101]

From this viewpoint, the most conspicuous modern instance of a man who was instrumental in working great and beneficial changes from the most purely selfish motives was Napoleon. "With all his egotism", Green argued,

> his individuality was so far governed by the action of the national spirit in and upon him, that he could only glorify himself in the greatness of France; and though the national spirit expressed

[97] *Ibid.*, sect. 90, II, p. 407.
[98] *Ibid.*, sect. 90, II, pp. 407–8.
[99] *Ibid.*, sect. 92, II, p. 409.
[100] *Ibid.*, sect. 125, II, p. 438.
[101] See *ibid.*, sect. 128, II, p. 439.

itself in an effort after greatness which was in many ways of a mischievous and delusive kind, yet it again had so much of what may
be called the spirit of humanity in it, that it required satisfaction in
the belief that it was serving mankind.[102]

Despite appearances, Green did not want to revive the
Hegelian World-Historical Individuals. Green's starting point
was entirely antithetical to Hegel's. Hegel thought that the
Idea (the universal) was prior to the particular, and was convinced it paid "the penalty of determinate existence and of cor-
ruptibility, not from itself, but from the passions of
individuals."[103] In Hegel's view the hero, who was exempted
from moral judgment, could do violence to the particular.[104]
By contrast, for Green, the particular was antecedent to the
universal, and particularity and universality were so intrinsically connected that only God could separate them. Green's
exceptional individuality was embodied not in the hero but in
the philosopher-saint. Green, who would have deserved the
accusation of Thersitism, i.e. of judging heroes from a moral
viewpoint,[105] identified his exceptional individuality with a
figure able to emancipate History from exactly the Hegelian
inclination to abstract from the concreteness of life. At the
same time, by insisting that reason could stimulate men to conceive their perfection as an end in itself, Green kept himself
aloof from Hume too. In case of conflict of sovereignty, Green
suggested that the way out was to examine one's conscience,
and that the good result of a political movement derived from
the number of good citizens engaged in it.[106] Significantly,
Green maintained that the success of Napoleon was due
mainly to the contribution of other, unknown men. "If we
would understand the apparent results of his action", Green
argued, "we must bear in mind how much besides his particu-

---

[102] *Ibid.*, sect. 128, II, p. 440.
[103] Hegel, *The Philosophy of History*, p. 33.
[104] "This", Hegel observed, "may be called the *cunning of reason* – that it sets the
passions to work for itself, while that which develops its existence through
such impulsion pays the penalty, and suffers loss. For it is *phenomenal* being
that is so treated, and of this, part is of no value, part is positive and real. The
particular is for the most part of too trifling value as compared with the general: individuals are sacrificed and abandoned" (*ibid.*).
[105] *Ibid.*, pp. 31–2.
[106] 'Lectures on the Principles of Political Obligation', sect. 111, II, pp. 424–5 and
sect. 112, II, p. 426.

lar agency has really gone to produce them, so far as they were good; how much of unnoticed effort on the part of men obscure because unselfish, how much of silent process in the general heart of man."[107]

In Green's view, the impossibility of distinguishing between universality and particularity contributed both to the fact that great men, under certain conditions, could favour the advent of the general will and to the fact that, though right was much more important than force, it could not exist independently of force. Nonetheless, force had always to be subject to right:

> Nothing is more real than a right, yet its existence is purely ideal, if by 'ideal' is meant that which is not dependent on anything material but has its being solely in consciousness. It is to these ideal realities that force is subordinate in the creation and development of states.[108]

In this sense, Russia could be counted a state, i.e. an institution which expresses the general will, only "by a sort of courtesy on the supposition that the power of the Czar, though subject to no constitutional control, is so far exercised in accordance with a recognised tradition of what the public good requires as to be on the whole a sustainer of rights."[109] Green believed those states were superior in which the general will embodied itself in representative institutions. Of course, from his perspective, the representative state too should develop itself according to the evolution of the general will.[110] The inclination, which Green inherited from Vane, to subordinate political to moral obligation led him to think that in the context of the modern representative state new rights would arise. "And", Green argued,

> as new rights arise in the state once formed, so further purposes are served. It leads to a development and moralisation of man

---

[107] *Ibid.*, sect. 130, II, p. 441.
[108] *Ibid.*, sect. 136, II, pp. 446–7.
[109] *Ibid.*, sect. 132, II, p. 443.
[110] Barker observed of Green: "We know from his actual career, and we may gather from the logic of his own principles, that he believed in representative government and a wide franchise. But it is what the State can do and should do with its powers that interests him more than its machinery" (E. Barker, *Political Thought in England, 1848–1914* (London, 1915), pp. 39–40).

beyond the stage which they must have reached before it could be possible.[111]

For instance, by limiting itself to establishing that no man should be used by other men as a means against his will, the law left it pretty much a matter of chance whether a man was "qualified to fulfil any social function, to contribute anything to the common good, and to do so freely."[112] Here at present the law did not go far enough, and it was the role of the social reformer to suggest what new rights would enable men to acquire the necessary qualifications.

8. Common Sense and Self-realization

In Green's view, an educational democracy would enable the people to form "certain qualities, not as a means to anything ulterior which the possession of these qualities might bring about, but simply for the sake of that possession; ... inducing in them habits of action on account of the intrinsic value of those habits, as forms of activity in which man achieves what he has it in him to achieve, and so far satisfies himself."[113] At the same time, the democratic character emphasised by Green resulted, not from abstract principles, but from habits and imagination. Green's starting point was definitely empirical and deeply imbued with common sense:

> when the soul is suddenly called upon to face some awful moment, to which are joined great issues for good or evil in its moral history, it is not by "going over the theory of virtue in one's mind", not by any philosophical consideration of the origin and validity of moral ideas, that the right determination can be given. A judgment of the sort we call intuitive — a judgment which in fact represents long courses of habit and imagination founded on ideas — is all that the occasion admits of.[114]

Consistently with his dialectic, which tended to avoid the risk of discerning too clearly and therefore in an abstract way, the universal from the particular, Green candidly admitted that man

> has other faculties indeed than those which are directly exhibited in the specifically moral virtues — faculties which find their

---

[111] 'Lectures on the Principles of Political Obligation', sect. 135, II, p. 446.
[112] *Ibid.*, sect. 155, II, p. 465.
[113] *Prolegomena to Ethics*, sect. 243, IV, p. 261.
[114] *Ibid.*, sect. 320, IV, p. 350.

expression not in his dealings with other men, but in the arts and sciences — and the development of these must be a necessary constituent in any life which he presents to himself as one in which he can find satisfaction.[115]

Thus Sidgwick could easily question the non-competitive character of Green's conception of the common good. Sidgwick pointed out that in this case the possible conflict concerned "books, pictures, prolonged education, varied travel, opportunities of intellectual society."[116] By contrast, for Green, the Hedonistic theory was inadequate because of its inability to treat the perfecting of the will as the end in itself, as the ultimate good for man.[117]

Nevertheless, Green openly acknowledged the value of Utilitarianism:

in most cases where a man has to decide how he may best promote the greatest good of others, it makes little practical difference in regard to the line of action to be taken, whether he considers their greatest good to lie in the possession of a certain character, as an end not a means, or in the enjoyment of the most pleasure of which they are capable.[118]

At the same time, though, Green appreciated the egalitarian bent of Utilitarianism.[119] He affirmed that "*for practical purposes*" the principle embodied in the Utilitarian formula, that every one should count for one and no one for more than one, "yields very much the same direction" as the Kantian categorical imperative.[120] However, he noted how the very calculation

---

[115] *Ibid.*, sect. 370, IV, p. 415.

[116] H. Sidgwick, 'Green's Ethics', *Mind*, 9 (1884), p. 183. See also Sidgwick, *Lectures on the Ethics of T.H. Green, Mr. Herbert Spencer, and J. Martineau* (London, 1902), p. 70.

[117] *Prolegomena to Ethics*, sect. 380, IV, p. 425.

[118] *Ibid.*, sect. 332, IV, p. 365.

[119] "There is no reason", Ritchie observed, "why the Idealist, after making clear his objections to Hedonism, should not join hands with the Utilitarian" (*The Principles of State Interference*, p. 145). See also I.M. Greengarten, *Thomas Hill Green and the Development of Liberal-Democratic Thought* (Toronto, 1981), pp. 131–41; D. Weinstein, 'The Discourse of Freedom, Rights and Good in Nineteenth-Century English Liberalism', *Utilitas*, 3 (1991), pp. 256–9. On the relationship between Green, Mill, and Sidgwick, see Weinstein, 'Between Kantianism and Consequentialism in T.H. Green's Moral Philosophy', *Political Studies*, 41 (1993), pp. 618–35. For a different interpretation, see A. Simhony, 'Was T.H. Green a Utilitarian?', *Utilitas*, 7 (1995), pp. 121–44.

[120] *Prolegomena to Ethics*, sect. 214, IV, p. 226 (italics mine).

of the felicific consequences prevented the Utilitarians from going beyond the limits of a merely formal equality.[121]

Green aimed to justify his theory of positive freedom without running the danger of making liberty coincide either with contingency or with an idolizing version of the state. He recognized that Sidgwick's Hedonistic doctrine represented a step forward beyond the egoistic Hedonism of some Utilitarian thinkers. At the same time, in Green's view, Sidgwick's position could crush any impulse to go beyond that reasonableness typical of common sense as Hume thought of it.[122] Sidgwick had good reason to state that Green used two different conceptions of human good, "the one liberally comprehensive, but palpably admitting competition, the other non-competitive but stoically or puritanically narrow."[123] Nonetheless, Sidgwick was wrong because he did not realize that Green wanted to make these different conceptions perfectly consistent.[124]

Green thought that there was no contradiction between common sense, which made itself explicit in conventional morality, and the awareness that the only principle able to encourage the development of an effective democracy was afforded by "the theory of ultimate good as a perfection of the human spirit resting on the will to be perfect."[125] "To most people", Green wrote

> sufficient direction for their pursuits is afforded by claims so well established in conventional morality that they are intuitively recognised .... But the cases we have been considering are those in which some 'counsel of perfection' is needed.[126]

A true democracy resulted from giving everyone the possibility of morally improving himself.

---

[121] *Ibid.*, IV, p. 227.
[122] *Ibid.*, sects 365–70, IV, pp. 408–15.
[123] Sidgwick, 'Green's Ethics', p. 184.
[124] For a criticism of Green's conception of the common good like that formulated by Sidgwick, see C.A. Smith, 'The Individual and Society in T.H. Green's Theory of Virtue', *History of Political Thought*, 2 (1981), pp. 187–201; R. Bellamy, *Liberalism and Modern Society* (Oxford, 1992), pp. 45–7. For a confutation of Sidgwick's viewpoint, see A. Simhony, 'T.H. Green's Theory of the Morally Justified Society', *History of Political Thought*, 10 (1989), pp. 481–98. See also T.H. Irwin, 'Eminent Victorians and Greek Ethics: Sidgwick, Green, and Aristotle' in B. Schultz, ed., *Essays on Henry Sidgwick* (Cambridge, 1992), pp. 279–310.
[125] *Prolegomena to Ethics*, sect. 382, IV, p. 427.
[126] *Ibid.*

9.   The Right of Property

Pursuing his aim of reconciling empiricism with idealism and mitigating idealism with empiricism,[127] Green saw property on the one hand as an appendix of personality and therefore as an inalienable right; on the other hand, however, he doubted whether the forms in which the right of property expressed itself historically should be regarded as absolute and unquestionable. In order to prevent society falling under the domination of the strongest, custom and reason should be considered as elements which could develop. Mill, in his *Principles of Political Economy*, affirmed that the distribution of wealth "depends on the laws and customs of society"[128] and, universalizing the criteria of individual interest, argued that the exercise of the right of property must not result in harm to others. "With property in moveables, and in all things the product of labour: over these", Mill observed, "the owner's power both of use and exclusion should be absolute, except where positive evil to others would result from it."[129] Mill was not interested in inquiring into the generation of human opinions:

> They are part of the general theory of human progress .... We have here to consider, not the causes, but the consequences, of the rules according to which wealth may be distributed.[130]

By contrast, although Green was convinced of the importance of custom, he did not want to confine himself to inquiring into the consequences of human actions. Green was interested in causes.

When Green contended that "the foundation of the right of property lies in the will, that property is 'realised will'", he was probably making reference to Hegel.[131] "Since my will", Hegel

---

[127] Because some critics ignored Green's peculiar dialectic, they believed they discerned in his position a conflict between utilitarianism and idealism: see for instance C.B. Macpherson, *Democratic Theory: Essays in Retrieval* (Oxford, 1973), pp. 4–5, P. Hansen, 'T.H. Green and the Moralization of the Market', *Canadian Journal of Political and Social Theory*, 1 (1977), pp. 91–117, and Vincent and Plant, *Philosophy, Politics and Citizenship*, pp. 31–3.

[128] Mill, *Principles of Political Economy*, bk II, ch. i, sect. 1, p. 200.

[129] *Ibid.*, bk II, ch. i, sect. 6, p. 231.

[130] *Ibid.*, bk II, ch. i, sect. 1, p. 200.

[131] 'Lectures on the Principles of Political Obligation', sect. 217, II, p. 523. This interpretation is consistent both with that of Gerald F. Gaus (*The Modern Liberal Theory of Man* (London, 1983), p. 240) and with that of Peter Nicholson, who specified (*The Political Philosophy of the British Idealists*, p. 103): "Green's is sometimes called a 'personality' or 'expressive' theory of property, as is

observed, "as personal and hence as the will of an individual [*des Einzelnen*], becomes objective in property, the latter takes on the character of *private property*."[132] Like Hegel, Green maintained that the will on which property rests is "not the momentary spring of any and every spontaneous action, but a constant principle, operative in all men qualified for any form of society."[133] Nevertheless, in order to underline the social origin of property, Green insisted that another condition must be fulfilled. Fichte stated that

> original right consists essentially in an ongoing reciprocal interaction, dependent only on the person's own will, between the person and the sensible world outside of him. In the property contract, a particular part of the sensible world is allocated exclusively to each individual as the sphere of his reciprocal interaction with it; and this part of the sensible world is guaranteed to each individual under two conditions: (1) that he refrain from disturbing the freedom of all others in their spheres, and (2) that, in the event that these others are transgressed against by some third party, he will contribute towards their protection.[134]

Similarly Green argued that property stemmed from social recognition, "the recognition by others of a man's appropriations as something which they will treat as his, not theirs, and the guarantee to him of his appropriations by means of that recognition."[135] Mill's criteria of individual interest were not deep enough. Social injustice resulted from a wrong conception of property, not simply from the attitude to interference with the interest of others. Property originated, as did any other right, in a social context. Everyone, therefore, must be allowed the opportunity of becoming a possessor of property:

Hegel's, which clearly is its principal inspiration. The label is appropriate, provided due regard is paid to the dual meaning of 'personality'. One might be tempted to think of 'the expression of personality' entirely in terms of individuality, giving vent to what is idiosyncratic and peculiar to the particular person: so that personality means, as it seems to in Mill, what is distinct and unique. This particularity is part of what Hegelians mean, but there is also another side to it, personality in a general or universal sense. All persons, besides being different from one another, are the same in other respects ... All human beings are persons, self-conscious 'I's, and this universality of moral personality is the ground of their right to property."

[132] Hegel, *Elements of the Philosophy of Right*, sect. 46, p. 77.
[133] 'Lectures on the Principles of Political Obligation', sect. 217, II, p. 523.
[134] *Foundations of Natural Right*, ed. F. Neuhouser, trans. M. Baur (Cambridge, 2000), sect. 210, p. 183.
[135] 'Lectures on the Principles of Political Obligation', sect. 214, II, p. 520.

> The rationale of property, in short, requires that everyone who will conform to the positive condition of possessing it, viz. labour, and the negative condition, viz. respect for it as possessed by others, should, so far as social arrangements can make him so, be a possessor of property himself, and of such property as will at least enable him to develop a sense of responsibility, as distinct from mere property in the immediate necessaries of life.[136]

Notwithstanding this, Green's view of the right of property does not involve any egalitarian conclusion. "Considered as representing the conquest of nature by the effort of free and variously gifted individuals, property", Green noted, "must be unequal."[137] Green was undoubtedly against any restriction of free trade, as he rejected any regulation of the freedom of bequest. Apart from the special case of land, whose characteristics required the abolition of the right of primogeniture, Green maintained the necessity of freedom of bequest.[138] This leaves the possibility that, with the aim of getting a return for the security it gives to it, the state may tax inherited wealth.[139] Nevertheless, the abolition of the right of primogeniture itself does not stem from any abstract or absolute principle: as Green emphasised, "it depends on circumstances."[140]

Unlike both Mill and Hegel, for Green custom and reason operated together. In this sense, Green regarded social recognition as a "customary recognition, founded on a moral or rational will."[141] The constant search for a balance between custom and reason led Green to say that, though will cannot exist without force, in its turn force should never prevail over will. From the operation of force, which could make the wild beast in man yield obedience to the rational will,

> there result many characteristics of the institution of property, as it actually exists, which cannot be derived from the spiritual principle which we have assigned as its foundation. Still without that principle it could not have come into existence, nor would it have any moral justification at all.[142]

Thus, the prevalence of force could be seen as the breaking down of the social recognition on which the state itself is

---

[136] *Ibid.*, sect. 221, II, p. 526.
[137] *Ibid.*, sect. 223, II, p. 527.
[138] *Ibid.*, sect. 225, II, pp. 529–30.
[139] *Ibid.*, sect. 224, II, p. 528.
[140] *Ibid.*, sect. 231, II, p. 534.
[141] *Ibid.*, sect. 217, II, p. 523.
[142] *Ibid.*

grounded. On the other hand, the prevalence of force revealed that an antisocial dogmatic conception of right had imposed itself. Just because it was based on the principle of customary social recognition, the right of property could not be made an absolute dogma either by those who were against any kind of state intervention, or by those who thought state intervention was the only way out.[143]

The denial of the opportunity of becoming a possessor entailed the denial of social life itself, and since no right can be conceived legitimately apart from social relations, Green did not hesitate to affirm that "in that case it may truly be said that 'property is theft'."[144] At the same time, Green, who probably shared Mill's view about the dangers of Communism, St. Simonism and Fourierism, clearly rejected any kind of state planning:

> The artist and man of letters require different equipment and apparatus from the tiller of land and the smith. Either then the various apparatus needed for various functions must be provided for individuals by society, which would imply a complete regulation of life incompatible with that highest object of human attainment, a free morality; or we must trust for its provision to individual effort, which will imply inequality between the property of different persons.[145]

Green did not accept any kind of regulation — or non-regulation — of the right of property which might hinder individuals from freely developing their moral faculties.

---

[143] Green was undoubtedly a liberal, and his position can be hardly described as socialist. He rejected not only collectivism but also any kind of state intervention which could undermine human dignity. Thus, his theory of property can be regarded as compatible with socialism provided that socialism becomes liberal, i.e. favours the development and the extension of private property rather than its annihilation: see C. Tyler, 'Context, Capitalism and the Natural Right to Private Property in the Thought of Thomas Hill Green' in I. Hampsher-Monk and J. Stanyer, ed., *Contemporary Political Studies 1996, Volume III* (Oxford, 1996), pp. 1412–4. On the right of property in Green, see also C.B. Macpherson, ed., *Property: Mainstream and Critical Positions* (Toronto, 1987), pp. 101–17 and J. Morrow, 'Property and Personal Development: An Interpretation of T.H. Green's Political Philosophy', *Politics: Journal of the Australian Political Science Association*, 18 (1981), pp. 84–92.

[144] 'Lectures on the Principles of Political Obligation', sect. 221, II, p. 526.

[145] 'Lectures on the Principles of Political Obligation', sect. 223, II, pp. 527–8. For Mill see *Principles of Political Economy*, bk II, ch. i, sects 3 and 4.

10. Vane and Positive Freedom

Probably it was Vane who gave Green the clue which enabled him to work out the distinction between positive and negative freedom.[146] Vane maintained that the realm of Christ was marked out by the positive and negative precepts of the divine law. Where Christ reigned undisturbed — the conscience — the magistrate was not allowed to exercise any coercion: where the divine law stated the prevalence of Christ, at the same time it denied the supremacy of the magistrate.[147] The magistrate should not interfere with the religious power, because that concerned the conscience from which stemmed the ethical growth of the individual. In Vane's view, liberty involved the emancipation of conscience from any kind of rule, and it was grounded on the guarantee that the civil law would not thwart the divine law. Vane thought that the state should be an instrument for the ethical development of men.

Seen in the light of the dialectic inherited from Baur, Green's position seems to be so deeply characterized by a consideration for the practical or empirical aspects, that it could never be used to justify any form of despotism or oppression. Although in the case of the regulation of the liquor traffic Green favoured stronger state intervention than did Mill, he specified that state intervention could be justified only on the ground of facts, and that, the sacredness of the inner life being understood, only a thorough examination of the circumstances could prove the suitability of state intervention. Green maintained that the Poor Law hindered the development of the moral faculties, and he was definitely against any regulation of testamentary succession (except in the case of landed estates) because it restricted free trade. The distinction between positive and negative freedom Green elaborated was based on the assumption of the inviolability of conscience and

[146] On the relationship between progressivism and religion, see M. Bevir, 'Welfarism, Socialism and Religion: On T.H. Green and Others', *The Review of Politics*, 55 (1993), pp. 642–61; see also Francis and Morrow, *A History of English Political Thought in the Nineteenth Century*, pp. 272–3. By contrast, Ulam saw a contradiction between Green's admiration for Cromwell and Vane and Idealism: *Philosophical Foundations of English Socialism*, pp. 29–30.

[147] See P. Harris, 'Henry Vane's Arguments for Freedom of Conscience', *Political Science*, 40 (1988), pp. 34–48. For a comparison with Hobbes, see D. Parnham, 'Politics Spun Out of Theology and Prophecy: Sir Henry Vane on the Spiritual Environment of Public Power', *History of Political Thought*, 22 (2001), pp. 69–82.

the firm belief that conscience was inclined to moral growth. While positive freedom concerned the inner life, negative freedom regarded the outward man and should be subordinated to the possible evolution of the ethical life.[148] Moreover, negative freedom was useful to preserve that social impulse characteristic of human beings which, originating from the divine law, bore witness to the equality of men.

Vane's viewpoint was confirmed by Fichte's. Fichte too was convinced of the necessity of conceiving society separately from that empirically determined form of society which could be identified with the state. Like Vane, Fichte thought that the state did not embody "a part of the absolute purpose of human life (whatever a great man may have said to the contrary); but it is, under certain conditions, a possible means towards the formation of a perfect Society."[149] The state constantly tends to its own annihilation: "the ultimate aim of all government is to make government superfluous."[150] Again like Vane, Fichte maintained that society was prior to the state. "The Social Impulse", Fichte observed,

> thus belongs to the fundamental impulses of man. It is man's vocation to live in Society — he *must* live in Society; — he is no complete man, but contradicts his own being, if he lives in a state of isolation.[151]

For Green, freedom could be meant both negatively and positively. Negative freedom implied the equality of men and was instrumental to the realization of positive freedom. Likewise, the Social Impulse outlined by Fichte was determined both

---

[148] Nicholson rightly saw that both Green and Mill limited state intervention on the bases of their inductive method (*The Political Philosophy of the British Idealists*, pp. 181–94). However, the Greenian distinction between negative and positive freedom gave rise to many influential criticisms, of which the most authoritative is that formulated by Berlin (see Berlin, 'Two Concepts of Liberty' reprinted in *Four Essays on Liberty* (Oxford, 1969), pp. 118–72). For a confutation of Berlin's viewpoint, see B. Wempe, *T.H. Green's Theory of Positive Freedom: From Metaphysics to Political Theory* (Exeter, 2004), pp. 211–9; A. Simhony, 'On Forcing Individuals to be Free: T.H. Green's Liberal Theory of Positive Freedom', *Political Studies*, 39, 1991, pp. 303–20; R. Bellamy, 'T.H. Green, J.S. Mill and Isaiah Berlin on the Nature of Liberty and Liberalism' in H. Gross and R. Harrison, ed., *Jurisprudence: Cambridge Essays* (Oxford, 1992), pp. 257–85. On Green and positive freedom see also W.H. Greenleaf, *The British Political Tradition, Volume Two: The Ideological Heritage* (London, 1983), pp. 124–41 and Gaus, *The Modern Liberal Theory of Man*, pp. 163–5.

[149] Fichte, *The Vocation of the Scholar*, p. 30.

[150] *Ibid.*

[151] *Ibid.*

"negatively" and *"positively"*, and the first, that required *"co-ordination"*, was to pave the way to the second.[152] Indeed, *"positively"* regarded, the Social Impulse was bent on encouraging the improvement of humanity. Like Vane, Fichte maintained that, though individuals were deeply different, they shared their ultimate aim, i.e. what Green called their self-realization. "All the individuals who compose the human race differ", Fichte argued, "from each other; there is only one thing in which they entirely agree; — that is, their ultimate end — perfection."[153]

11. A New Liberalism

In his 'Lecture on Liberal Legislation and Freedom of Contract,' given at Leicester early in 1881 under the auspices of the Liberal Association, Green, having mentioned some cases of the regulation of freedom of contract, said:

> When we speak of freedom as something to be so highly prized, we mean a positive power or capacity of doing or enjoying something worth doing or enjoying, and that, too, something that we do or enjoy in common with others. We mean by it a power which each man exercises through the help or security given him by his fellow-men, and which he in turn helps to secure for them.[154]

Indeed, the progress of society resulted from the amount of moral growth favoured by positive freedom, i.e. "by the increasing development and exercise on the whole of those powers of contributing to social good with which we believe the members of the society to be endowed; in short, by the greater power on the part of the citizens as a body to make the most and best of themselves."[155] Green was explicit how the moral growth of society had been encouraged, expressing his satisfaction. "Happily", he observed, "a sense of the facts and necessities of the case got the better of the delusive cry of liberty."[156] The new Liberalism — its inclination to avail itself of state intervention with the aim of improving the condition of children and women — bore witness to the lack of any kind of

---

[152] *Ibid.*, pp. 33–4.
[153] *Ibid.*, p. 34.
[154] 'Lecture on Liberal Legislation and Freedom of Contract', *Works*, III, p. 371.
[155] *Ibid.*
[156] *Ibid.*, III, p. 385.

abstract philosophical schema or system which claimed to set aside human suffering.

Green appreciated the idea of the state on which Hegel's position was grounded insofar as it was comparable to that of the Greek philosophers, whose aim was to secure "the common good of the members of the society" and enable them to make the best of themselves.[157] At the same time, true to the dialectic inherited from Baur, he accused Hegel of ignoring the difference between the ideal and the actual. Hegel seemed to speak of tendencies "as if they were accomplished facts."[158] The conception of freedom which Hegel thought was realized in the state seemed, Green argued, "hard to square with facts."[159] "To an Athenian slave", Green added, "who might be used to gratify a master's lust, it would have been a mockery to speak of the state as a realisation of freedom; and perhaps it would not be much less so to speak of it as such to an untaught and under-fed denizen of a London yard with gin-shops on the right hand and on the left."[160]

Facts always ought to prevail over the dogmatism both of those who idolized the state and of those who, idolizing liberty, rejected any kind of state intervention. To Hegel, and to those who believed that a society which could solve its problems spontaneously was better than one which needed state intervention, Green objected that they lacked realism. "We must", Green observed, "take men as we find them."[161] Green's elaboration of Baur's dialectic led him to identify his starting point with the actual condition of men and, at the same time, not to limit himself to a sceptical or resigned report of the facts. In this sense, state intervention was subordinated to the development of conscience and, therefore, made instrumental to positive freedom. Until society had reached a condition in which public health was duly protected and necessary education properly provided for by the spontaneous action of individuals, it was "the business of the state to take the best security it can for the young citizens' growing up in such health and with so much knowledge as is necessary for their

---

[157] 'On the Different Senses of 'Freedom' As Applied to Will and to the Moral Progress of Man', *Works*, II, sect. 4, p. 312.

[158] *Ibid.*, II, sect. 6, p. 314.

[159] *Ibid.*

[160] *Ibid.*

[161] 'Lecture on Liberal Legislation and Freedom of Contract', III, p. 375.

real freedom."[162] But, Green specified: "In so doing it need not at all interfere with the independence and self-reliance of those whom it requires to do what they would otherwise do for themselves."[163] Green's doctrine of positive and negative freedom cannot be regarded simply as a justification of state intervention. It has to be seen in relation to circumstances. From Green's perspective, conservatism and progressivism become two dynamic categories, and the difference between them is essentially a different view of the importance of facts. By underestimating the importance of facts and therefore being thoughtless of human suffering, conservatism was undoubtedly prone to preserve the status quo. Progressivism, on the contrary, revolved around the belief that moral energies must be freed from economic dependence. In the context of Baur's dialectic, the dynamic towards the universal moved from the particular. Facts came first and progress could not disregard them.

According to this outlook, for Green, no contract should be regarded as valid in which human persons, willingly or unwillingly, were dealt with as commodities. Such contracts, Green observed, "of necessity defeat the end for which alone society enforces contracts at all."[164] The consequences of Green's doctrine were obvious:

> Labour, the economist tells us, is a commodity exchangeable like other commodities. This is in a certain sense true, but it is a commodity which attaches in a peculiar manner to the person of man. Hence restrictions may need to be placed on the sale of this commodity which would be unnecessary in other cases, in order to prevent labour from being sold under conditions which make it impossible for the person selling it ever to become a free contributor to social good in any form.[165]

Green thought that society would be within its right not only in prohibiting the labour of children beyond certain hours, but also, unlike Mill, that of women. Every injury to the health of the individual, like every impediment to the development of his social relationships, should be considered "deduction

---

[162] *Ibid.*
[163] *Ibid.*
[164] *Ibid.*, III, p. 373.
[165] *Ibid.*

from our power, as members of society, to make the best of ourselves."[166]

Green contended that the Liberal Party should be, in his own times as it had been fifty years before, the Party of the "social good against class interests."[167] There was therefore a continuity between the old and the new Liberalism. While the first, beginning with the reform of Parliament (1832), and extending to Sir Robert Peel's administration, was marked by the struggle of free society against close privileged corporations and monopolies, the second started with the first Parliament (1868) able to take efficient measures for enforcing the restraints which previous legislation had in principle required. These measures, such as education and factory laws, implied a greater interference with freedom of contract.[168] A more popular suffrage required a greater attention to the influence of facts and circumstances.

---

[166] *Ibid.*
[167] *Ibid.*, III, p. 367.
[168] *Ibid.*, III, pp. 367–9.

Conclusion

Green was more interested, as Barker observed, in what "the State can do and should do with its power", than in its machinery.[1] Though Green favoured a wide franchise including women, pressed for decentralization to make ordinary people's common sense stand out in a way that could overcome ideological and party divisions, and a reform of the House of Lords, he did not outline any theory specifically concerning institutions. Despite his awareness that a higher degree of representative government could be hoped for, Green foresaw that those who had opposed representative government at first would do their best later to empty representation of its content. Democracy was at risk of retiring into its shell and becoming a weapon which its adversaries would use against its champions. Green's view can, therefore, be compared with Tocqueville's or J.S. Mill's, authors who knew that democracy should not be regarded as a panacea for all evils and that, as the ancient Greeks had experienced, it was a regime which valued quantity more than quality and which could easily yield to corruption. Like Tocqueville and J.S. Mill, Green thought that morality provided the only way out. Democracy was based on moral virtues. Moral virtues could exist apart from democracy; but a democracy without moral virtues was bound to change into its opposite, a tyranny, even if one exercised on behalf of a majority. Green agreed with Aristotle that if a good citizen was not necessarily a good man, a good man was inevitably a good citizen. In this sense, virtuous men were the last hope for democracy.

Nevertheless, virtue and facts cannot clash: if that were not the case, democracy was under sentence of death. As the Tory Hume showed in his *History of England*, the English revolution was just such an incursion of virtue which turned into blood-

---

[1]   Barker, *Political Thought in England, 1848–1914*, p. 40.

shed and a dictatorship. Though Green shared Hume's position about the impossibility of forcing a course of events, he did not blame the leaders of the Commonwealth: Cromwell was his favourite character. It was only the inadequacy of the Puritan philosophy that Green revealed. For him, Puritan thought tended to be too abstract (without "matter") because it inclined to set reason against facts. That is why the revolutionaries gave rise to a democracy without a demos, and the great Milton himself expressed at once the deepest contempt for the high ranks of the court and a detachment towards a people seen as being at the mercy of sensual degradation. It is important to bear in mind that Green distinguished between the Puritan philosophy and the intentions which inspired its leaders. The latter should be judged intrinsically democratic. They would be revived by an idealist philosophy made compatible with the English philosophical tradition, that is, with empiricism.

Though Luther favoured the invisible church, the degeneration of the Lutheran Reformation soon reaffirmed the primacy of the visible one, and the idealism (Green meant Hegel's) that stemmed from the Lutheran Reformation was consequently prone to see state and church as two sides of the same coin. It tended therefore to mistake the real for the ideal, and to become a serious hindrance to any kind of improvement. On the other hand, Green maintained that Kant himself was wrong when he sustained the distinction between noumenon and phenomenon. However, Hegel made as great a mistake in getting rid of this distinction, so that, for Green, the remedy was worse than the disease. More like Fichte, Green believed that any dichotomy between the real and the ideal must be rejected, yet at the same time that the difference between them must not be blurred. Moreover, idealism sprang from a character (the German character) which was bent on abstracting its mind from external considerations and pushing its opinions to their utmost consequences. For Green, there was a double risk: idealism might confirm the *status quo*, and it might reinvigorate that antithesis between *hommes d'état et hommes à principes* which Hegel himself deprecated. Either outcome would prevent real reform from being put into practice. Green drew a parallel between the Parliament purged by Pride in 1648 and the Parliament elected after the 1832 Reform Act. In order to avert the danger that the democratic reforms supported by the

Puritans would be thwarted once again, a new idealist philosophy was required. Idealism should be revised in the light of the Puritan belief that reality, despite its dynamic character and therefore its tendency to make real the ideal, should not be confused with the ideal.

Puritanism was already a controversial and ambiguous term in Green's time. He clearly stated that it referred to the Independents or Congregationalists, that is, the sect which counted among its members people such as Cromwell, Vane and Milton and which was fed by Robinson's exhortation to privilege the liberty of conscience implied in the pre-eminence of the invisible church. Green's view of democracy was deeply influenced by the Puritan belief that the dynamism of reality came from a Divine seal which was impressed in man's conscience. From this perspective, very unlike Kant and very like Vane, Green viewed institutions as at once distinct from and instrumental to the moral development of men. He held that not even the definition of "the state" could omit the aims pursued by the state. Green thought that Russia could hardly be regarded a state. Citizenship itself followed from the fact that the state was able to accomplish the function, as Green put it, of removing obstacles. People should be placed in a position to realize themselves morally. If they were not, they were justified in disregarding the state even though they were formally part of it. Again, according to Green, war was the result of the state failing to fulfil its task of being instrumental to the moral growth of its members. States were prone to go to war insofar as were inadequate in this respect. Green also referred to this dynamic when opposing his conception of the *jus naturae* to that of the contract theory.

This dynamic, generated by the Divine, never coincided with human institutions, so that if they stopped it, society became a lifeless mechanism carried along the path of necessity by the mere force of circumstances. While Hegel's version of idealism confirmed the superiority of the visible church, the philosophy Green needed would be based on the primacy of the invisible church. Furthermore, the dangerous Hegelian tendency to abstract from facts should be amended in the light of the typical English disposition to compromise: the English were usually more concerned about the possible outcomes of their doctrines than were the Germans. In just this sense, the Puritan philosophy was a notable exception. Significantly, though Green showed his own solidarity with religious dissent, he disliked the tone and the spirit of its following. He always regarded himself as a member of the Anglican Church, maintaining that a man was not justified in rejecting what does not commend itself to his own private reason. In this case, instead of the Puritan tendency to prefer reason to facts, the wisdom of the English character had to be preserved. That is why the new idealist philosophy would be based not only on the Puritan primacy of the invisible church, but also on the reassessment of the value of that empirical bent which was underrated by Puritan philosophy. Once again, it was necessary to distinguish the Puritan philosophy from the concrete Puritan way of living and thinking which, on the contrary, supported that practical habit characteristic of English history. "Our Norman aristocracy", Green wrote,

> ruling a half-conquered people, were soon obliged to secure their position by compromises with the burghers of the towns, and throughout English history, there seem to have been two well-balanced parties, whose interests must alike be respected in legislation. A similar effect is produced among us by the freedom and influence of public opinion.[2]

Green's task was incredibly difficult. His viewpoint implied the possibility of a compromise between idealism and empiricism. It is likely that in 1863 Green was thrilled about his stay at Heidelberg just because only then had he realized that Baur's dialectic could allow him to mediate between two views which were usually regarded as entirely antithetical. He was convinced that idealism and empiricism taken on their own were both lacking. While the first was not concerned about ordinary people's common sense, the second was a prisoner of common sense. However, thanks to Baur, common sense could be made rational. Indeed, in the light of Baur's position, and of his own critique of Hegel, Green was able to propose an unusual interpretation of Aristotle as well: it produced thought which, unlike the Puritan philosophy, could rightly be regarded as concrete. Reason was not opposed to facts, and "matter" and "form" were so intertwined that "form" could not be conceived apart from "matter". It was impossible to abstract completely from reality because there was always a

---

[2]   'The English National Character Compared with that of the Germans' (see Appendix).

residuum of facts that testified to the need for improvement. Green's political activity itself was always moved by facts. Indeed, Green's philosophy cannot be fully appreciated without considering his political activity.

Democracy was a regime that was not to be judged independently of facts. In Green's eyes democracy was probably more than a simple institutional structure. Green wanted to shape a philosophy which was not over-identified with representation, and which could support harsh criticism of democracy as well. Green believed that if Rousseau had been able to emancipate himself from the presuppositions of natural right he would have affirmed that even the decree of a monarch or of an aristocratic assembly might, under certain conditions, be the organ of the general interest. According to Green, the administration controlled by the Czar, British rule in India and even the condition of Northern Italy under Austrian domination, could express a general will which reflected the needs and lifestyle of ordinary people. At any rate, Green saw in habitual obedience something which would reveal when the sovereign moved away from the general will: it was nothing more than the general sense of what is equitable and necessary. In this sense, "empirical general will" is a suitable expression for a view like Green's, which while it made democracy its basic value, had no explicit institutional reference.

This "empirical general will" would be moulded and remoulded by the Divine dynamism which operated within human history. It was this kind of general will which, rationalized, needed help from the state. Since this rationality was deeply imbued with common sense and revealed itself through it, Green stressed the importance of facts whenever he pressed for some state intervention. Those who opposed state intervention were seen by Green as people who either ignored the facts or undervalued them, depending on the circumstances of the case. State intervention should never depend on an ideal requirement conceived independently of facts. Thus as soon as circumstances changed, state intervention might not only be useless but even harmful to the development of moral faculties. Green probably realised that indiscriminate state intervention could become a source of privileges like those created in a society which dogmatically rejected any kind of interference. Education, land, relationships between workers and employers and the sale of liquor needed to be regulated in a different manner from that provided for by freedom of contract, but only because of the particular situation of the time. However, the state should never be allowed to go beyond the limit which distinguishes the outward from the inward man; and whenever the inward man was put in a position, as Green said, "to realise himself", the state had accomplished its task. Green's position on the right of property clearly proved this. While on the one hand Green saw property as a right concerning the inward man and therefore inalienable, on the other hand he maintained that the forms in which the right of property expressed itself historically must not be treated as absolute. Hence, if property should not be abolished and if inequality should be considered a stimulus for the improvement of society, the right of property should be regulated in a way that allowed everybody to become a possessor.

One can easily grasp that, for Green, there was an unambiguous link between improvement in the capability of the state to remove obstacles, and the widening of democracy. Green's conception of an "empirical general will" led him to affirm that, although right could not exist independently of force, force had always to be subject to right. Consistently with Vane's inclination to subordinate political to moral obligation, a state was only a state for Green insofar as it was able to express its general will. That is why Green had more confidence in representative states than in Russia, where there was no parliament and the people could not go to the polls. At the same time, states unable to display a general will were destined to decline and the first sign of this was the failing of the requisite habitual obedience. Force should be used to encourage the growth of the common good and not to repress the source from which it sprang, that is, man's conscience. In this sense the common good, which flourished when man's conscience was set free, would be more developed with the advent of representation. However, in Green's view, citizenship would become a mere formal and empty right unless every extension of the suffrage brought more "positive freedom". As institutions never fully embodied the Divine but always could be improved and perfected — and democracy was no exception to the rule — "positive freedom" was the one essential instrument for preventing states from regressing and therefore stopping the dynamism Green considered vital.

If a democratic government was more likely than a despotism to express its society's general will because of its representative system, so too "positive freedom" benefitted a democracy by correcting its faults and by increasing the amount of the common good. While a state that was unable to embody a general will did not deserve even the name of state, a democracy which wished to flourish necessarily had to resort to "positive freedom". "Positive freedom" was not simply an item to include in the political agenda when some momentous question arose, but an absolute priority for those who fought to defend democracy against those set on sabotaging it. In this sense, either democracy became a "Puritan" democracy or it ceased to be a democracy at all. The strength of a democracy should be judged not only on whether people went to the polls and the suffrage was universal and free, but also on the common good which resulted from it. Therefore, for Green, it was beyond doubt that the Conservatives should be seen as the party of vested interests while the Liberals could be identified as the party of the common good. Green thought the Conservatives would do their best to hinder the progress of democracy. The Liberals, on the contrary, would devote all their energies to making society more and more democratic and to stimulating people to behave with the common good in mind.

Green's "Puritan" democracy was founded on the conviction that a common good was needed. At the same time, Green's idea of the common good, consistently with his Puritan background, rejected any kind of identification with a fossilized universal (the visible church) which could be thought apart from facts. A dogmatic individualism, equally with a dogmatic idea of a society abstractly conceived and setting aside individual impulses, would destroy social life. By contrast, for Green the common good resulted from preserving the dynamism which, as Vane observed, stemmed from the inward man. Vane maintained that the common rational nature of men boasted a Divine seal. It followed that those societies which tended to protect themselves by defending their own privileges were denying the substantial equality of men, and were doomed to die. In this sense, "positive freedom", just because it favoured the moral growth of societies, was instrumental to the constant extending of the common good. Even so, it had to be used carefully: it should be very responsive to the fact that what was regarded as unjust and was reformed, could later easily produce a privilege. Green's common good required unselfishness. Men must prevail who, without any hidden agenda, were prepared to see institutions not as ends in themselves but only as symbols of a spiritual government, that is, as means to a further end.

Such men, who should be regarded as the guardians of democracy, were the "saints". They struggled to free history from its tendency to stiffen into dogmas, and to escape the risk of institutions becoming vehicles of exclusion. Cromwell and Vane were men like this, and such selfless people caused the success of Napoleon. While the "saint" embodied a sort of exceptional individuality which was deeply democratic and therefore did not sacrifice the particular and the individual for the universal, the Hegelian hero left individuals to their fate. Unlike the Hegelian World-Historical Individuals and unlike Carlyle's hero, intent on getting above ordinary people, the democratic character of the "saint" was confirmed by his being subject to circumstances in the same way as ordinary people. At the same time, in Green's eyes, this was exactly the weak side of the Puritan philosophy, which was unable to see the wisdom that lurked in circumstances. That is why, despite its being democratic in principle, the English Revolution resulted in a dictatorship. Just as a new idealist philosophy was needed in order to put the democratic intentions of the Puritan leaders into practice, so the figure of the "saint" had to be revised in the light of the teaching of the "philosopher" who could see the reason which lay hidden in the facts. Yet there was an undeniable continuity between the first and the second, so that Green asserted that the "philosopher" had to find room for the "saint". If the "saint" had to point out the way, the "philosopher" had to say how the political aspirations of the "saint" could be put into practice. However, as it turned out, democracy was reinforced by unselfishness: only selfless men did not idolize institutions. Green clearly stated that the success of a political movement sprang from the number of disinterested people involved in it.

The strength of democracy came from moral virtues. Green hoped that once working class people managed to gain an education, they would return to the place where they grew up in order to teach and help children who could follow their example. Unselfishness would also be reflected in an increase in political participation and a growth of political awareness. Citizens should always have the chance of expressing themselves both in the case of education and in that of the liquor traffic. The selection of Liberal candidates itself should not be left in the hands of cliques but should be the concern of all potential Liberal voters. Green opened a coffee tavern where former drunkards could be free from temptation and become used to living according to unselfish values. "Positive freedom" was to be used as a lever to diminish selfishness. Green was probably refering to a misuse of "positive freedom" when he blamed the Liberals for the 1874 defeat. Greater prosperity led to a general moral decline which the Liberals did not manage to check. They failed to offer the new voters a suitable political and moral training. The Conservatives, by contrast, succeeded in their attempt to undermine the moral sense of the masses and thereby subvert democracy into an oligarchy. Thanks to drink the few could continue to oppress the many. The lower classes were undeniably more likely than wealthy people to succumb to heavy drinking. Green's battle against drunkenness was not only a moral but also a political one. Alcohol was a most potent weapon available to those who aimed to sabotage democracy because it made people dependent. Once people were unable to resort freely to their own reason, they could no longer discern their real interests. Green was not surprised that the Conservatives were against both any regulation of the liquor traffic and any reform of education that would have deprived the Anglican Church of its monopoly. The Conservatives defended the interests of the landowners as well. Moreover, the Conservatives understood that nationalism could be very useful to blunt the claims of the working classes. Wars quietened popular discontent because they encouraged the belief that threats were posed only by external enemies.

"Saints", that is, men who did not use institutions as a means of justifying their own egoism, were the only resource for democracy. By leading associations and stimulating that social impulse from which democracy sprang, such men could prevent the outbreak of imperialist wars, end the exploitation of labour, and transform political parties — including the Liberal Party itself — from centres of power for defending their own interests exclusively. Green's exceptional individuality was to be embodied by the "philosopher" who, though he had to be first of all a "saint", knew that reason does not have to be set against facts. He was aware for instance that, in some situations, the corruption of the electoral system was unavoidable. The "philosopher" was conscious that the masses were weak, so exposed to the temptation of selling their vote in exchange for a job that they had to be regarded as utterly unreliable. In the context of modern democracy, characterized by mass political participation, a democracy dedicated to the improvement of humanity would be hard to establish: but, for the "philosopher", it alone deserved to be called democratic. The "philosopher" was above all a believer: a man with hope. In Green's view, faith was the principal ingredient of democracy. From Green's analysis one can draw the conclusion that any possible crisis of democracy should be traced to a religious and ethical crisis. Undoubtedly, democracy was and still is the product of a firm faith in the progress of man.

A Selection of Green's Undergraduate Essays

The Spirit of Poetry

We should naturally expect that the spirit of poetry would remain essentially the same, till the introduction of some new element into that inner life of man, of which it is the reflex. The imagery which it borrows from external nature may vary with the variations of circumstance, but the difference between ancient and modern poetry seems to lie deeper than this, and to be only accounted for by alteration in those religious feelings, which, if they do not cause, at any rate qualify the human joys and sorrows, which it is the province of poetry to express. The common remark that ancient poetry is more objective, and modern more subjective, is incorrect if it be taken to mean that we are less sensible of the outer world than the ancients, but most true if it merely imply that we regard it in a different light. The antagonism between the two worlds in which man lives — the transient world of sin and sorrow, and the eternal world of righteousness and peace, — which Christianity has made one of the chief elements of modern poetry, has no place in the ancient. "The obstinate questionings of sense and outward things" had not then arisen. Men regarded themselves as parts of the great mechanism of natural existence, able sometimes to reflect the whole in their own minds, but unable to separate themselves from it, or rise above it. And thus, though their copy of external nature might be more correct than ours, they were less able to exercise upon it that modifying and combining power of the imagination, which places the little on a level with the great, and reads even in the apparent confusion of human life the mercy of a beneficent God.

The Advantages and Disadvantages of Diffusive Reading

The advantages and disadvantages of diffusive reading are very differently balanced at different stages of the growth of the same mind. In early youth, before the mind has acquired any settled principle, which may explain and give harmony to the various information it receives, and before it has sufficiently purged out its own habits of vague and erroneous thought, diffusive reading is but another name for a play upon the surface of the mind, which can bring no good thing to perfection, but which nourishes to a more fertile growth the errors which prejudice and the ambiguities of language implant in every mind. Those errors which Bacon terms the phantoms of the market-place, — vagueness of thought and an ignorance of the native power of words, — which spring from the communications of thoughtless men on matters of wide extent and requiring careful thought, spring no less in the case of individuals from their meddling with many subjects of various importance before they have been trained to discern their complexities or appreciate their full force. In this stage of mental growth it is far better that the attention should be centred on a single branch of knowledge, that so the mind may have a more simple task in discerning its own operations when they are all directed to the same point, and at the same time may learn the greater power of words and the deeper significance of facts, when it can no longer flit from the surface of one subject to the surface of another. But in another stage of the mind the case is reversed. A thoughtful and religious man has a basis of principles sufficiently firm to prevent his diffusive reading becoming vague and shallow. He has that power within him which supplies an index to all that he reads, and enables him to be master of it instead of being carried away by it, and to assimilate to his mind all the external knowledge he receives, so that the fruit remains though the knowledge itself be forgotten. And though by ranging over a variety of subjects he is less able to enter into the intricacies of any single one, yet what he learns of each gains a new life from the light which all his other knowledge combines to shed upon it, and if his learning be less, his acquaintance with truth is greater for he can see it on every side. It may be doubted indeed whether a very deep and exclusive knowledge of one particular science, however useful it may be to his hearers or readers, is very beneficial to the man of learning himself. It sometimes proves a lifeless mass with little power over the man's own mind, nor can it be said to be true to him, unless he regard it in a true state of mind, — a state against which the alienation of his thoughts from all other branches of knowledge greatly militates. Moreover in his exclusive and intense attention to this one science/subject he is apt to forget the great Author from Whom it came, and its bearings on the life of man; while the diffusive reader, by the brighter light which his other knowledge enables him to throw on it, at every step learns something more of the ways of God, and is quickened into warmer sympathy with his fellow-man. To take Astronomy as an instance. The man who has drunk deeply of this science, but has scarcely tasted any other, is apt to push on his investigations in the laws of nature, with little thought either of the Author or the subjects of them. But the man who can bring a knowledge of History to bear on his study of Astronomy, may be roused, among other things, by the thought of the old Sabianism, to greater thankfulness to Him, by the farther knowledge of whose laws the heavenly powers, so fearful to the ancients, have been shown us as regularly-ordained instruments of our good, and to greater love for mankind, under whose superstitions there lurked so much that was beautiful and true. But it is to the man of action, rather than to the man of learning, that diffusive reading, if controlled by a vigorous mind, is especially advantageous. It is sometimes urged that for a man leading a busy life it is necessary that there should be some one branch of knowledge, with which he should form a special acquaintance, and to which he should refer all other information that reaches his mind, that it may not wander loosely about, but may find something with which to connect itself. But surely the only knowledge which ought to be thus employed is the knowledge of man, — his history, his modes of thought, and his destiny, — for this alone is complete in itself, and would not give that one-sided aspect to the information we may obtain, which it must receive if referred to any one separate science. And this knowledge of mankind we can best acquire by diffusive reading, by communing with the minds of the various representatives of mankind as they are manifested in their written works, — a practice especially needful to those men of action whose daily walk and conduct is among the cares and turmoils of life. But the man of learning and science cannot dispense with it. The

Political economist, for instance, if unrestrained by the acquaintance with mankind which diffusive reading ought to produce, may push his doctrines to an excess/extent in which they are opposed to the moral laws which should regulate our dealings with one another, and would produce oppression and mutual distrust. In short the various branches of knowledge are so closely connected and bear so much on one-another that an acquaintance with any one of them is little worth, unless accompanied by a general acquaintance with the rest, such as diffusive reading should confer. The different branches of science are sometimes compared to mines of inexhaustible treasure, to fathom any single one of which might well demand the labours of a whole life, and this is true, but the precious ore we may extract will be of little service to us unless we gain light to discern its qualities from the open atmosphere of general knowledge, and from the same source form/obtain some notion of/insight into the chain by which each treasure of human thought and Divine operation is linked to every other.

The Comparative Value of Fact and Fiction in Education

Both fact and fiction seem to be equivocal terms, and to be contrasted by different persons in very different senses. In the language of some men 'fact' is used as equivalent to the highest kind of truth. It includes all that a wise man can know and be sure of, — not merely those outward phenomena, whether in the history of men or in the world around us, from which the so-called matter-of-fact man derives his title to the name, but the deeper spiritual meaning which is hidden under those palpable phenomena, as well as those higher ideas of the mind, which are as truly facts in the nature of man as the mere habits that appear on the surface. Fiction, when contrasted with fact as used in this sense, would express those subterfuges to which vain and false minds resort to escape from the burden of truth which is irksome to them, and to force themselves into a world of shadows, where the[y] may indulge their idle pastime, till the truth of life is forced back upon them in some way that cannot be mistaken. It is in this sense, I suppose, that the word is applied to the common mass of novels and romances. But, using the words in these senses, it would be absurd to doubt for a moment which is the best instrument of education. We must resort to that different meaning of the words in which 'fact' is confined to those truths which are the objects of science, and those events which have been, or are actually and visibly transacted among men, while 'fiction' expresses those ideal truths which are apprehended by the power that views history in artistic form, discovers the beauty hidden under the facts of science, and abstracts from the mind of man those pollutions of passion and sense, which seem inseparable to the eye of the common observer. Fact would refer to those things which actually have been or are; fiction to those which are ideally true to nature, though in act they never existed. It would seem at first sight as if fiction, in this sense of the word, must certainly be the best means of education. In youth, it seems more essential that a man should learn the broad lessons of all branches of knowledge than the details of any, more important that he should discern the ideal principles of action as they are in themselves than that he should study their effects as applied to the business of life. Till he has acquired these first elements all knowledge will be a riddle to him. History for instance if studied as a series of facts would appear to an inexperienced man an interminable waste, full of contradictions and confusion, with various chains of events, starting from no similar causes, guided by no similar system, and tending to no common ultimate end. The lives of the chief actors in it would seem full of inconsistencies. But the influence of poetry presents it to us in a new aspect. By bringing out the cardinal principles of human nature which are the same in all ages, it imparts a unity of design to the history of man. It enables us to discern that events, apparently such a confused turmoil, are really "orbing themselves to a perfect end", and it sets before us the men of past ages at once as our brethren and our examples, by discovering all that was vital and noble in their characters, and which they had in common with ourselves, while it discards all that was temporary superficial or mean. And thus fiction gives a far deeper and more comprehensive view of history than any knowledge of facts can do, and at the same time encourages high principles by displaying their operation on the world and in great men, unalloyed by baseness and human frailty or inconsistency. Thus it seems to serve the chief ends of education, and that not in history only, but in reference to natural science and the study of the human mind. For it is surely more important to be trained to reverence for the signs of infinite power around us, than to know the order and courses of the stars; far more ennobling for the thought to dwell on the purest exercise of the affections, and on the mysteries of man's nature as they are displayed in the great crises of his life, than to study those facts which indicate little more than his outward habits, and which if taken by themselves would lead us to regard him as a kind of intelligent machine, generally out of order, and marked by irregularity and a sordid littleness.

But though this is true, there is another side to the question. We do not live in an ideal world, but all around us and in ourselves we find good struggling with evil, greatness and meanness strangely blended together, and we must be familiar with the evil as well as with the good, with the meanness as well as the greatness, or we shall not know how to remedy them. A man who has been trained chiefly in fiction, with little attention to facts, will probably find himself cruelly disappointed, as well as useless, in the business of the world. He may be familiar with the ideas of the good and the true, but between them and the fulfilment of worldly duties there is a gulf fixed, which only painful practice, and a strict attention to the world as it is, can enable him to pass. He cannot fulfil his duty to his neighbour or to himself without regular habits of routine, and a neglect to pay his bills may bring him into as utter ruin as the belief that money is the only solid good in the world. This gradual discovery of the littleness in himself and others may lead him on to a selfish cynicism, — an hopeless contempt for himself and others, — and this in its turn may lead to worse forms of self-indulgence. Or if he avoid these worst effects, he will yet find himself unfitted, by his want of practical knowledge, to be such a teacher of others, as his lofty qualities of mind might otherwise have constituted him. Indeed, simply with a view to intellectual excellence, fiction should never in education be separated from fact, for at best it can give but one aspect of truth and human life at a time, and a man ought to have a wide knowledge of facts to qualify his several ideas, and exhibit them in their general bearings. Nor without this can he have that impression of the complexity of life, which tends especially at once to exalt and humble the mind. In short, as in nature "the ideal everywhere underlies the actual", so in education a knowledge of facts should be built upon a training in fiction, that there may neither be high motives without the power of putting them to practical use, nor skill in the business of life without high ideas to ennoble and purify it.

The Character and Opinions of Samuel Johnson

It is far more easy to write of Johnson's character than of his opinions, for while the latter are scattered up and down in his conversation, or hidden amid masses of artificial dross in his writings, his character shines out with more or less fullness in all his pithy sayings and social peculiarities, in every blow he deals at stupidity and in every act of rude kindness. In his case especially we see the truth of the saying, that the man is more and other than his opinions, when we reflect that, while his personal influence was so great over his contemporaries, and continues to be so over us, embalmed, as it is, in his written life, his moral and philosophical writings are now known only to the curious. One great secret of his power over us is, no doubt, the outspoken sincerity of his nature. Partly from the consciouness of his own mental strength, partly from his social geniality, partly perhaps from his contempt for the world, which made him see the folly of wearing a mask, to be soon put off when we quit the stage for ever, he was at no pains to conceal whatever was uppermost in his mind. When Wilkes appeased his wrath by offering him "some of the brown" of the veal at dinner, he was not too philosophical to conceal his enjoyment; if he felt his blood flow quicker in travelling, he was not ashamed to say that "he felt his own vacuity less in a post-chaise"; and thus we feel that he too was a child of Adam, we seem to commune more freely with one like ourselves, but greater, and are somewhat flattered at the same time to see our own weaknesses joined with so much strength. This genuine sincerity of mind might seem inconsistent with the artificial style, and fictitious splendour of most of his written works. But these faults probably arose from a quite different cause. His mind was utterly wanting in purity of taste, but it possessed remarkable vigour in all its more mechanical and constructive faculties, those which go to make up what we call a clever man, in the lower sense of the term. This is evident from the speed with which he wrote his papers for the Rambler, and from the amount of intellectual toil demanded by his Dictionary. It was natural that these powers, combined with his strong English feeling of the necessity of labouring at whatever he had in hand, and regulated by no purity of taste should lead him to disguise in a dress of artificial splendour sentiments, which would have had far more force if they had been stated simply with his natural perspicacity. He did this painfully and ingeniously, and thus satisfied at once his notion of the value of labour, and his own intellectual power. We see the same sentiment, that beauty consists in a laborious accumulation of ornaments, appearing in his admiration of the Duke of Argyle's Palace; "what I admire here, Sir, is the entire disregard/regardlessness of expense". This also is what an English millionaire admires, who feels a deep satisfaction in spending his hardly-won money on some gorgeous but unsightly mansion. In these respects Johnson was a kind of intellectual manufacturer. Somewhat similar was the exclusive value he set on matters of antiquity and research, as opposed to speculation, and on versification as opposed to poetry. He set little store by anything that was not a tangible piece of knowledge, which all men would recognize, and he seems quite to have ignored those products of the mind which it works out by meditation on itself, without direct mechanical labour. In society and travelling he did not seek to inform his mind by external impressions, but to store it with odd facts, and if he read books of travel, as he seems often to have done, he did not set any picture before his mind of foreign lands, but carefully retained details, which he could bring forward in conversation. When the King inquired if he were preparing a new work, Johnson replied, that he had told the world all he knew, and he must acquire fresh knowledge before he could write again. Nowadays, we should scarcely admit this necessity in a professed poet. When Boswell asked his opinion on Berkeley's philosophy, he replied with scorn by kicking his foot against a stone. This anecdote however might illustrate a nobler feature in his character than his prosaic love of the mere details of knowledge. He knew that it was with the stubborn facts of life that he had to deal, — with a body full of hypochondrical humours, with a garret at eighteen pence a week, with his own yearning for indolence, and with the miseries of the afflicted whom he took under his care. And if, with a heroic feeling of the importance of his practical duties, he had a constant dread of falling into a world of ideas and abstractions, we can only admire his stern temper. There appears to have been a gulf of despairing doubt at the bottom of his own mind, which was kept down by his stern sense of duty and his resignation to a superior will, but which would yet sometimes rise to the surface. He once said that the whole of Hume's scepticism had passed through his own mind long before; "his great business was to escape from himself"; and, when asked if there was not sufficient proof of the being of God, he replied that "he wished for more". And thus, finding little peace in his obedience to the will of God, but obeying none the less, he applied the same feeling to his earthly relations. The dignities of this world had done nothing for him, he had himself given the signal for rebellion against literary patronage, yet he required in himself and others an entire, though unloving, submission to "the powers that be". When applied to men in general, this feeling passed into an almost savage desire to see the silly people kept in order by a strong hand above them. In this desire, arising, as it did, from his contempt for the folly of men, he reminds one of his great admirer, Carlyle. "By popular delusion illiterate writers would rise into renown", by popular delusion Wilkes was thought a great man, and such a mad world had no right to question the Divine authority of its rulers. Much less had it the right to expect him to conform to its foolish ways, which it yet thought men insane for disregarding. "Kit Smart was sent to Bedlam because he asked people to pray with him in the street, but it is not nearly so foolish to pray in the street, as not to pray at all, which is the case with most people. For my own part I had as lief pray with Kit Smart as anyone". But, with all this scorn, Johnson's nature was essentially a social and genial one. He esteemed himself "a good-natured fellow", and the good-will of men was "inexpressibly dear to him". In his youth he wasted his time in discoursing to groups of students at the gate of Pembroke college, and in his age he thought that to look down the Strand was to see the finest sight in the world. This tendency was indeed constantly kept in check by his bodily infirmities, and by that hatred for human dullness which made him advise some conceited puppy not to marry, "lest he should propagate the want of understanding". But still, in whatever society he was living, whether he was talking to his king, to Highland Lairds, or to men "who lived in London and hung loose upon society", he could speak as a man to men, with his social impulse unchecked by the accidents of temporary circumstance.

On Thackeray's Novels

Everything that is very good of its kind is at any rate pleasing and satisfactory, even if it be not admirable. But if a thing makes professions which it does not fulfil, and raises expectations which it does not answer, or if the excellence of one part of it is out of all proportion to that of another, we at once perceive the incongruity and want of harmony, and something jars on the mind in the contrast between its faults and its excellence. But whatever is complete and perfect, so far as it goes, and satisfies all the requirements which of itself it prompts us to make, this we at once set down as something good of its kind, without troubling ourselves to compare its merits with those which an higher standard might require. It is thus with Thackeray's novels. In them everything flows smoothly on, — the style, the incidents, and the sentiment alike. There is no effort to be witty, no straining after grandiloquence, none of the self-assertion, which most novel-writers exhibit, when, in dwelling on the virtues of their hero, they seem constantly reflecting on their own, and magnify themselves in the eyes of the reader by the high moral aspirations of their men of sentiment. He fixes our thoughts on the fleeting incidents of social life which he describes, but it is because they are life-like, not because they are "thrilling"; he brings out even his unimportant characters in the most distinct individuality, but it is their manners, not their minds that he paints; he never touches on the deepest principles of action, seldom even on our strongest emotions, but with him the common feelings and actions of every-day life are all in their just proportion and too true to the life to be uninteresting. Hence we do not complain that the pleasant level lies too low, nor do we feel the want of a high moral tone in these books, for where it has scarcely ever appeared at all it is not likely to be missed. It is not till we raise our thoughts to an higher standard of literary excellence, and measure Thackeray's novels by it, that we can fully appreciate their moral character. All the lessons, which Thackeray has given the world, seem only variations of the old song "vanitas vanitatum". The moral of his writings is of only purely negative character. They are all satires in one form or another, but they never seem to attain to that clear moral indignation, which is the first step towards the correction of the evil satirized. When, by the most gentle process of dis[s]ection, he has laid bare some monstrous social evil, and kindled our wrath against it, he immediately turns round on us, lest we should rest complaisant in our own superiority, to show that it only arises from some weakness inherent in mankind, of which we ourselves, like all others, are partakers. There is as much vanity displayed in a church as in a ball-room, the poor man who cringes before a noble-man has as mercenary a spirit as the rich man who sells his daughter to improve his mercantile connection. Every one has his stall in Vanity-fair, and if through favourable circumstances my trade is an honester one than my neighbour's, yet I cannot tell what I might have become, if I had been tried by his difficulties, and I am not the man to throw a stone at him. This view of the common weakness of men has no doubt its true side, but if it be separated from hope, from the consideration of the good that is wrought out of evil and of the final perfection to which all things are tending, it reduces life to an aimless existence, which we must make the best of, so long as we are cursed with it, remaining as indifferent as possible to the external evils which mar our comfort. Thackeray's nobility of feeling prevents him from altogether submitting to this conclusion, but he seems often to come near it. He makes happiness the great end of man, but he has too keen an eye not to see that our happiness is in a great degree at the mercy of external circumstances, that few enjoy it permanently, and often the best men least of all. He seems to lose sight of the blessings that result from suffering, and makes hopeless submission our only plan. We are puppets in the hand of our Maker, and his way is dark; we must bow before the Divine Will, and, for the rest, let us seek what comfort we can in innocent enjoyment, being careful only to retain our finer feelings, or, as he himself expresses it, "let all, pray Heaven, be gentlemen". He quite ignores any possibility of a spiritual union and harmony between the mind of man and the Divine Will — nor should we complain of such an omission in a novel, were it not that he often touches on religious sentiments, which are profaned by being merely handled on the surface. The truth is that it is with the manners of men that he deals, and with their minds, only so far as they are expressed in the superficial intercourse of common society. He brings in religious feelings, as they are seen on the surface, to form parts of the many-coloured picture of life which he loves to contemplate. To harmonize the more intense struggles of

the spirit in one dramatic whole requires greater power than
his.

"Quondam etiam victis redit in praecordia virtus." What is the Truth of This, as Viewed in the Light of History?

Every one must feel strongly inclined, at first sight, to regard
this maxim as expressing a law which regulates the rise and
fall of nations. It seems, a priori, more natural to suppose that
prosperity and adversity, and the mental states from which
they proceed, should succeed each in alternate cycles, than
that ruin and corruption should be the permanent fate of any
nation. One argues from the analogy of individuals that defeat
is but a purifying affliction, and that national sufferings are
but that eruption of disease on the surface which is the first
step towards loosening its hold within. But the analogy of
individuals likewise teaches us that there are cases when punishment is inflicted as the just vengeance for sins, with the
prospect, so far as man can see, of only ingraining more deeply
the wickedness of the offender. It is with punishments of this
stamp that the conquest of nations seems generally to correspond. Every nation requires occasional defeats, and checks in
its progress, to bind its members together and rouse them to
activity, these may sometimes amount to a temporary subjection to a foreign power, but a permanent subjection generally
implies a degree of corruption as its cause, to which punishment is indeed due, but to which it can bring only increased
misery and sin. But it is as difficult to determine by any general
rule in what cases the punishment of subjection is a curse, and
in what it becomes a purifying chastisement, as to decide
whether a criminal should be consigned to a reformatory, or to
perpetual confinement. And when, in looking back on history,
we see that some nations have sunk under foreign oppression
into hopeless inactivity and sensuality, while others have risen
under the trial to a nobler patriotism and a more united public
spirit, we assume some diversity either in the oppressor or the
oppressed to account for the different results, but are scarcely
able to point out where it lies. It seems most natural however
that the evils which occasion the conquest, should be perpetuated by it. The great cause of the decline of nations is selfishness. Disunion and mutual suspicion among private men, and

corruption among officials, necessarily follow from the habit of putting ourselves first, and our fellow-citizens last; and when men have come to regard their own interests as everything, and those of the state as nothing, the state practically ceases to exist and is the prey of the first-comer. This selfishness is naturally intensified and perpetuated by foreign oppression, which sweeps away even the shadow of a state, and leaves not so much as the name of an higher duty to disturb men in the undivided pursuit of private gain. The intrusion of police or something similar into the private relations of life, and the defection of the most selfish to the dominant power, which follow of necessity in the train of conquest, increase the restless suspicion and fear of treachery; the heavy weight of an immovable class of oppressive officials represses all expectation of rising in this world; and men give themselves up to a sensual pursuit of momentary pleasure and comfort, with no hope for the future of themselves or their country. There may be occasional spasmodic bursts of rebellion against excessive outrage, but the time for an united patriotism is gone forever. Greece or Italy, both past and present, might serve to exemplify this aggravation of evils. Athens fell before the power of Macedon because her generals had become soldiers of fortune, her statesmen rhetoricians who merely sought the display of their own cleverness, and her citizens traders who sought to get money for themselves, and then enjoy it. But after her fall this selfishness was aggravated. The rhetoricians then lost even the food which a fancied patriotism offered to the imagination, and became paid declaimers. It is said that the modern Greek, however much he may hate his oppressors, has no patriotic love for his countrymen, and that cowed into that servile fear, which is next of kin to fraud and treachery, is content if he may be left alone to seek his private gain. These observations, of course, will not apply to those cases, if any such there be, in which nations are conquered without any deep-seated corruption on their part. But such cases would lie beyond the scope of the question, for virtue cannot be said to 'return' when it has never been lost. There are other cases however in which subjugation to foreigners seems to arise rather from the corruption of the governing classes than from that of the people, and the sting of oppression may rouse an energy among the people which was previously dormant rather than lost. But even this benefit is not unmixed with evil, for the violent interruption in the quiet course of a nation's life disorders those countless private projects for good of which the Historian takes no account, and a passionate outburst of national hatred, though it excites the imagination and forms a grand picture in history, cannot but produce those turbid effects, which we always expect from a similar outburst in an individual. The nation moreover, driven from its natural course into an excited abhorrence of foreign oppression, is ready to submit to any national tyranny that may be imposed on it. Thus Napoleon's conquest of Prussia, though it called forth a noble burst of enthusiasm, resulted in the Holy Alliance, — a renewal of that very system of government which may be said to have led to the conquest.

The English National Character Compared with that of the Germans

The degrees of diversity in the characters of nations vary greatly in extent. In some cases the difference is so wide, that, while we are unable to find any adequate cause for it within the limits of known history, we can yet be sure that the points of difference are real, though we are unable to ascribe them to any common principle. In the cases of the English and Germans, on the other hand, it is the fundamental resemblance between the two characters that is most strongly marked, and we can only satisfy ourselves that the diversities which we detect are not fleeting and accidental, by finding some cause in the different circumstances of the two nations to which we may ascribe them. When it is races that are opposed in character, we may regard them as distinct families, and suppose that they have perpetuated the dissimilar tempers of their first progenitors, which we know to be the case with the descendants of Jacob and Esau. But when we find two streams from the same spring, each retaining the properties of the original source, we must find some external feature of difference in their several courses, to account for their differences of quality, if we would be certain that they are anything more than "flashes on the surface". It is vain to seek for such a cause in laws and institutions, which are in themselves only effects, though they tend to perpetuate the national feeling in which they have their rise. But in geographical position, and in the action/influence of foreign states, we may find external causes, the influence of which in moulding a nation's character is undoubted, if it be not paramount. Almost every Englishman has a notion that his countrymen are practical, while the Germans are speculative. This notion has become so rooted among us that, in common language, to be a German and to be unpractical are equivalent terms, and if any one wishes to condemn a political or religious theory, he calls it a German abstraction. Though we have no right to regard them as inferior to ourselves, because they are different, yet, when we remember that no nation has shown greater freedom of thought or greater courage in asserting their national liberty, we must assume a certain slowness to act and an indifference to their present condition, to account for the unworthiness of their political state. This difference between the nations will seem more natural and essential, when we consider the position of Germany in the heart of the continent, as opposed to the insulation of England. The neighbourhood of the sea tempted Englishmen to commerce, prone to it as they naturally were from the infusion into their veins of the blood of Danish adventurers, and their commercial habits have tinged not merely their common life, but even their science and literature. The English, no less than the Germans, are a reflecting and forecasting people, but in fact they live much more for the present, for, while the German is brooding idly over the stories and memories of the past, or speculating as to the future of himself and his children, the Englishman is combining his past observations with a view to some more or less commercial enterprise, which, though future, demands all his present energy to make the needful preparations. So those branches of science are most tempting to Englishmen, which seem to produce the most immediate practical effect; in Mathematical and physical science we have generally had the lead of the Germans, and we adopt their metaphysical theories at second hand, to mould them into a practical form, and thus give them marketable value in England. Similar tendencies may perhaps be discovered in the religious inclination of the two countries, for it is at least remarkable that the Calvinistic doctrines, which in England have been generally popular with the trading classes, and especially so among the Scotch, the most commercial and grasping in spirit of all the Anglo Saxons, they have never obtained much hold on the Germans. The Lutheran doctrines, allowing a larger domain to mystery, and appealing

more to the heart and imagination, and less to the understanding, than those of Calvin, are more compatible with the con-
templative and reverential spirit of the Germans than with
that republican spirit of which there has always been a considerable element in England, and which is fostered by the personal independence natural to a commercial life. If we look to
the temper of the English people before the Reformation, we
shall find that, apart from the higher spirit of religion which
marked some of its leaders, the popular feeling out of which
the movement arose was one of resistance to Easter dues and
mortuaries, and of rebellion against interference in religion as
a personal wrong. In Germany, on the other hand, the pile, to
which Luther applied the torch, had been prepared for the
burning by a general scorn for monkish stupidity and impu-
rity, natural to men whose eyes had been opened by the
revival of literature, and who had learnt to aspire towards an
intellectual, if not a spiritual, elevation, from the teaching of
the Theosophists and Mystics. The progress of the Reformation in the two nations illustrates another feature of diversity
in their characters. In Germany the religious opinions of the
reformed attained a much greater completeness than in England, but the people and their different governments
remained very widely divided in religious matters, and no
permanent ecclesiastical system was established. But we have
to turn to Germany, if we would study the religious theories of
the reformation, while England produced hardly any purely
doctrinal writers, though many on ecclesiastical matters. With
us the reformation, as soon as it began to prevail extensively
among individuals, effected a corresponding work on the state
and the government. This arose partly from the fact that the
English government and church were, from their position, less
open to external influences, but also from the compromising
tendency of the English mind. This tendency is more manifest
in political than in any other matters, (though in all things an
unbending rule is odious to Englishmen), and perhaps arises
in some degree from the mixture of other nations with the English. Our Norman aristocracy, ruling a half-conquered people,
were soon obliged to secure their position by compromises
with the burghers of the towns, and throughout English history, there seem to have been two well-balanced parties,
whose interests must alike be respected in legislation. A similar effect is produced among us by the freedom and influence

of public opinion. An Englishman is in many ways more independent in feeling, and less anxious for sympathy than a German (a difference which is natural between a wealthy and an oppressed nation), but when he is writing or studying, he has always public opinion, and generally the public good, before his eyes, and hence he promulgates far fewer extravagances of opinion, than a German, who writes under protection of a court with a view merely to his fellow-students, and who is therefore better able to abstract his mind from external considerations, and push his opinions to their furthest consequences.

The Character of Mahomet

There seem to be two principal causes which prevent us from gaining a clear insight into the character of Mahomet. In the first place it is almost impossible to ascertain the state of religion among his countrymen at the time when the great Prophet arose; and secondly, our ways of thinking are utterly alien from those of a people, widely separated from us in time and race, of whose literature no vestige has reached us, and whose character was in no way affected by any of those special influences, which have helped to mould the character of European nations. We cannot tell how much the teaching of Mahomet improved or degraded or superseded the religion which had before prevailed, till we know what that religion was; nor can we decide on the question of his sincerity, till we understand, through a certain degree of sympathy, how far his heavenly visions were the natural expressions — or even the natural vehicle, of mental and spiritual impressions. Nor is it fair to judge Mahomet as an impostor on account of Mahometanism, as it at present exists. We know indeed that God may give men over "to a strong delusion, that they should believe a lie", but such a delusion would seem to lie rather in a system of religion into which men gradually sink, than in a new faith which they welcome with enthusiasm as a deliverance from bondage: we may admit that Mahometanism is, and has been, a lie to those who hold by it, and yet suppose that to its founder and his first followers it was the result of an honest struggle to escape from a worse delusion. Up to the time of Mahomet Arabia remained probably in a state of virtual paganism. The worship of the Black stone was going on under his eyes, and, if it be true that his father was devoted to appease the wrath of heaven, it was but the sign of a common superstition. Christianity had indeed spread considerably in Arabia, but it seems to have lost its true character by mixture with the relics of heathenism, as indeed was natural in a country remote from the main body of Christendom, and out of the reach of those influences which preserved the purity of the rest of the Church. Arabia was the ready receptacle for those grosser heresies, which could not be tolerated by the central authority of the Church, — among others that of Deifying the Virgin, — and it is quite conceivable that both Tritheism and an idolatrous worship of saints may have corrupted the Christianity which Mahomet saw about him. The influence of the Jews on the Arabians lay merely in directing that reverence for patriarchs, to which they were naturally prone on certain of the prophets and lawgivers of the Jewish nation. We know that Mahomet, though a man of noble birth and natural authority, lived a life of seclusion and stern frugality till he was 40, and this combined with the simplicity of his first revelation, "there is but one God and Mahomet is his prophet", conveys the notion of a man who had long brooded in silence over the complex idolatries and follies of his countrymen, and at last resolved that the only remedy was a simple dependence on one Divine power, which he was himself appointed to proclaim among men, as alone having the will to do so. There is a simple grandeur in this utterance which would ill accord with the artificial pretensions of an impostor, and if he maintained that the truth had been revealed to him in heavenly visions, he was doing no more than was natural to an Eastern. In Oriental History we find many cases in which the knowledge of important truths and the high resolution as to future duties, which we ascribe to spiritual insight or the enlightment of conscience, are spoken of as communicated in trances and heavenly visions, nor is there any reason to suppose that one way of speaking, under the circumstances, is less correct than the other. The other fundamental doctrine, which Mahomet inculcated, had probably a similar origin. It was the natural expression of a consciousness that he was not his own master or doing his own work, but was appointed by God to lead his countrymen to a better life. But Mahomet could not long retain his purity of motive, or confine his work to its proper limits. He was driven from Mecca by persecution, and from that time he seems to have been carried away by mental intoxication, mingled unconsciously, as fanaticism often is, with a parallel intoxication of the senses and a cunning accomodation to the popular taste. If it be true that among the Eastern Churches the acceptance of Christianity sometimes led, in its first excitement, to a sensual licentiousness strangely corresponding to the new spiritual freedom, this may explain, in some measure, how Mahomet with his Eastern temper should pass from the passionate fanaticism of his new mission to a passionate sensuality, both in his acts and in his teaching. But he doubtless gave a looser rein to this tendency from that desire of accomodating himself to the people which now began to mark all his conduct. Several facts show that he himself knew how to spare, but to animate his soldiers he proclaimed the duty of exterminating unbelievers, and for the same purpose degraded his earlier doctrine of fatalism into a destiny of future enjoyment and a consequent disregard of present circumstances. It is probable however that he continued through life honestly to regard himself as the inspired messenger of Heaven, for in those days of unconsciousness men were little given to analyse their motives, and the same impulse, which roused him at first, seemed to carry him through to the end, though its purity was soiled day by day. It is one of the distinguishing features of fanaticism that, while it begins with a genuine love for some high principle it ends with a love for the party or cause which represents the principle, and is itself unconscious of the change. Mahomet began with declaring that there was one God, and Mahomet was his prophet, and in word he maintained it to the end, but in fact he daily merged the former clause more and more in the latter.

Enthusiasm

The word "enthusiasm" is used in many different senses, which may however be brought under two general heads. In common language it is used to denote zeal and warmth of feeling of any kind, while at the same time it denotes more specifically an intenser bending of the mind towards some one end, which is invested with undue importance, in disregard of the greatness of other objects. The character of the enthusiasm will thus depend very much on the character of the object towards which it is directed. If it look with singleness of aim towards the highest object of all, — the glory of God, — it loses all its deformity, if not all its danger. But even when thus directed, it is incompatible with that "quietness of thought", which belongs to him whose mind is truly stayed on God, and therefore can only be regarded as the impulse towards a state not yet fully attained. And though it is of course impossible that an undue importance can be attached to such an object, if only its extent and fullness be adequately understood and appreciated, yet it is the characteristic of enthusiasm that it only discerns one side or aspect of it. It looks merely to some one particular mode of glorifying God, in forgetfulness of others equally important, and hence it produces that hurried activity and that violence to one's own feelings no less than those of others, which are inseparable from a partial view of that which should satisfy every want of man's nature. We may see this one-sided tendency running through all the forms of religious enthusiasm. The fanatic, with his eye fixed on his own narrow path of conduct, cares not through what immorality it may lead him, if only it tends to the desired end of the glory of God, for not fully discerning the extent and comprehensiveness of that end, he does not see that any act of immorality repels him from it far more than his enthusiasm helps him on. He condemns, as 'the world', all those who may happen to be surrounded with different religious associations from himself; he can tolerate no diversity of opinion, no doctrine that is not hammered on his own anvil, because he gazes so intensely and abstractedly on his own track, that he cannot see that others may be leading in the same direction. From the same narrowness of vision he often falls into self-seeking and self-deceit. Seeking the glory of God only through the medium of some particular church or creed, he passes by an easy transit to a habit of glorifying this church or creed, and himself as their champion, in forgetfulness of the end to which they are a means. Or he fancies that he has still a godly zeal, when it is in truth only his enthusiasm that he retains, diverted from its original object, and likely soon to pass from a spiritual excitement into an intoxication of the senses. The mystic, with a like partiality of view, seeks, by an assimilation of his own spirit with the Divine, to rise to communion with God, while he forgets his bodily nature and his earthly duties. He seeks to quiet the contest between the spirit and the flesh by ignoring the resistence of the latter, instead of satisfying his fleshly wants and fulfilling his earthly duties in subjection to the spirit. Hence there is great danger lest in practice the power which he ignores should become his ordinary master, only shaken off at times of special spiritual excitement, or lest his teaching should be generally useless from its taking no account of those common duties of life, in which the religion of the mass of men must be manifested, or not at all. In a similar way the enthusiast deludes himself by shutting his eyes to the real state of things around him, and regarding the peculiar facts of his own inward experience as proper to the universal nature of man. To his eyes everything takes its colouring from his own highly-wrought feelings, and he judges of truth by the evidence of his own idiosyncracies. Perhaps he falls in with men who can sympathize with him, and he founds a sect, which will continue to exist when the notions, which had a peculiar truth to the first disciples on account of their peculiar experiences, have become barren forms or false superstitions. So it has been with the Quakers and Irvingites and all other sects, whose founders have mistaken the facts of their individual consciousness for truths of universal application. But sometimes an enthusiast of this stamp takes a different course. Judging of the world without by the world within he forms an ideal of it, very different from the reality, and impossible to be attained, since it supposes man to be actuated by motions peculiar to the enthusiast himself. He has a passion for reforming the world, but the world will not listen to him, and sooner or later he discovers his mistake. He falls out with mankind and they with him, and he is thrown back even more than before to brood on his own consciousness. He shuts himself out from all the good influences current in the world, quarrelling with religion because it does not make men better, and even with morality because it shackles the free exercise of his own high impulses. In narrower minds, and with lower objects, enthusiasm will sometimes produce still more ruinous effects, especially if its course is checked by external violence or persecution. In such cases the object in view seems to absorb the mind into itself, and deprive it of its free agency. However good it may be in itself, unless it is the highest object of all, it blinds its victim to all other considerations, and if violent resistance stand in his way, he gradually comes to think that every thing which does not directly advance his progress, must be trampled under foot till he reach the goal. Sir Walter Scott's

Balfour of Burley might serve as an instance of this character, as well as some of the most blood-stained leaders in the French Revolution, who seem to have been rather enthusiasts, maddened by fear of domestic treachery and foreign invasion, than men who loved bloodshed for its own sake.

Bibliography

I: T.H. Green

Published by Green

'The Force of Circumstances' (1858), reprinted in R. L. Nettleship, ed., *Works of Thomas Hill Green: Vol. III. Miscellanies and Memoir* (London, 1888), pp. 3–10.

'An Estimate of the Value and Influence of Works of Fiction in Modern Times' (1862), reprinted in Nettleship, *Works*, III, pp. 20–45.

'The Philosophy of Aristotle' (1866), reprinted in Nettleship, *Works*, III, pp. 46–91.

'Popular Philosophy in its Relation to Life' (1868), reprinted in Nettleship, *Works*, III, pp. 92–125.

(Edited with T.H. Grose), *The Philosophical Works of David Hume*, 4 vols (London, 1874–5). Green's contributions, the 'General Introduction' and 'Introduction to the Moral Part of the Treatise', are reprinted in R.L. Nettleship, ed., *Works of Thomas Hill Green: Vol. I. Philosophical Works* (London, 1885), pp. 1–371.

'Mr. Spencer on the Relation of Subject and Object' (1877), reprinted in Nettleship, *Works*, I, pp. 373–409.

'Mr. Spencer on the Independence of Matter' (1878), reprinted in Nettleship, *Works*, I, pp. 410–41.

'Lecture on "Liberal Legislation and Freedom of Contract"' (1881), reprinted in Nettleship, *Works*, III, pp. 365–86.

'Lecture on "The Work to be done by the new Oxford High School for Boys"' (1882), reprinted in Nettleship, *Works*, III, pp. 456–76.

Published Posthumously

Prolegomena to Ethics, ed. A.C. Bradley (Oxford, 1883). Cited by section and page.

The Witness of God and Faith: Two Lay Sermons, ed. A. Toynbee (London, 1883).

'On the Different Senses of "Freedom" As Applied to Will and to the Moral Progress of Man' in R.L. Nettleship, ed., *Works of Thomas Hill Green: Vol. II. Philosophical Works* (London, 1886), pp. 308–33.

'Lectures on the Principles of Political Obligation' in Nettleship, *Works*, II, pp. 335–553. Cited by section and page.

'Essay on Christian Dogma' in Nettleship, *Works*, III, pp. 161–85.

'Fragment of an Address on Romans x. 8, "The word is nigh thee"' in Nettleship, *Works*, III, pp. 221–9.

'Four Lectures on the English Revolution' in Nettleship, *Works*, III, pp. 277–364.

'The Elementary School System of England' in Nettleship, *Works*, III, pp. 413–55.

'Life and Immortality brought to light by the Gospel' in P. Nicholson, ed., *Collected Works of T. H. Green: Vol. 5 Additional Writings* (Bristol, 1997; re-issued 2003 as a separate book, T. H. Green, *Miscellaneous Writings, Speeches and Letters*), pp. 57–81.

'The State of Religious Belief among the Jews at the time of the Coming of Christ', in Nicholson, *Collected Works*, 5, pp. 83–104.

Undergraduate Essays

The manuscripts published in the Appendix to this book are among Green's undergraduate essays, in the Green Papers, Balliol College, Oxford. They are contained in two notebooks (White Notebook and Blue Notebook), classified by Geoffrey Thomas as 1 and 2 (see Thomas, *The Moral Philosophy of T. H. Green*, pp. 282–3) and date to a period between 1855 and 1859.

There is another selection of Green's undergraduate essays in P. Nicholson, ed., *Collected Works of T. H. Green: Vol. 5 Additional Writings* (Bristol, 1997; re-issued 2003 as a separate book, T. H. Green, *Miscellaneous Writings, Speeches and Letters*), pp. 1–53.

Speeches

Green's principal speeches, as reported in the press, and his letters to the press, are printed in P. Nicholson, ed., *Collected Works of T. H. Green: Vol. 5 Additional Writings* (Bristol, 1997).

Letters

Some of Green's letters are printed in P. Nicholson, ed., *Collected Works of T. H. Green: Vol. 5 Additional Writings* (Bristol, 1997). Others are quoted from the Green Papers, Balliol College, Oxford.

II: Other Books and Articles

Abbagnano, N., *L'idealismo inglese contemporaneo* (Naples, 1926).

—, *Il nuovo idealismo inglese e americano* (Naples, 1927).

Anderson, O., 'The Feminism of T. H. Green: A Late-Victorian Success Story?', *History of Political Thought*, 12 (1991), pp. 671–93.

Aristotle, *The Nichomachean Ethics*, with an English translation by H. Rackham (Cambridge, Mass., 1956).

Balfour, A.J., 'Green's Metaphysics of Knowledge', *Mind*, 9 (1884), pp. 73–92.

Barker, E., *Political Thought in England, 1848–1914* (London, 1915).

Barth, K., *Protestant Theology in the Nineteenth Century: its Background and History* (London, 1972).

Baur, F.C., *Symbolik und Mythologie, oder die Naturreligion des Alterthums*, 2 vols (Stuttgart,1824–1825).

—, *Die christliche Gnosis, oder die christliche Religions-Philosophie in ihrer geschichtlichen Entwicklung* (Tübingen, 1835).

—, *Die christliche Lehre von der Dreienigkeit und Menschenwerdung Gottes in ihrer geschichtlichen Entwicklung*, 3 vols (Tübingen, 1841–3).

—, *Lehrbuch der christlichen Dogmengeschichte* (Stuttgart, 1847).

—, *Die Epochen der kirchlichen Geschichtsschreibung* (Tübingen, 1852).

—, *Geschichte der christlichen Kirche*, 5 vols (Tübingen, 1853-63).

—, *Vorlesungen uber die christliche Dogmengeschichte*, ed. F.F. Baur, 4 vols (Leipzig, 1865–7).

—, *The Church History of the First Three Centuries*, trans. Rev. A. Menzies, 2 vols (London and Edinburgh, 1878–9).

Bebbington, D.W., *Evangelicalism in Modern Britain: A History from 1730 to the 1980s* (London, 1989).

Bellamy, R., 'A Green Revolution? Idealism, Liberalism and the Welfare State', *Bulletin of the Hegel Society of Great Britain*, 10 (1984), pp. 34–9.

—, 'Hegel and Liberalism', *History of European Ideas*, 8 (1987), pp. 693–708.

—, 'T.H. Green and the Morality of Victorian Liberalism' in Bellamy, ed., *Victorian Liberalism: Nineteenth Century Political Thought and Practice* (London, 1990), pp. 131–51.

—, 'T.H. Green, J.S. Mill and Isaiah Berlin on the Nature of Liberty and Liberalism' in H. Gross and R. Harrison, ed., *Jurisprudence: Cambridge Essays* (Oxford, 1992), pp. 257–85. Reprinted in his *Rethinking Liberalism* (London and New York, 2000), pp. 22–46.

—, *Liberalism and Modern Society: An Historical Argument* (Oxford, 1992).

Bellini, O., 'La società civile secondo Thomas Hill Green', *Nuovi Studi Politici*, 6 (1976), pp. 101–19.

Berlin, I., 'Two Concepts of Liberty' reprinted in *Four Essays on Liberty* (Oxford, 1969), pp. 118–72.

Bevir, M., 'Welfarism, Socialism and Religion: On T.H. Green and Others', *The Review of Politics*, 55 (1993), pp. 639–61.

Biagini, E.F, *Liberty, Retrenchment and Reform: Popular Liberalism in the Age of Gladstone, 1860–1880* (Cambridge, 1992).

Bongioanni, F.M., 'I Prolegomena to Ethics di T.H. Green', *Rivista di Filosofia*, 27 (1936), pp. 118–48.

Boucher, D., 'British Idealism, the State, and International Relations', *Journal of the History of Ideas*, 55 (1994), pp. 671–94.

—, 'British Idealist International Theory', *Bulletin of the Hegel Society of Great Britain*, no. 31 (Spring-Summer 1995), pp. 73–89.

—, ed., *The British Idealists* (Cambridge, 1997).

Bourne, K., *The Foreign Policy of Victorian England, 1830–1902* (Oxford, 1970).

Bradley, A.C., *Shakespearean Tragedy* (London, 1965).

Briggs, A., *The Age of Improvement, 1783–1867* (London and New York, 1979).

Brinton, C., *English Political Thought in the Nineteenth Century* (New York, 1962).

Buckle, H.T., *History of Civilisation in England*, 2 vols (London, 1857–1861).

Burrow, J.W., *A Liberal Descent: Victorian Historians and the English Past* (Cambridge, 1991).

Caird, E., 'Professor Green's Last Work', *Mind*, 8 (1883), pp. 544–61.

Calderwood, H., 'Another View of Green's Last Work', *Mind*, 10 (1885), pp. 73–84.

Camporesi, C., *L'uno e i molti: l'idealismo britannico dal 1830 al 1920* (Florence, 1980).

Carlyle, T., *On Heroes, Hero-Worship and the Heroic in History: Six Lectures* (London, 1841).

—, 'Boswell's Life of Johnson' in his *Critical and Miscellaneous Essays in Five Volumes*, vol. III (London, n.d.), pp. 62–135.

—, ed., *Oliver Cromwell's Letters and Speeches: with elucidations*, 2 vols (London, 1845).

Carter, M., *T.H. Green and the Development of Ethical Socialism* (Exeter, 2003).

Chadwick, O., *The Victorian Church*, 2 vols (London, 1966–70).

Collini, S., 'The Idea of "Character" in Victorian Political Thought', *Transactions of the Royal Historical Society*, 35 (1985), pp. 29–50.

—, *Public Moralists: Political Thought and Intellectual Life in Britain, 1850–1930* (Oxford, 1991).

Collingwood, R.G., *An Autobiography* (London, 1939).

Davies, H., *Worship and Theology in England: From Watts and Wesley to Martineau, 1690–1900* (Cambridge, 1996).

Davis, J.C., 'Against Formality: One Aspect of the English Revolution', *Transactions of the Royal Historical Society*, Sixth Series, 3 (1993), pp. 265–88.

Dimova-Cookson, M., *T.H. Green's Moral and Political Philosophy: A Phenomenological Perspective* (Basingstoke and New York, 2001).

—, 'A New Scheme of Positive and Negative Freedom: Reconstructing T. H. Green on Freedom', *Political Theory*, 31 (2003), pp. 508–32.

Dingle, A.E., *The Campaign for Prohibition in Victorian England: the United Kingdom Alliance, 1872–1895* (London, 1980).

Embree, A.T., 'Christianity and the state in Victorian India: confrontation and collaboration' in R.W. Davies and R.J.

Helmstadter, ed., *Religion and Irreligion in Victorian Society* (London and New York, 1992), pp. 151–65.

Emy, H.V., *Liberals, Radicals and Social Politics 1892–1914* (Cambridge, 1973).

Ensor, R.C.K., *England, 1870–1914* (Oxford, 1936).

Faber, G., *Jowett, a Portrait with Background* (London, 1957).

Fairbrother, W.H., *The Philosophy of Thomas Hill Green* (London, 1896).

Feuchtwanger, E.J., *Democracy and Empire: Britain 1865–1914* (London, 1985).

Fichte, J.G., *The Vocation of the Scholar*, trans. W. Smith (London, 1847).

—, *The Popular Works of J.G. Fichte translated from the German (the Vocation of the Scholar – The Nature of the Scholar – The Vocation of Man – Characteristics of the Present Age – the Way towards a Blessed Life - Outlines of the doctrine of Knowledge)*, with a memoir of the author by W. Smith (London, 1848–9).

—, *The Vocation of Man*, trans. by W. Smith (Chicago, 1906).

—, *Foundations of Natural Right*, ed. F. Neuhouser, trans. M. Baur (Cambridge, 2000).

Firth, C.H., *Cromwell's Army* (London, 1962).

Forster, J., *Sir Henry Vane the Younger. Eminent British Statesmen*, Vol. IV (London, 1838).

Francis, M. and Morrow, J., *A History of English Political Thought in the Nineteenth Century* (London, 1994).

Freeden, M., *Rights* (Milton Keynes, 1991).

Frosini, V., 'Sul problema dell'obbligazione politica nel pensiero di Green' in T. H. Green, *L'obbligazione politica*, trans. G. Buttà (Catania, 1973), pp. 47–93.

—, *La ragione dello stato: Studi sul pensiero politico inglese contemporaneo* (Milan, 1976).

—, 'T.H. Green come educatore', *I problemi della pedagogia*, 41 (1995), pp. 217–26.

Gardiner, A.G., *The Life of Sir William Harcourt*, 2 vols (London, 1923).

Gash, N., *Politics in the Age of Peel: A Study in the Technique of Parliamentary Representation 1830–1850* (London, 1953).

—, *Reaction and Reconstruction in English Politics, 1832–1852* (Oxford, 1965).

Gaus, G.F., *The Modern Liberal Theory of Man* (London, 1983).

Gordon, P. and White, J., *Philosophers as Educational Reformers: The Influence of Idealism on British Educational Thought and Practice* (London, 1979).

Goretti, C., 'La metafisica della conoscenza in Thomas Hill Green', *Rivista di Filosofia*, 27 (1936), pp. 97–117.

Greaves, R.L., *The Puritan Revolution and Educational Thought: Background for Reform* (New Brunswick, 1969).

Green, E.H.H., *The Crisis of Conservatism: The Politics, Economics and Ideology of the British Conservative Party, 1880–1914* (London, 1995).

Greengarten, I.M., *Thomas Hill Green and the Development of Liberal-Democratic Thought* (Toronto, 1981).

Greenleaf, W.H., *The British Political Tradition, Volume Two: The Ideological Heritage* (London, 1983).

Hamer, D.A., *Liberal Politics in the Age of Gladstone and Rosebery: A Study in Leadership and Politics* (Oxford, 1972).

—, *The Politics of Electoral Pressure: A Study in the History of Victorian Reform Agitations* (Hassocks, 1977).

Hanham, H.J., *Elections and Party Management: Politics in the Time of Disraeli and Gladstone* (London, 1959).

Hansen, P., 'T.H. Green and the Moralization of the Market', *Canadian Journal of Political and Social Theory*, 1 (1977), pp. 91–117.

Harris, F.P., *Neo-Idealist Political Theory: Its Continuity with the British Tradition* (New York, 1944).

Harris, P., 'Green's Theory of Political Obligation and Disobedience' in A. Vincent, ed., *The Philosophy of T.H. Green* (Aldershot, 1986), pp. 127–42.

—, 'Henry Vane's Arguments for Freedom of Conscience', *Political Science*, 40 (1988), pp. 34–48.

Harris, P. and Morrow, J., ed., *T.H. Green: Lectures on the Principles of Political Obligation and Other Writings* (Cambridge, 1986).

Harrison, B., *Drink and the Victorians: the Temperance Question in England, 1815–1872* (London, 1971).

Harrison, J.F.C., *Learning and Living, 1790–1960: A Study on the History of the Adult English Movement* (London, 1961).

—, *Late Victorian Britain 1875–1901* (London, 1990).

Harvie, C., *The Lights of Liberalism: University Liberals and the Challenge of Democracy, 1860–1886* (London, 1976).

Hearnshaw, F.J.C., *The Life of Sir Henry Vane the Younger, Puritan Idealist* (London, 1910).

Hegel, G.W.F., *The Philosophy of History*, with Prefaces by C. Hegel and the Translator, J. Sibree, and a New Introduction by Professor C. J. Friedrich (New York, 1956).

—, 'On the English Reform Bill' in *Political Writings*, ed. L. Dickey and H.B. Nisbet, trans. H.B. Nisbet (Cambridge, 1999).

—, *Elements of the Philosophy of Right*, ed. A. W. Wood, trans. H.B. Nisbet (Cambridge, 1991).

Helmstadter, R. and B. Lightman, ed., *Victorian Faith in Crisis: Essays on Continuity and Change in Nineteenth-Century Religious Belief* (Palo Alto, 1990).

Heyck, T.W., *The Transformation of Intellectual Life in Victorian England* (London, 1982).

Hilton, B., *The Age of Atonement: The Influence of Evangelicalism on Social and Economic Thought, 1785–1865* (Oxford, 1995).

Himmelfarb, G., *Poverty and Compassion: The Moral Imagination of the Late Victorians* (New York, 1992).

Hinchliff, P., *Benjamin Jowett and the Christian Religion* (Oxford, 1987).

Hodgson, P.C., *The Formation of Historical Theology* (New York, 1966).

Hosmer, J.K., *The Life of Young Sir Henry Vane* (London, 1888).

Houghton, W.E., *The Victorian Frame of Mind 1830–1870* (New Haven, 1957).

Hume, D., *The Philosophical Works of David Hume*, ed. T.H. Green and T.H. Grose, 4 vols (London, 1874–5).

Irwin, T.H., 'Eminent Victorians and Greek Ethics: Sidgwick, Green and Aristotle' in B. Schultz, ed., *Essays on Henry Sidgwick* (Cambridge, 1992), pp. 279–310.

Jellamo, A., 'Il principio dell'obbligazione politica: Riconoscimento e bene comune nel pensiero di Thomas Hill Green' in B. Romano, ed., *Relazione giuridica, riconoscimento e atti sociali* (Rome, 1991), pp. 307–56.

— , 'Da Mill a Green: osservazioni su liberty e freedom', *I problemi della pedagogia*, 41 (1995), pp. 197–216.

— , *Interpretazione del bene comune: Saggio su Thomas Hill Green* (Milano, 1993).

Jenkins, R., *The Victorians and Ancient Greece* (Oxford, 1980).

Jenkins, T.A., *Gladstone, Whiggery and the Liberal Party, 1874–1886* (Oxford, 1988).

Jowett, B., *The Epistles of St. Paul to the Thessalonians, Galatians and Romans*, 2 vols (London, 1855).

Judson, M.A., *The Political Thought of Sir Henry Vane the Younger* (Philadelphia, 1969).

— , *From Tradition to Political Reality: A Study of Ideas Set Forth in Support of the Commonwealth Government in England, 1649–1653* (Hamden, 1980).

Kant, I., *Groundwork of the Metaphysics of Morals*, trans. M. Gregor (Cambridge, 2002).

Kelly, D., 'Idealism and Revolution: T.H. Green's Lectures on the English Commonwealth' (paper for the International Conference on Anglo-American Idealism, 20–25 August 2003, Pyrgos, Greece).

Kelly, T., *A History of Adult Education in Great Britain* (Liverpool, 1992).

Kitson Clark, G., *The Making of Victorian England* (London, 1962).

— , *Churchmen and the Condition of England, 1832–1885: A Study in the Development of Social Ideas and Practice from the Old Regime to the Modern State* (London, 1973).

Knight, W., *Memoir of John Nichol* (Glasgow, 1896).

Lamont, W.D., *Introduction to Green's Moral Philosophy* (London, 1934).

Lamont, W., *Puritanism and Historical Controversy* (Montreal, 1996).

Lang, T., *The Victorians and the Stuart Heritage: Interpretations of a Discordant Past* (Cambridge, 1995).

Laslett, P., ed., *Philosophy, Politics and Society* (Oxford, 1956).

Leighton, D.P., *The Greenian Moment: T.H. Green, Religion and Political Argument in Victorian Britain* (Exeter, 2004).

Levine, G., *Darwin and the Novelists* (Cambridge, 1988).

Lewis, H.D., 'Was Green a Hedonist?', *Mind*, 65 (1936), pp. 193–8.

Lindsay, A.D., 'T.H. Green and the Idealists' in F.J.C. Hearnshaw, ed., *The Social and Political Ideas of Some Representative Thinkers of the Victorian Age* (New York, 1933), pp. 150–64. Reprinted in T.H. Green, *Lectures on the Principles of Political Obligation*, with a preface by B. Bosanquet (London, 1941), pp. vii–xix.

Mabbott, J.D., *The State and the Citizen: An Introduction to Political Philosophy* (London, 1967).

Machin, G.I.T., *Politics and the Churches in Great Britain, 1832–1868* (Oxford, 1977).

MacCunn, J., *Six Radical Thinkers: Bentham, J. S. Mill, Cobden, Carlyle, Mazzini, T.H. Green* (London, 1907).

MacPherson, C.B., *Democratic Theory: Essays in Retrieval* (Oxford, 1973).

—, ed., *Property: Mainstream and Critical Positions* (Toronto, 1978).

Mandelbaum, M., *History, Man, & Reason: A Study in Nineteenth-Century Thought* (Baltimore & London, 1971).

Martin, R., 'Green on Natural Rights in Hobbes, Spinoza and Locke' in A. Vincent, ed., *The Philosophy of T.H. Green* (Aldershot, 1986), pp. 104–26.

Martineau, J., *A Study of Religion: Its Sources and Contents*, 2 vols (Oxford, 1889).

Mastellone, S., *Mazzini and Marx: Thoughts Upon Democracy in Europe* (London, 2003).

Matthew, H.C.G., *Gladstone. 1809–1874* (Oxford, 1986).

Mayhew, A., *Christianity and the Government of India* (London, 1929).

Mazzini, G., 'On the Genius and Tendencies of the Writings of Thomas Carlyle' in *Life and Writings of Joseph Mazzini: Vol. IV, Critical and Literary* (London, 1891).

Mill, J.S., *A System of Logic: Ratiocinative and Inductive*, ed. J. M. Robson, Introduction by R.F. McRae, 2 vols (Toronto, 1978).

—, *Principles of Political Economy, With Some of Their Applications to Social Philosophy*, ed. J.M. Robson, Introduction by V. W. Bladen, 2 vols (Toronto, 1965).

—, *An Examination of Sir William Hamilton's Philosophy*, ed. J.M. Robson, Introduction by A. Ryan (Toronto, 1979).

—, *On Liberty* in *Essays on Politics and Society*, ed. J.M. Robson, Introduction by A. Brady (Toronto, 1977).

—, 'Civilization' in *Essays on Politics and Society*, ed. J.M. Robson, Introduction by A. Brady (Toronto, 1977).

—, 'On Genius' in *Autobiography and Literary Essays*, ed. J.M. Robson and J. Stillinger (Toronto, 1981).

Milne, A.J.M., *The Social Philosophy of English Idealism* (London, 1962).

Monro, D.H., 'Green, Rousseau and the Culture Pattern', *Philosophy*, 26 (1951), pp. 347–57.

Moore, J.R., ed., *Religion in Victorian England* (Manchester, 1991).

Morley, J., *The Life of William Ewart Gladstone*, 2 vols (London, 1905–6).

Morrow, J., 'Property and Personal Development: An Interpretation of T.H. Green's Political Philosophy', *Politics: Journal of the Australian Political Science Association*, 18 (1981), pp. 84–92.

—, 'Liberalism and British Idealist Political Philosophy: A Reassessment', *History of Political Thought*, 5 (1984), pp. 91–108.

—, 'Heroes and Constitutionalists: The Ideological Significance of Thomas Carlyle's Treatment of the English Revolution', *History of Political Thought*, 14 (1993), pp. 205–23.

Muirhead, J.H., *The Service of the State: Four Lectures on the Political Teaching of T.H. Green* (London, 1908).

Nettleship, R.L., *Memoir* in Nettleship, ed., *Works of Thomas Hill Green: Vol. III. Miscellanies and Memoir* (London, 1888).

New, J.F.H., *Anglicans and Puritans: The Basis of Their Opposition, 1558–1640* (Stanford, 1964).

Nicholson, P., 'Philosophical Idealism and International Politics: A Reply to Dr Savigear', *British Journal of International Studies*, 2 (1976), pp. 76–83.

—, 'T.H. Green and State Action: Liquor Legislation', *History of Political Thought*, 6 (1985), pp. 517–50. Reprinted in A.Vincent, ed., *The Philosophy of T.H. Green* (Aldershot, 1986), pp. 76–103.

—, *The Political Philosophy of the British Idealists: Selected Studies* (Cambridge, 1990).

—, 'T.H. Green's Doubts About Hegel's Political Philosophy', *Bulletin of the Hegel Society of Great Britain*, no. 31 (1995), pp. 61–72.

—, 'T.H. Green and the Burden of Christian Citizenship', *Balliol College Annual Record 1998* (1998), pp. 15–22.

O'Brien, R. Barry, *John Bright* (London, 1910).

Palazzolo, C., *Idealismo e liberalismo: La filosofia pratica di T.H. Green* (Carrara, 1983).

—, 'Liberalismo e filosofia dei diritti in Green', *I problemi della pedagogia*, 41 (1995), pp. 179–196.

Parnham, D., *Sir Henry Vane, Theologian: A Study in Seventeenth-Century Religious and Political Discourse* (Denver, 1997).

—, 'Politics Spun Out of Theology and Prophecy: Sir Henry Vane on the Spiritual Environment of Public Power', *History of Political Thought*, 22 (2001), pp. 69–82.

—, 'The Nurturing of Righteousness: Sir Henry Vane on Freedom and Discipline', *Journal of British Studies*, 42 (2003), pp. 1–34.

Parry, J.P., *Democracy and Religion: Gladstone and the Liberal Party, 1867–1875* (Cambridge, 1989).

Parsons, G., 'Irish Disestablishment' in G. Parsons, ed., *Religion in Victorian Britain* (Manchester, 1988), pp. 124–146.

Passerin d'Entreves, A., 'Il problema dell'obbligazione politica nel pensiero inglese contemporaneo', *Rivista Internazionale di Filosofia del diritto*, 8 (1928), pp. 25–43. Reprinted in Passerin d'Entreves, *Saggi di storia del pensiero politico*, ed. G.M. Bravo (Milan, 1992), pp. 325–40.

Passmore, J., *A Hundred Years of Philosophy* (London, 1957).

Plamenatz, J.P., *Consent, Freedom and Political Obligation* (London, 1968).

Prest, J., 'The Death and Funeral of T. H. Green', *Balliol College Annual Record 1998* (1998), pp. 23–5.

Prichard, H.A., *Moral Obligation and Duty and Interest: Essays and Lectures* (London, 1968).

Quinton, A., 'Absolute Idealism', *Proceeding of the British Academy*, 57 (1971), pp. 303–29. Reprinted in Quinton, *Thoughts and Thinkers* (London, 1982), pp. 186–206 and in A. Kenny, ed., *Rationalism, Empiricism and Idealism: British Academy Lectures on the History of Philosophy* (Oxford, 1986), pp. 124–50.

Reardon, B.M.G., *From Coleridge to Gore. A Century of Religious Thought in Britain* (London, 1971).

—, 'T.H. Green as a Theologian' in A. Vincent, ed., *The Philosophy of T.H. Green* (Aldershot, 1986), pp. 36–47.

Richter, M., 'T.H. Green and his Audience: Liberalism as a Surrogate Faith', *Review of Politics*, 18 (1956), pp. 444–72.

—, *The Politics of Conscience: T.H. Green and his Age* (London, 1964).

Ritchie, D.G., *The Principles of State Interference: Four Essays on the Political Philosophy of Mr. Herbert Spencer, J.S. Mill and T.H. Green* (London, 1891).

Robbins, P., *The British Hegelians, 1875–1925* (London, 1982).

Routh, D.A., 'The Philosophy of International Relations: T.H. Green *versus* Hegel', *Politica*, 3 (1938), pp. 223–35.

Schueller, Herbert M. and Robert L. Peters, ed., *The Letters of John Addington Symonds. Volume II: 1869–1884* (Detroit, 1968).

—, *The Letters of John Addington Symonds. Volume III: 1885–1893* (Detroit, 1969).

Scott, F. Newton, ed., *T.H. Green: An Estimate of the Value and Influence of Works of Fiction in Modern Times, With Introduction and Notes* (Ann Arbor, 1911).

Sell, A.P.F., *Philosophical Idealism and Christian Belief* (Cardiff, 1995).

Seth, A., *Hegelianism and Personality* (London, second edition, 1893 [1887]).

Shannon, R., *The Crisis of Imperialism 1865–1915* (London, 1974).

Sidgwick, H., 'Green's Ethics', *Mind*, 9 (1884), pp. 169–87.

---, *Lectures on the Ethics of T.H. Green, Mr. Herbert Spencer and J. Martineau* (London, 1902).

Sikes, G., *The Life and Death of Sir Henry Vane* (London, 1662).

Simhony, A., 'T.H. Green's Theory of the Morally Justified Society', *History of Political Thought*, 10 (1989), pp. 481–98.

—, 'Idealist Organicism: Beyond Holism and Individualism', *History of Political Thought*, 12 (1991), pp. 515–35.

—, 'On Forcing Individuals to be Free: T.H. Green's Liberal Theory of Positive Freedom', *Political Studies*, 39 (1991), pp. 303–20.

—, 'T.H. Green: The Common Good Society', *History of Political Thought*, 14 (1993), pp. 225–47.

—, 'Was T.H. Green a Utilitarian?', *Utilitas*, 7 (1995), pp. 121–44.

—, 'T.H. Green and Henry Sidgwick on the "Profoundest Problem of Ethics"' in W.J. Mander, ed., *Anglo-American Idealism, 1865–1927* (Westport, Conn., 2000), pp. 33–50.

Smith, C.A., 'The Individual and Society in T.H. Green's Theory of Virtue', *History of Political Thought*, 2 (1981), pp. 187–201.

Spencer, H., *The Principles of Ethics*, 2 vols (London, 1892).

Thomas, G., *The Moral Philosophy of T.H. Green* (Oxford, 1987).

Trevelyan, G.M., *The Life of John Bright* (London, 1993).

Trevor-Roper, H.R., 'The General Crisis of the Seventeenth Century', *Past and Present*, 16 (1956), pp. 31–64.

Turner, F.M., *The Greek Heritage in Victorian Britain* (London, 1981).

Tyler, C., 'Context, Capitalism and the Natural Right to Private Property in the Thought of Thomas Hill Green' in I. Hampsher-Monk and J. Stanyer, eds., *Contemporary Political Studies 1996, Volume III* (Oxford, 1996), pp. 1406–14.

—, *Thomas Hill Green (1836–1882) and the Philosophical Foundations of Politics: An Internal Critique* (Lampeter, 1997).

Ulam, A.B., *Philosophical Foundations of English Socialism* (Cambridge, 1951).

Vane, H., *The Retired Man's Meditations* (London, 1655).

—, 'A Healing Question propounded and resolved, upon occasion of the late publique call to humiliation, in order to love and union' in *Somers Tracts* (London, 1811), pp. 303–15.

Vincent, A., 'T.H. Green and the Religion of Citizenship' in Vincent, ed., *The Philosophy of T.H. Green* (Aldershot, 1986), pp. 48–61.

Vincent, A. and Plant, R., *Philosophy, Politics and Citizenship: The Life and Thought of the British Idealists* (Oxford, 1984).

Walsh, W.H., 'Green's Criticism of Hume' in A. Vincent, ed., *The Philosophy of T.H. Green* (Aldershot, 1986), pp. 21–35.

Walzer, M., *The Revolution of the Saints: A Study in the Origins of Radical Politics* (Cambridge, 1965).

Ward, Mrs H., *Robert Elsmere*, 3 vols (London, 1888).

—, *A Writer's Recollections* (London, 1918).

Webb, C.C.J, *A Study of Religious Thought in England from 1850* (Oxford, 1933).

Weinstein, D., 'The Discourse of Freedom, Rights and Good in Nineteenth-Century English Liberalism', *Utilitas*, 3 (1991), pp. 245–62.

—, 'Between Kantianism and Consequentialism in T.H. Green's Moral Philosophy', *Political Studies*, 41 (1993), pp. 618–35.

Wempe, B., *T.H. Green's Theory of Positive Freedom: From Metaphysics to Political Theory* (Exeter, 2004).

Worden, B., *Roundhead Reputations: the English Civil Wars and the Passions of Posterity* (London, 2001).

Wordsworth, W., 'Ode to duty' in M. Arnold, ed., *Poems of Wordsworth* (New York, 1880), pp. 193–4.

Wordsworth, W., *Lyrical Ballads*, ed. M. Mason (London and New York, 1992).

Index